The Uses of Johnson's Criticism

The Uses of Johnson's Criticism

Leopold Damrosch, Jr.

University Press of Virginia
Charlottesville

THE UNIVERSITY PRESS OF VIRGINIA
Copyright © 1976 by the Rector and Visitors
of the University of Virginia

First published in 1976

Library of Congress Cataloging in Publication Data

Damrosch, Leopold.
  The uses of Johnson's criticism.

  Includes index.
  1. Johnson,   Samuel,   1709-1784--Knowledge--Literature.   I.   Title.
  PR3537.L5D3   801'.95'0924   75-19431   ISBN 0-8139-0625-3

Printed in the United States of America

To Sheila

Acknowledgments

I AM GRATEFUL to those friends who very kindly commented on preliminary drafts of this work. Various parts of the manuscript were read by Martin C. Battestin, Ralph Cohen, T. Walter Herbert, Jr., E. D. Hirsch, William W. Kerrigan, Richard Waswo, and Paul C. Wilson, each of whom made valuable suggestions; and I owe special thanks to Irvin Ehrenpreis, who read a complete draft with uncommon care and sympathy. I only wish that the book could be more worthy of them.

My work was greatly assisted by a year's leave from teaching duties, made possible by a Younger Humanist fellowship from the National Endowment for the Humanities and a concurrent Sesquicentennial fellowship from the University of Virginia.

Contents

Abbreviations

Adventurer Johnson, Samuel, *The Idler and The Adventurer.* Ed. W. J. Bate, John M. Bullitt, and L.F. Powell. In Yale *Works.* Vol. II. 1963.

Biographia Coleridge, Samuel Taylor. *Biographia Literaria.* Ed. J. Shawcross. 2 vols. Oxford, 1907.

Dictionary Johnson, Samuel. *A Dictionary of the English Language.* 2 vols. 1755.

Discourses Reynolds, Joshua. *Discourses on Art.* Ed. Stephen O. Mitchell. New York, 1965.

Idler Johnson, Samuel. *The Idler and The Adventurer.* Ed. W. J. Bate, John M. Bullitt, and L.F. Powell. In Yale *Works.* Vol. II. 1963.

Letters *The Letters of Samuel Johnson.* Ed. R.W. Chapman. 3 vols. Oxford, 1952.

Life Boswell, James. *The Life of Samuel Johnson, LL.D.* Ed. G.B. Hill. Rev. L.F. Powell. 6 vols. Oxford, 1934, 1950.

Lives Johnson, Samuel. *The Lives of the Poets.* Ed. G.B. Hill. 3 vols. Oxford, 1905. [These are cited as *Life of . . .* except when the specific *Life* is already evident from the context.]

Miscellanies *Johnsonian Miscellanies.* Ed. G.B. Hill. 2 vols. Oxford, 1897.

Rambler Johnson, Samuel. *The Rambler.* Ed. W.J. Bate and Albrecht Strauss. 3 vols. In Yale *Works.* Vols. III, IV, V. 1969.

Rasselas Johnson, Samuel. *The History of Rasselas, Prince of Abissinia.* Ed. Geoffrey Tillotson and Brian Jenkins. Oxford, 1971.

Savage Johnson, Samuel. *Life of Savage.* Ed. Clarence Tracy. Oxford, 1971.

1825 *Works* *The Works of Samuel Johnson, LL.D.* 9 vols. Oxford, 1825.

Yale *Works* *The Yale Edition of the Works of Samuel Johnson.* Ed. Allen T. Hazen et al. New Haven, 1958–.

Preface Johnson, Samuel. *Preface to Shakespeare.* In Yale *Works.* Vol. VII. 1968.

I dare not flatter myself, that the freedom with which I have declared my opinions concerning both his theory and his defects . . .will be satisfactory or pleasing to *all* [his] admirers and advocates. More indiscriminate than mine their admiration may be: deeper and more sincere it can not be.

Coleridge, *Biographia Literaria*

The Uses of Johnson's Criticism

Introduction

A HUNDRED YEARS ago Leslie Stephen wrote of the *Lives of the Poets*, "The criticism, like the politics, is woefully out of date."[1] More recent writers have taught us to see how flexible, imaginative, and resistant to abstract categories Johnson really is. But his criticism has not altogether shared in the modern rehabilitation of his moral and political writing. One has the impression that many readers, particularly those with no special commitment to eighteenth-century studies, continue to perceive him as cold, censorious, and myopic.

> Lo the Bat with Leathern wing
> Winking & blinking
> Winking & blinking
> Winking & blinking
> Like Doctor Johnson.[2]

Students of Johnson the moralist have been able to intimate that we have lost the ability to read that sort of writing, so that it is we who are at fault, not Johnson, if we find him forbidding. And as we now ask his questions about human life in very different terms, we are content to judge them on their own assumptions: the psychologist will appreciate proto-Freudian hints in Johnson without deploring his Lockean theory of mind; the agnostic will admire the vigor and richness of his Christian moralizing without debating its ultimate truth. But such suspension of judgment (which Johnson himself would probably have despised) is impossible when we turn to the criticism, which we expect to tell what is true about literature, not simply to express a historically dated way of apprehending it.

Against the assumption of readers like Stephen that Johnson is a struldbrugg of criticism, his admirers have naturally tended

---

[1]"Dr. Johnson's Writings," *Hours in a Library, Second Series* (London, 1876), p. 232.

[2]William Blake, *An Island in the Moon, The Poetry and Prose of William Blake*, ed. David V. Erdman (New York, 1965), p. 448.

to act as defenders and to explain away whatever they could not explain. As Lawrence Lipking shrewdly remarks, "Those who know the delights of reading Johnson have often seemed to be engaged in a perpetual rescue operation, saving him from the prejudices of his enemies and himself, and from their own possessive affection."[3] In particular this has led to a concerted effort to establish theoretical bases for Johnson's literary views, and in some cases even an objective and self-consistent Johnsonian system. Such an approach reflects the tendency of post-Coleridgean criticism to examine itself and to formulate theories, and also the hope that Johnson's more notorious judgments, like the denunciation of *Lycidas*, can be explained or excused in the context of his larger assumptions.

A great deal of valuable discussion has resulted from this procedure, especially in the work of Jean H. Hagstrum and William R. Keast, but recent investigations have yielded diminishing returns. I wish to do something rather different: to look at what Johnson can tell us about actual authors and works, and beyond that about the relation between literature and life. In a way I am responding to an appeal made by Donald J. Greene twenty years ago: "Can we not have, at least to begin with, an analysis of Johnson's criticism that is simply an analysis of Johnson's criticism?"[4] I propose to study it not as formal poetics but as a way of reading: criticism as an act in which the reader shares, not as a body of doctrine and adjudications. I shall argue that Johnson's criticism has to be read in context, not as isolated insights or aesthetic principles; that the much-quoted *Rambler*s and the *Preface to Shakespeare*, where he is most theoretical, do not show him at his best; and that his finest achievement is a union of moral, biographical, and critical analysis in the *Lives of the Poets*.

In suggesting that Johnson has much to say about the relation between literature and life, I am aware that I refer to the very point at which he has been said to be weakest. A number of influential writers, in histories of criticism and elsewhere, have mounted sustained attacks on Johnson's critical position and have intimated strongly that he can be read today only as a

---

[3] *The Ordering of the Arts in Eighteenth-Century England* (Princeton, 1970), p. 406.
[4] Review of Hagstrum's *Samuel Johnson's Literary Criticism*, *Review of English Studies*, NS 5 (1954), 201.

historical curiosity. I wish to alter the battlefield and to show that his criticism taken as a whole suffers much less than might be supposed from the alleged inadequacy of his poetics. In spite of all objections it continues to live.

In large measure this is because Johnson distrusts abstract theory: the contradictions in his general pronouncements often reflect an admirable attempt to be honest about his real impressions of literary works. He instructs the reader both in his proper humility—he is carried away by a great author, he is *interested*—and in his proper pride—he should always be willing to express his true feelings, to admit that he is confused or offended or simply bored. Criticism in our own era, though not so obviously moralistic as Johnson's, often seems to stress instruction at the expense of delight, for it implies that anything complex (or organically unified, or whatever) is by definition worth reading, and that if it fails to give delight the reader must take the blame. Modern criticism has also tended to separate moral issues from critical ones, or to claim to deduce the adequacy of a poet's moral vision from the quality of his imaginative gifts, and has obscured important matters which Johnson makes us face directly, even if we disagree with his conclusions.

It may be thought that more should have been said about Johnson's relations to English and Continental criticism in the eighteenth century. I have preferred not to do this for two reasons. There are already many histories of criticism that survey Johnson (not always fairly) from wider perspectives. And it could furthermore be shown that he was indifferent or hostile to most of the prevailing interests of critics in his time. Genre theory plays only a negative part in his analysis of literary works; he does not have much to say about the nature of artistic creation; connections between the various arts do not occur to him at all. While he does respond to other critics on specific points, as we shall often notice, many of his contemporaries regarded him as old fashioned. What fascinated Johnson was literary history: not the internal dynamics of form, but the successive performances of a host of human beings. Even his (very traditional) technical interests are subsumed in this. What sort of mind could adapt the classical epic to justify the ways of God to men? How is the heroic couplet a fitting expression of Dryden's or Pope's powers? What unlucky choices and emphases underlie Gray's odes?

I must emphasize as well that I do not attempt a complete survey of Johnson's criticism, which would only be to do again what others have done well. In the first chapters I address a series of topics that have excited controversy and try to make a case for Johnson's continuing usefulness. In the final chapters I consider in detail the special excellence of the *Lives of the Poets*. In thus emphasizing Johnson's usefulness, I have naturally sought to evaluate as well as to describe. While I am far from imagining that modern criticism has all the answers—my theme, indeed, is that it can learn much from Johnson—I believe that we cannot really appreciate his value if we shy away from value judgments and quarantine him with Dennis and Hurd and the Wartons in the safe precincts of "eighteenth-century criticism." And perhaps I ought to state frankly my opposition to the scholarly tendency to impose ambitious theoretical structures on the literature of the past, meanwhile demanding that the reader abdicate his natural tendency to make judgments of value. The attempt to understand the past in its own terms is essential; for that reason I have quoted comments by Johnson's contemporaries whenever they seemed useful. But the historical approach must be a starting point and not a conclusion, unless one accepts the proposition that the reader must become a scholar for whom everything in the past has equal importance. On his own terms Rymer is a great critic; Akenside, on his own terms, is a great poet. To the degree that this book has a polemical bias, it is in praising Johnson's resistance to abstract theory and his attempt to unite the critic and scholar with the common reader. The writer I most often invoke for comparison is not one of Johnson's contemporaries, but Coleridge—the next really great English critic, who sought to define an aesthetic radically different from Johnson's, but agreed with him at many points and continued to ask many of the same questions.

Perhaps I should say something further in defense of my procedure, more familiar in history or philosophy than in literary study, of criticizing the views of modern writers who have dealt with Johnson. A study of imaginative literature may well aspire to win assent by the simple force of its own arguments: its subject is the poems or plays or novels, not the interpretations that other people have given them. But to study a critic is to enter a debate on the nature and value of criticism, and Johnson has received close attention from influential critics whose views seem to call for—in his own phrase—rational opposition. While Johnsonians have been adjusting the details of his opinions, more general writers have tended to dismiss him to the disused chambers of literary paleontology. His criticism was not written, if any criticism ever is, to furnish a chapter in the history of ideas. It was written to tell the truth about poets and poems. In emphasizing its *uses* I want to throw light on the ways in which Johnson still speaks to us as a living voice, and to show that his faults, though real, are not crucial obstacles to his continuing greatness.

1   *The Limitations of Theory*

IT IS . . .THE TASK OF CRITICISM," Johnson declares in *Rambler* 92, "to establish principles; . . .criticism reduces those regions of literature under the dominion of science, which have hitherto known only the anarchy of ignorance, the caprices of fancy, and the tyranny of prescription" (IV, 122). Almost three decades later we find him still using the same language: "Dryden may be properly considered as the father of English criticism, as the writer who first taught us to determine upon principles the merit of composition" (*Life of Dryden*, I, 410). Dryden himself shared this view. "Having thus shewn that imitation pleases," he wrote in a late essay, "and why it pleases in both these arts   [poetry and painting], it follows that some rules of imitation are necessary to obtain the end; for without rules there can be no art, any more than there can be a house without a door to conduct you into it."[1]

In the days when "neoclassicism" was thought to be a monolith, these remarks were easily interpreted as expressions of what was sometimes called "the neoclassical creed." Johnson's "principles" and Dryden's "rules" were simply two versions of the same thing, in further illustration of which one could expect to be told a good deal about Rymer and Dennis and to hear several couplets quoted from Pope's *Essay on Criticism*: "Those RULES of old *discover'd,* not *devis'd,* / Are *Nature* still, but *Nature Methodiz'd*" (ll. 88-89).

More recently we have begun to notice that writers and readers in the eighteenth century, as in any other, resist our natural impulse to categorize them. Pope may have written earnestly about the rules in his youthful attempt at critical syncretism, but it is hard to see that he followed them much in his later poems or that he felt great respect for the pigmy rules-critics who clog the footnotes of the *Dunciad*. He certainly went on believing in principles of a general sort, just as Dryden did, whom Robert D.

[1] *Parallel of Poetry and Painting* (1695), in *Of Dramatic Poesy and Other Critical Essays*, ed. George Watson (London, 1962), II, 194.

Hume properly calls a critical absolutist who "believes in, looks for, and works from what he regards as unchanging standards."[2] But as Hume shows in detail, what is unchanging in Dryden is a theory of imitation, not a series of prescriptive rules by which poems can be composed. Indeed Dryden, like Eliot, is a type of the critic who asks and answers his questions under the pressure of an ongoing poetic career.

As the immutability and authority of "the rules" came to be questioned, Johnson's remarks about "principles" were explained rather differently. In an important and deservedly influential essay William R. Keast sought to define "The Theoretical Foundations of Johnson's Criticism"[3]—the underlying structure, like bedrock beneath a landscape, that could be deduced from his deliberately untheoretical critical writings. Investigations of this kind have produced valuable results, but they have emphasized certain aspects of Johnson's criticism at the expense of others and in some respects have made it appear less impressive than it really is. For this Johnson himself is partly to blame, since he made a large number of general pronouncements—particularly in the *Rambler*—that seem ideally suited to the definition of his tacit critical system. Such a codification, as I shall argue presently, does him a disservice; and it can be shown in addition that his own theoretical statements define the limits of criticism in a highly skeptical manner.

We need furthermore to distinguish, not merely between Johnson's theory and practice, but between his statements about theory and the theories themselves. We do not always remember that a critic—or even a systematic aesthetician, which Johnson was not—may make claims for his theories that do not correspond to his actual results. No one could *want* principles more than Johnson does, or speak more ardently about his intention to develop them. But this is a psychological fact; it describes what Johnson wishes criticism were rather than what he finds it capable of being. For as soon as he takes up any specific topic, his fundamental common sense and honesty prevail: he becomes irritated (sometimes enraged) at the pretensions of earlier

[2]*Dryden's Criticism* (Ithaca, N.Y., 1970), p. 229.
[3]In *Critics and Criticism,* ed. R. S. Crane (Chicago, 1952), pp. 389-407.

theorists and proceeds to trample their shapely systems. It would not be right to say that he deliberately sets out to demolish principles or to reduce them to the narrowest possible compass, yet again and again that is exactly what happens.

With this in mind I should like to return to the quotation from *Rambler* 92 that opened the chapter and to consider it in its context. "It has long been observed," Johnson begins, "that the idea of beauty is vague and undefined, different in different minds, and diversified by time or place"; and he goes on to approve Boileau's view that the best evidence of excellence is simply "the test of time."

It is, however, the task of criticism to establish principles; to improve opinion into knowledge; and to distinguish those means of pleasing which depend upon known causes and rational deduction, from the nameless and inexplicable elegancies which appeal wholly to the fancy, from which we feel delight, but know not how they produce it, and which may well be termed the enchantresses of the soul. Criticism reduces those regions of literature under the dominion of science, which have hitherto known only the anarchy of ignorance, the caprices of fancy, and the tyranny of prescription.

This passage does sound impressive, but it is subject to several qualifications. First, it is not obvious that Johnson means to be dismissive about "the enchantresses of the soul"; as I shall try to show in discussing the common reader, he had an unusually active sense of this aspect of literature. Moreover, critical "science" is opposed not only to ignorance and fancy but also to "the tyranny of prescription"—that is to say, to most of the arbitrary positions of previous critics. And, finally, the passage introduces a discussion of nothing more general than onomatopoeia and is part of a larger sequence of papers (86, 88, 90, 92, 94) on the narrow topic of versification. Johnson is clearly saying that the reasons why poetry pleases must probably remain obscure—Boileau's test of time measures results, not causes—but that we can at least hope to be more precise in the analysis of metrical harmony and the dubious claims of sound echoing sense.

This is cautious and moderate, yet it is Johnson at his most theoretical. As I have argued elsewhere, the program of the *Rambler* as a whole is to teach the reader to think critically, whether about literature or society or (most frequently) morality.[4] The last thing Johnson means to do is to replace prescriptive criticism with a comprehensive theory of his own. Rather than elaborating a theory of literature, these papers effectively cancel out most of the questions—since they are shown to have no useful answers—that theory is ordinarily concerned with.

To be sure, this pruning operation is intended to get results, with "complications analised into principles, and knowledge disentangled from opinion" (*Rambler* 156). Critical rules are very helpful if carefully managed: "The eye of the intellect, like that of the body, is not equally perfect in all, nor equally adapted in any to all objects; the end of criticism is to supply its defects; rules are the instruments of mental vision, which may indeed assist our faculties when properly used, but produce confusion and obscurity by unskilful application" (*Rambler* 176, V, 166-67). The crux, then, is the scope that Johnson will allow to proper use; and whenever his general pronouncements are examined in context, they will be found to have a very limited function. Criticism, he says in the final *Rambler* (No. 208), "is only to be ranked among the subordinate and instrumental arts." In this subordinate role he has done his best to be precise: "Arbitrary decision and general exclamation I have carefully avoided, by asserting nothing without a reason, and establishing all my principles of judgment on unalterable and evident truth" (V, 319). Taken simply as assertion, this is unexceptionable, and also vague enough to apply to anything; it could easily be endorsed by Rymer or Voltaire. Taken in the context of the *Rambler*s as a whole, it means refusing to state principles that are not logically demonstrable *even though* this means giving up the hope of theorizing about most of what matters in literature. In teaching the reader to think critically, Johnson is teaching him to distrust theory, not to make it.

Thus the account already quoted of "complications analised into principles" introduces a carefully limited defense of tragicomedy. Every principle Johnson puts forward depends on logic and only on logic. He scoffs at the rule that there should be no more than five acts, but defines "act" so narrowly as to mean nothing more by it than "scene": "An act is only the representation of such a part of the business of the play as proceeds in an

[4]"Johnson's Manner of Proceeding in the *Rambler*," *ELH*, 40 (1973), 70-89.

unbroken tenor, or without any intermediate pause . . . Whenever the scene is shifted the act ceases, since some time is necessarily supposed to elapse while the personages of the drama change their place" (*Rambler* 156, V, 68). This is only to say that a play may have any number of scenes (or acts), without trying to make sense of the common idea that an act is somehow a unit of structural or psychological importance. "There are other rules more fixed and obligatory, " Johnson says a little later, and explains himself again on purely logical grounds: "It is necessary that of every play the chief action should be single; for since a play represents some transaction, through its regular maturation to its final event, two actions equally important must evidently constitute two plays" (p. 69). This kind of reductionism is all very well for abstract theory, but when Johnson deals with actual works he knows that the bigger questions have to be faced: a play *can* have any number of "acts," but is it right that *Antony and Cleopatra* has so many? Two actions constitute two plays, but can the double plot in *King Lear* be set aside simply by calling it double? In cases like these Johnson knows perfectly well that he is straying, as he must, from the certainties to which critical theory aspires: if they are indeed certain, then they must be very simple indeed. As for tragicomedy, Johnson's conclusion is that Shakespeare was so good at it that he has made it seem natural, but that writers of lesser genius may find it works badly. We can say with certainty that a play may contain many "acts" but only one action; we cannot say with certainty that tragicomedy is or is not excellent.

In *Rambler* 158 Johnson dismantles and rejects two more "rules." The first, rather strangely, is actually a rule in favor of disconnected writing in the lyric and in essays (presumably those of Montaigne); it is dismissed not because it is mistaken on structural grounds but because it subverts "the great prerogative of man," which is "to proceed from one truth to another, and connect distant propositions by regular consequences" (V, 78). That is, this rule in favor of misrule is not so much inappropriate to art—Johnson might not despise every poem that followed its assumptions—as it is a disservice to human nature. The principle is moral as much as aesthetic. Johnson then goes on to dismiss another rule of the more usual kind, a foolish prescription for the opening lines of epic poems, and to replace it with simple common sense: "The intent of the introduction is to raise expectation, and suspend it; something therefore must be discovered, and something concealed" (p. 80).

To give a final example, *Rambler* 125 takes the view that there are an indefinite number of kinds of comedy and that even inductive definitions have little value since "every new genius produces some innovation, which, when invented and approved, subverts the rules which the practice of foregoing authors had established." Johnson distrusts theories of genre for precisely this reason, that they oversimplify reality. So he defines comedy simply by its "effects upon the mind," and finds that its only universal characteristic is in being "such a dramatic representation of human life, as may excite mirth." This is so vague a definition as to preclude theoretical minuteness, but Johnson sees little point in more elegant theories that produce "absurdities," not just in criticism but also in actual plays, whose authors have been misled by the theory that comic characters are low into assuming that only low characters are comic. Thus we are shown Dryden writing a scene in *Aureng-Zebe* in which "every circumstance concurs to turn tragedy to farce" and which is "sufficient to awaken the most torpid risibility." The critic may abandon the ambition of defining comedy in elaborate detail, but in practice he sees well enough that Dryden's scene is comic.

The other critical *Ramblers* mostly treat general topics, often marginal literary forms like biography (No. 60) or letter writing (No. 152), where as no rules exist Johnson is willing to hazard some. When he examines a specific work, *Samson Agonistes*, the point is to show that it doesn't measure up to the simple requirement that a drama have a beginning, middle, and end (No. 139).[5] The most dogmatic of the literary *Ramblers*, No. 4 on the novel, develops along purely moral lines. And what one remembers most clearly from the *Rambler* is not "principles," but rather the frequent discussion—looking forward to the *Lives*—of the role of the writer, his hopes, anxieties, and disappointments. Many papers (Nos. 137 and 154, for example) deal with aspects of

[5]Johnson makes a great point of following Aristotle here, but it seems likely that he does so mainly for tactical reasons. Elsewhere he shows little veneration for Aristotle's authority.

learning and the ambitions of "the heroes in literature," with obvious relevance to the project of the *Dictionary*, in which Johnson was then engaged.

The whole issue of criticism in the *Rambler* may be seen finally as an attempt to assert its proper dignity by teaching it to moderate its claims. There was plenty of prejudice in the eighteenth century against critics as pedantic quibblers. The definitions of "critick" in the *Dictionary* nicely discriminate the two aspects:

1. A man skilled in the art of judging of literature; a man able to distinguish the faults and beauties of writing.
2. A censurer; a man apt to find fault.

Critics are afflicted like other men with "the treachery of the human heart" (*Rambler* 93) and are always in danger of judging shortsightedly and maliciously, of becoming snarlers instead of judicious examiners. At the very start of the series, in *Rambler* 3, Johnson offered a wry allegory of the decay of criticism. It begins in ideal splendor: "Criticism . . .was the eldest daughter of Labour and of Truth: she was, at her birth, committed to the care of Justice, and brought up by her in the palace of Wisdom" (III, 16) —an edifice not, in Johnson's view, to be approached by the road of excess. But the sequel is that Criticism learns to despair of accurate judgment, breaks her scepter, and abandons the field to the slow but conclusive decisions of Time.

Johnson's resistance to theory is further illustrated by his indifference to the ambitious program of the (mostly Scottish) psychologizing aestheticians. On the face of it their inquiry might have been expected to appeal to him: if all knowledge is derived from the senses and if Lockean epistemology offers a comprehensive insight into the human mind, then this new kind of scientific psychology ought to explain exactly how and why works of art give pleasure. Abandoning the old, more or less Aristotelian ways of describing the structure of literary works, these writers tried to show how literary works correspond to the structure of the mind. Lord Kames introduces thus his massive *Elements of Criticism*: "The man who aspires to be a critic in these arts must . . . acquire a clear perception of what objects are lofty, what low, what proper or improper, what manly, and what mean or trivial. Hence a foundation for reasoning upon the taste of any individual, and for passing sentence upon it: where it is conformable to principles, we can pronounce with certainty that it is correct; otherwise, that it is incorrect, and perhaps whimsical. Thus the fine arts, like morals, become a rational science; and, like morals, may be cultivated to a high degree of refinement."Curiously, the method, though strenuously empirical in its analysis of mind, is dogmatically antiempirical in its virtual rejection of literature as evidence for analysis.

Bossu, a celebrated French critic, gives many rules; but can discover no better foundation for any of them, than the practice merely of Homer and Virgil, supported by the authority of Aristotle: Strange! that in so long a work, he should never once have stumbled upon the question, Whether, and how far, do these rules agree with human nature? It could not surely be his opinion, that these poets, however eminent for genius, were entitled to give law to mankind; and that nothing now remains, but blind obedience to their arbitrary will: If in writing they followed no rule, why should they be imitated? If they studied nature, and were obsequious to rational principles, why should these be concealed from us?

Johnson always denounced blind obedience to authority, but he was much less optimistic than Kames about the comprehensiveness of the "rational principles" that were likely to be discovered. As he remarked to Boswell (in a passage somewhat softened in the *Life of Johnson*), "Lord Kames's *Elements* is a pretty essay and deserves to be held in some estimation, though it is chimerical."[6]

One obvious weakness of Kames's kind of study is its resistance to mere literature; passages are quoted in abundance, but always to support a preconceived theory. Kames's cousin David Hume, though himself interested in similar matters in "Of Tragedy" and "Of the Standard of Taste," had warned twenty years earlier of the dangers of critical abstraction. Hume points out that Fontenelle's essay on pastoral is full of fine generalities that could have been composed by Virgil himself, but that Fontenelle's own poems show how inadequate his understanding of pastoral really was. "No criticism can be instructive," Hume con-

---

[6] Henry Home, Lord Kames, Introduction, *Elements of Criticism* (Edinburgh, 1762; 9th ed., 1817), I, 6, 11-12. I quote from Boswell's *London Journal*, ed. F.A. Pottle (New York, 1950), p. 261. Thirty years later in the *Life of Johnson* Boswell altered "it is chimerical" to "much of it is chimerical" (I, 394).

tinues, "which descends not to particulars, and is not full of examples and illustrations. It is allowed on all hands, that beauty, as well as virtue, always lies in a medium; but where this medium is placed is a great question, and can never be sufficiently explained by general reasonings."[7]

Jean H. Hagstrum and later writers have fully demonstrated Johnson's commitment to a Lockean theory of mind, which pervades the *Rambler* and is implicit in the statement that in Shakespeare's time "speculation had not yet attempted to analyse the mind, to trace the passions to their sources, to unfold the seminal principles of vice and virtue, or sound the depths of the heart for the motives of action" (*Preface*, p. 88). But Johnson seems to have believed that what he accepted as an adequate theory of knowledge could not easily be extended to poetics. At any rate he was willing to recognize the vagrant, unpredictable, and extralogical quality of aesthetic response and to accept, as the Scottish thinkers would not, the force of *De gustibus non est disputandum*.

The significance of this position deserves to be emphasized, since it leaves Johnson open to many difficulties that a more absolutist theory would avoid or at least evade. It might appear that he has abandoned himself to all the paradoxes implicit in the *je ne sais quoi* or the "grace beyond the reach of art." But it is really these formulations that are at fault rather than the thing they describe, for it may equally be urged that Johnson deliberately remains open to the great realm of uncertainty in art, whereas other writers try to minimize it by dismissive phrases like *je ne sais quoi*.

Let us return to the statement that "Dryden may be properly considered as the father of English criticism, as the writer who first taught us to determine upon principles the merit of composition" (*Life of Dryden*, I, 410). What exactly does this mean? And how is it to be reconciled with the attack almost at the same time on "the cant of those who judge by principles rather than perception" (*Life of Pope*, III, 248)? Again we have to see that all "principles" are not of equal magnitude or authority. In the

---

[7]"Of Simplicity and Refinement in Writing" (1742), in *Of the Standard of Taste and Other Essays*, ed. John W. Lenz (New York, 1965), p. 45.

latter case Johnson has in mind the narrow and rather silly "principle" that a poet could somehow be too uniformly musical. In the case of Dryden he means, I think, that we are shown (as in the *Rambler*) how to seek truth for ourselves. This is the burden of the comparison between Dryden and the doctrinaire Rymer: "With Dryden we are wandering in quest of Truth, whom we find, if we find her at all, drest in the graces of elegance; and if we miss her, the labour of the pursuit rewards itself: we are led only through fragrance and flowers. Rymer, without taking a nearer, takes a rougher way; every step is to be made through thorns and brambles, and Truth, if we meet her, appears repulsive by her mien and ungraceful by her habit. Dryden's criticism has the majesty of a queen; Rymer's has the ferocity of a tyrant" (*Life of Dryden*, I, 413).

To be sure, Johnson pays particular tribute to Dryden's generalizations: "In his general precepts, which depend upon the nature of things and the structure of the human mind, he may doubtless be safely recommended to the confidence of the reader; but his occasional and particular positions were sometimes interested, sometimes negligent, and sometimes capricious" (I, 413). This seems essentially an admission of what cannot be denied, that Dryden is often motivated by self-interest and prejudice and is frequently hasty and careless; as Johnson says elsewhere, "To the critical sentence of Dryden the highest reverence would be due, were not his decisions often precipitate and his opinions immature" (*Life of Butler*, I, 217). But we expect more of a critic than general "precepts," which we are somehow better able to apply than he is. As the contrast with Rymer suggests, Dryden teaches by example a mode of civilized, rational thought about literature that springs from specific problems and pretends to no immutable verity.

In the end what Dryden or any other critic does is to persuade us into agreement—whether with general "principles" or specific opinions—by contagion rather than proof. Here is where Johnson parts company with the Scottish aestheticians and with many modern theorists: he would *like* to achieve certainty just as much as they, and is eager to make criticism as clear and accurate as possible, but he knows the limits of this aspiration. "In all the parts of human knowledge," he says at the

beginning of *Taxation No Tyranny*, "whether terminating in science merely speculative, or operating upon life, private or civil,
are admitted some fundamental principles, or common axioms,
which, being generally received, are little doubted, and, being
little doubted, have been rarely proved." Yet it does not follow
that proof is therefore desirable, much less possible. "It is difficult to prove the principles of science; because notions cannot
always be found more intelligible than those which are questioned. It is difficult to prove the principles of practice, because
they have, for the most part, not been discovered by investigation, but obtruded by experience; and the demonstrator will
find, after an operose deduction, that he has been trying to make
that seen, which can be only felt" (1825 *Works*, VI, 224-25). This
account of politics applies perfectly to Johnson's view of literature. Those quasi-scientific principles that perhaps do exist have
the status of unprovable axioms, and the rest—which is surely
the main part of literature as we actually experience it—simply
has to be felt.

But if Johnson entertained so modest a view of the possibilities
of aesthetics, it need not follow that it is idle to define the terms of
his own criticism. Here we must distinguish between assumptions and system; it is only when Johnson's ideas are organized
into a solid structure that they lose their flexibility and scope.
Indeed such principles as do occur throughout his criticism are
so general that they hardly serve to distinguish him from other,
very different critics. The relation between the natural and the
new, for instance, is one of his favorite topics. "In this poem
there is no nature, for there is no truth; there is no art, for there
is nothing new" (*Life of Milton*, I, 163). The difficulty is that the
same formulation can be found in many other critics. Hume
writes in 1742: "Fine writing, according to Mr. Addison, consists
of sentiments which are natural, without being obvious. There
cannot be a juster and more concise definition of fine writing.
Sentiments, which are merely natural, affect not the mind with
any pleasure, and seem not worthy of our attention. . . .On the
other hand, productions which are merely surprising, without
being natural, can never give any lasting entertainment to the
mind." Or, again, we find Coleridge saying that "genius produces the strongest impressions of novelty, while it rescues the

most admitted truths from the impotence caused by the very circumstance of their universal admission." In planning *Lyrical Ballads*, Coleridge says, he and Wordsworth often discussed "the two cardinal points of poetry, the power of exciting the sympathy of the reader by a faithful adherence to the truth of nature, and the power of giving the interest of novelty by the modifying colours of imagination."[8]

Here, then, is a principle that really exists in Johnson's criticism—art must be both natural and new—but is so general as to tell us little about the system it is supposed to underlie. There are, of course, important differences in the ways that Addison, Hume, Johnson, and Coleridge use these terms; but they remain instances of conventional language whose specific meaning can only be explained by means of other terms, and by referring them to the whole of the critic's work. It follows that while they may be important to Johnson, they point to what he holds (at least partially) in common with other critics, rather than to what is distinctive in him.

A more serious objection to systematizing Johnson's thought is that the more precise the system becomes, the more it distorts or leaves out matters of great importance to him. A useful aspect of Keast's essay, for example, is its analysis of Johnson in terms of a fourfold scheme of author, work, nature, and audience. It is quite true that Johnson tends to emphasize two of these terms, author and audience, and to see a literary work as a means of communication between them rather than as a self-contained artifact. It is also true, as Keast suggests, that Johnson lacks any developed theory of genre. But he is bored with genre, not just because it is inadequate to the multifariousness of nature—the

---

[8]Hume, "Of Simplicity and Refinement in Writing," pp. 43, 44; Coleridge, *Biographia*, Ch. 4, I, 60; Ch. 14, II, 5. Hume has in mind the following passage from *Spectator* 345, in which Addison alludes to Adam's account of his feelings immediately after his creation: "These and the like wonderful Incidents, in this Part of the Work, have in them all the Beauties of Novelty, at the same time that they have all the Graces of Nature. They are such as none but a great Genius could have thought of, though, upon the perusal of them, they seem to rise of themselves from the Subject of which he treats. In a Word, though they are natural they are not obvious, which is the true Character of all fine Writing." Hagstrum discusses these passages in *Samuel Johnson's Literary Criticism* (Minneapolis, 1952), Ch. 8.

conclusion that emerges irresistibly from the fourfold
scheme—but because it is inadequate also to the multifariousness of literary works.

Thus although Johnson has a developed idea of the essential
Alexander Pope, he is also able to think clearly and critically
about individual poems. The *Essay on Man* is very different from
the *Dunciad*, and both from the *Rape of the Lock*; Johnson discriminates them with great clarity. This may seem obvious; yet
some modern commentators are much likelier than Johnson to
merge all of Pope's works, for example seeing the whole corpus
as reflecting "key" ideas in the *Essay on Criticism* or the *Essay on
Man*. While in some sense they may be right, they tend to forget
the ways—as Johnson does not—in which these are seriously
limited and perhaps even unsatisfactory *poems*. The point, then,
is that a preoccupation with the author can easily coexist in
Johnson with an interest in the uniqueness of individual poems,
refusing, indeed, to submerge the poems in collective generic or
thematic definitions. But a general theory of Johnson's criticism
tends to make us forget how flexible it can be.

I have not meant to suggest that Keast's argument is mistaken,
but rather that it is incomplete in ways that are determined by the
nature of its approach. What Keast has really discovered is a set
of theoretical *implications* of Johnson's criticism—assumptions
that help him to take hold of a topic or a literary work—rather
than *foundations* which represent his most important ideas and
without which the superstructure of analysis of specific works
would collapse. Another illustration may help to show how an
emphasis on theory, even when Johnson himself seems to invite
it, can get in the way of understanding what he has to say. Allen
Tate sets up his essay "Johnson on the Metaphysical Poets" by
discussing what Johnson considers the proper function of
metaphor: "I believe it is fair to say that Johnson liked his tenors
straight, without any nonsense from the vehicles." Although the
Life of Cowley abounds in specific examples, Tate concentrates so
much on Johnson's general pronouncements that he quotes only
one of them. This is a stanza from Cowley's "Of Wit," which
elicits Johnson's remark "Of all the passages in which poets have
exemplified their own precepts, none will easily be found of
greater excellence than that in which Cowley condemns exuber-

ance of Wit" (*Lives*, I, 36). After quoting the last four lines of the stanza—

> Several lights will not be seen,
> If there be nothing else between.
> Men doubt, because they stand so thick i'
>   th' sky,
> If those be stars which paint the galaxy.

—Tate declares, "If this does not exhibit the excess of conceit against which it was written, then one has wasted one's life in the concern for poetry (a possibility that must always be kept in view); but short of facing such a crisis one must regretfully impute to Johnson a lapse of judgment at a moment when his prejudice is flattered."[9] In other words, Johnson normally has no use for metaphysical wit, but condones its use here merely because he thinks Cowley is agreeing with him and fails to notice the way in which he does it.

It is hard to see the force of this interpretation. On the face of it Johnson is simply saying that Cowley's lines contain a successful image, one that does not much resemble Donne's "stiff twin compasses," Cowley's "A Lover's heart, a hand grenado" (*Cowley*, p. 30), or the other conceits that he holds up for derision. Tate could only arrive at his view by seeing Johnson in the light of a theory, in this instance a theory of metaphor that he has deduced from a notoriously odd remark about the "Though deep, yet clear" metaphor in the *Life of Denham*.[10] It would not be easy to develop a consistent, let alone a convincing, theory of metaphor in Johnson. When he wishes to abuse a poem (as we shall observe in a later chapter) he is fond of pretending that he can scarcely recognize a metaphor when he sees one. But if he sometimes writes, as he does about Denham's lines, as if the vehicle should have no existence independent of the tenor, at

[9]"Johnson on the Metaphysical Poets," *Collected Essays* (1949), rpt. in Donald J. Greene, ed. *Samuel Johnson: A Collection of Critical Essays* (Englewood Cliffs, N.J., 1965), pp. 91, 96.

[10]"The lines are in themselves not perfect, for most of the words thus artfully opposed are to be understood simply on one side of the comparison, and metaphorically on the other; and if there be any language which does not express intellectual operations by material images, into that language they cannot be translated" (*Life of Denham*, I, 78). This subject will be treated more fully in chapter 6, pp. 151 ff.

other times he expresses an equal distaste for vehicles that merge too completely in their tenors. "As a king would be lamented, Eleonora was lamented. . . . This is little better than to say in praise of a shrub that it is as green as a tree, or of a brook, that it waters a garden as a river waters a country" (*Life of Dryden*, I, 441).

Thus although Tate analyzes the Denham passage with great penetration, his analysis creates unnecessary difficulties if one wants simply to understand what Johnson thought was good and bad in metaphysical poems. Cowley's lines on wit are ingenious, but not *merely* ingenious, as the metaphor of the heart as hand grenade may be said to be. What irritates Johnson in these poets is that "in forming descriptions they looked out not for images, but for conceits" (*Life of Cowley*, I, 33). They force dissimilar ideas together; they *think* too much; they are like poetical Walter Shandies, forever overheating their brains with elaborate, useless intellectual energy. Another stanza of Cowley's "Of Wit" (the eighth) deserves particular notice:

> In a true piece of *Wit* all things must be,
>   Yet all things there *agree*.
> As in the *Ark*, joyn'd without force or strife,
> All *Creatures* dwelt; all *Creatures* that had *Life*.
>   Or as the *Primitive Forms* of all
>   (If we compare great things with small)
> Which without *Discord* or *Confusion* lie,
> In that strange *Mirror* of the *Deitie*.

Here is *concors* without *discordia*. If anything, Johnson's famous definition of wit countenances a more extreme dislocation of thought than Cowley's does.[11]

To approach Johnson in this way is no longer to ask whether he has an adequate theory of metaphor, or even whether he is fair to Cowley and Donne. It is rather to ask whether the defect he identifies in them is not worth our careful reflection, espe-

---

[11]"But Wit, abstracted from its effects upon the hearer, may be more rigorously and philosophically considered as a kind of *discordia concors*; a combination of dissimilar images, or discovery of occult resemblances in things apparently unlike" (*Life of Cowley*, p. 20).

cially as he supports his opinion with a series of shrewdly chosen quotations. As Helen Gardner observes,

Mr. Eliot spoke long ago of the blend of "levity and seriousness" in metaphysical poetry. This remains a brilliant brief description of its peculiar effect. We are avoiding its true seriousness and finding seriousness in its levity, if we concentrate upon the imagination's power to perceive analogies and neglect its primary power to apprehend and express what touches the mind and heart. Where this is lacking metaphysical poetry is tedious trifling, or, to use the language of its own age, the mere "itch of wit."[12]

That is a profoundly Johnsonian statement.

For Eliot and his followers, moreover, the metaphysical poets occupied the golden age before the Fall, located in the "dissociation of sensibility." They thought in images: Later poets could no longer unify thought and feeling, and their imagery was merely ornamental—in Frank Kermode's nice phrase, "the flower stuck in sand."[13] This of course sounds very much like Johnson's neoclassical position: language the dress of thought, poetry the means of conveying paraphrasable truth. Yet from Johnson's point of view it is precisely the metaphysicals whose imagery is ornamental, reflecting intellectual ingenuity rather than natural emotion. So it is not only that he sees what we see in the metaphysicals but values it differently. His discussion suggests also that his theoretical pronouncements, whether on metaphor or on language as the dress of thought, are more interesting and flexible in their practical application than theoretical summary would lead one to expect.

To locate and organize Johnson's principles, then, is not in the end the best way of getting at what he does best. The usual reason for his real or apparent self-contradictions is his admirable effort to respond fully to specific works, and to take account of elements in his response that may not agree with his response at other times to works that look similar. Consistency may be of the first importance for a philosopher, but it is not always a virtue

---

[12]*The Business of Criticism* (Oxford, 1959), p. 142.
[13]*Romantic Image* (London, 1961), p. 144. "The theory of the dissociation of sensibility is, in fact, the most successful version of a Symbolist attempt to explain why the modern world resists works of art that testify to the poet's special, anti-intellectual way of knowing truth" (p. 143).

in a critic. No one could be more consistent than Rymer. Whatever the adequacy of his explicit assumptions, Johnson constantly says interesting and valuable things about writers and works, sometimes because his active response as a reader transcends his explicit assumptions, at other times because he is responding to matters that lie near the outer edge of conventional literary criticism, notably the special relation between biography, moral judgment, and technical criticism that informs the *Lives of the Poets*. Insights like these depend on deducing implications from specific instances—authors' lives, or works, or both—and are therefore all but invisible to a general theoretical scheme.

I must emphasize as strongly as possible that I am not questioning the interest and importance of literary theory. Moreover, I fully appreciate that Johnson himself considered it interesting and important. My argument is simply that his theoretical discussions are not often his best and that his best criticism—thanks to his distrust of elaborate system—can be read with profit independently of the theories which it sometimes calls forth. A good test case is furnished by Johnson's most famous theoretical principle, the "grandeur of generality." Not only does he appeal to this principle at countless places in his writings, but he treats it in unusual detail in three separate set pieces: the tenth chapter of *Rasselas*, in which the poet is warned not to number the streaks of the tulip; the passage in the *Preface* in which Shakespeare's characters are said to represent species, not individuals; and the passage in the *Life of Cowley* that begins "Great thoughts are always general" (*Lives*, I, 21). What Johnson says so memorably can hardly be unimportant.

Of course it is important. No sensible reader could ignore it. But it does not follow that one should always *approach* Johnson's criticism from this direction, treating it as a long series of illustrations of the grandeur of generality. To put it differently, two questions may be usefully asked: What does Johnson mean by generality? and, What does he do with it when he is talking about specific literary works? The second question is surely the more fruitful in any attempt to *use* (rather than "place") Johnson's critical performance, but it is seldom asked.

If we pursue instead the first question, we enter one of the thorniest regions of eighteenth-century aesthetics. Clearly

Johnson's generality is a neoclassical principle, or, as William K. Wimsatt calls it, "the neo-classic universal." Must it not derive, then, from the mingled streams of classical philosophy, "an ambiguous junction of neo-Platonic largeness with the Aristotelian species"?[14] But to see it in this light, many scholars have thought, is to exaggerate Johnson's alleged love of abstraction, neglecting his Lockean epistemology that deduces the general from particulars and regards either as incomplete without the other.[15] If Johnson must be described in these terms, then it is true enough that he is a Lockean, not a Neoplatonist. But discussions that follow Locke confine themselves to the theory of knowledge and of mental images, elaborating the latter into a theory of poetry. So far as images go, Johnson certainly declares that "one of the great sources of poetical delight is description, or the power of presenting pictures to the mind" (*Life of Cowley*, I, 51), in contrast with Cowley's intellectualized conceits. But the discussion that follows shows that the "pictures" are not to be composed of much specific detail; and Johnson was not one of those critics who dwelt on the relationship of poetry and painting as sister arts. His friend the translator John Hoole recalled, "On the great defect of words to discriminate material objects, Dr. Johnson once observed to me, that no description, however accurately given, could impress any determinate idea of the different shapes of animals on the mind of one, who had never seen those animals. Hence it must be concluded, that the ap-

---

[14]W. K. Wimsatt, Jr., and Cleanth Brooks, *Literary Criticism: A Short History* (New York, 1964), Ch. 15, p. 333.

[15]As early as 1942 Arthur Friedman was making this point in a review of Wimsatt's *The Prose Style of Samuel Johnson*, in *Philological Quarterly*, 21 (1942), 211-13, and in a rejoinder to Wimsatt the following year, Vol. 22 (1943), 73-76. William R. Keast corroborated Friedman's position in a review of an article on generality and particularity by Scott Elledge, *Philological Quarterly*, 27 (1948), 130-32. Keast further documented his argument in "Johnson's Criticism of the Metaphysical Poets," *ELH*, 17 (1950), 59-70. The Lockean basis of Johnson's ideas was first expounded by Hagstrum in *Samuel Johnson's Literary Criticism* (1952) and was extended to embrace Johnson's moral thought in general by Robert Voitle, *Samuel Johnson the Moralist* (Cambridge, Mass., 1961), by Paul K. Alkon, *Samuel Johnson and Moral Discipline* (Evanston, Ill., 1967), and by Arieh Sachs, *Passionate Intelligence: Imagination and Reason in the Work of Samuel Johnson* Baltimore, 1967). Donald J. Greene gives a good restatement of the topic in *Samuel Johnson* (New York, 1970), pp. 200-205.

pearance of nature at large may be the province of poetry; but that the form of particular objects must belong to the painter."[16]

Even in the theory of mental images, then, Johnson emphasizes the general form rather than its source in specific sense impressions. And his criticism is that of a moralist rather than an epistemologist.[17] When he writes that "the most useful truths are always universal, and unconnected with accidents and customs" (*Idler* 66), he means exactly that: literary works that convey these truths may do so by means of vivid detail, or they may not, but in either case the truths themselves must remain clear and paraphrasable moral positions. Seen in this light, the balance between general and particular is heavily weighted toward the general. As Arieh Sachs says, "[The] association of unreason with the particular and of reason with the general is a cornerstone of Johnson's thought on many subjects."[18] However precise may be the particulars from which it is developed, the generality that rises above them is, for Johnson, the sign of a healthy mind.

What has happened here is that Johnson's admirers have tried to rescue him from the implications of a theory that contradicts post-Romantic aesthetics. But if Johnson refuses to be rescued, he need not be given up for lost. There is no need to trace his principle of generality back to its philosophical roots, tangled as those clearly are, for in fact it represents, *as theory*, a familiar commonplace that is by no means confined to dogmatic neoclassicism. Murray Krieger has pointed to a potential contradiction in the *Preface*, in which Johnson seems at one time to endorse the existence of universals ("just representations of general nature") and at another to praise tragicomedy as reflecting a "chaos of mingled purposes and casualties."[19] But Johnson simply means

[16] Biographical Preface to John Scott (of Amwell), *Critical Essays of Some of the Poems of Several English Poets* (1785), p. liii.

[17] Hagstrum rightly says, "In attempting to understand what Johnson meant by generality, it is well for us to remember that, except only in the realm of the most basic and universal moral and psychological truth, he was usually Lockean and empirical" (p. 87). The exception is crucial: Johnson constantly applied moral standards to literature—as we shall often remark throughout this book—and his moral psychology owed at least as much to the classical moralists as it did to Locke.

[18] *Passionate Intelligence*, p. 72.

[19] "Fiction, Nature, and Literary Kinds in Johnson's Criticism of Shakespeare," *Eighteenth-Century Studies*, 4 (1971), 184-98.

that the general (and unchanging) principles of human experience must be deduced from the chaos of mingled purposes and casualties in which we normally meet them. This is what is meant in the successive statements that "in the writings of other poets a character is too often an individual; in those of Shakespeare it is commonly a species" (*Preface*, p. 62) and that "characters thus ample and general were not easily discriminated and preserved, yet perhaps no poet ever kept his personages more distinct from each other" (p. 64). Similar observations can be found even in Blake, the champion of minute particulars. "The characters of Chaucer's Pilgrims are the characters which compose all ages and nations: as one age falls, another rises, different to mortal sight, but to immortals only the same. . . . Accident ever varies, Substance can never suffer change or decay."[20] On a more mundane level, nobody would seriously admire a compulsive counter of tulip streaks, like Jane Austen's egregious Mr. Collins, who pointed out every view "with a minuteness which left beauty entirely behind. He could number the fields in every direction, and could tell how many trees there were in the most distant clump" (*Pride and Prejudice*, II, 5).

The real point about generality is its use, not its source. In James Beattie's poem *The Minstrel* (1771), a young enthusiastic poet learns from a kindly sage to seek "modest truth" instead of indulging "Imagination's lawless rage," but having received this Johnsonian lesson, he does not abandon the Muse. Instead,

> From Nature's beauties, variously compared
> And variously combined, he learns to frame
> Those forms of bright perfection,

which Beattie describes in a footnote as "General ideas of excellence, the immediate archetypes of sublime imitation, both in painting and in poetry."[21] The source of these general ideas is the mind's power of combining and comparing, though Beattie does not invoke Locke: "See Aristotle's Poetics," he adds, "and

[20]William Blake, *A Descriptive Catalogue* (1809), *Poetry and Prose*, p. 523.
[21]*The Minstrel*, II. 358, 400, 519-21. Johnson does not seem to have mentioned this poem, and might have been offended by its "Gothic" effects and Spenserian stanza; but he liked Beattie, often praised his *Essay on Truth* written against Hume, and wept when reading "The Hermit" (*Life*, IV, 186).

the Discourses of Sir Joshua Reynolds." At any rate, it is Aristotelian rather than Platonic. But what is achieved, what men are
able to use, is "archetypes" that body forth "forms of bright
perfection." Generality, narrowly understood, may be a
psychological conception; perfection is a moral one. As Reynolds
observes, in very Johnsonian language:

As the senses, in the lowest state of nature, are necessary to direct us to
our support, when that support is once secure there is danger in
following them further; to him who has no rule of action but the
gratification of the senses, plenty is always dangerous: it is therefore
necessary to the happiness of individuals, and still more necessary to
the security of society, that the mind should be elevated to the idea of
general beauty, and the contemplation of general truth. . . . Whatever
abstracts the thoughts from sensual gratifications, whatever teaches us
to look for happiness within ourselves, must advance in some measure
the dignity of our nature.

And however much this process may begin in the senses, it ends
in conceptions—Beattie's archetypes—that go beyond the
senses. "The beauty of which we are in quest," Reynolds continues, "is general and intellectual; it is an idea that subsists only
in the mind."[22]

   Thus far we have seen that Johnsonian generality is a familiar
attitude, neoclassical but not narrowly so, whose moral emphasis
has as much in common with classical models as it does with
scientific epistemology. If Johnson is unusual, it is not for the
intellectual terms in which he states the principle, but rather for
the emotional urgency with which he seeks and practices it. In
trying to understand Johnson, we will do well, therefore, to
consider the implications of his practice. By whatever theory he
may have defined imagery as "pictures to the mind," he responded strongly to poetry almost wholly without imagery so
long as it appealed to his sense of truth. According to Mrs.
Thrale, "he was more strongly and more violently affected by the

----

[22]*Discourses*, No. 9, pp. 142-43. Reynolds clearly echoes Johnson's sentence in
the *Journey to the Western Islands*: "Whatever withdraws us from the power of our
senses; whatever makes the past, the distant, or the future predominate over
the present, advances us in the dignity of thinking beings" (Yale *Works*, IX,
148). But Johnson is talking about the piety that will "grow warmer among the
ruins of Iona," not about ideal beauty.

force of words representing ideas capable of affecting him at all, than any other man in the world I believe; and when he would try to repeat the celebrated *Prosa Ecclesiastica pro Mortuis*, as it is called, beginning *Dies irae, Dies illa*, he could never pass the stanza ending thus, *Tantus labor non sit cassus*, without bursting into a flood of tears."[23]

In Johnson's own poems the tendency to abstraction is a striking feature, all the way from *Irene*—where it occurs to a quite phenomenal degree—to the end of his life. Consider the opening lines of a translation written just before he died: "The snow dissolv'd no more is seen, / The fields, and woods, behold, are green" (Yale *Works*, VI, 343). The equivalent lines in Horace are not unusually particularized, and yet are more so than Johnson's: "Diffugere nives, redeunt jam gramina campis, / Arboribusque comae . . ." (*Odes* IV.vii). Horace's "grass" and "leaves" (in the dead metaphor of "hair") convey a feeling of observed objects more clearly than Johnson's universalizing "are green," and Johnson's use of "behold" exactly parallels Pope's usage, which, as William Youngren has observed, contributes to a sense of static tableau.[24] Indeed, Johnson's instinct is usually for greater generality than Pope's, granting that Youngren is right and that both poets strive to be general and particular at once. Consider the fine lines

> His fall was destin'd to a barren strand,
> A petty fortress, and a dubious hand;
> He left the name, at which the world grew pale,
> To point a moral, or adorn a tale.
> [*Vanity of Human Wishes*, ll. 219-22]

[23]*Miscellanies*, I, 284. The passage in question touches a theme that was deeply significant to Johnson, and runs as follows: "Recordare, Jesu pie, / Quod sum causa tuae viae: / Ne me perdas illa die. / Quaerens me, sedisti lassus, / Redemisti crucem passus; / Tantus labor non sit cassus." "Remember, merciful Jesus, that I am the cause of thine incarnation. Cast me not away on that day. When seeking me, thou didst sit down weary. Thou didst redeem me when thou hadst endured the cross. Let not such labour be in vain" (trans. Frederick Brittain in *The Penguin Book of Latin Verse* [1962], p. 240).

[24]"Generality in Augustan Satire," in *In Defense of Reading*, ed. Reuben A. Brower and Richard Poirier (New York, 1962), p. 215. The theoretical basis for Youngren's analysis is further developed in "Generality, Science, and Poetic Language in the Restoration," *ELH*, 35 (1968), 158-87, arguing that Renaissance and Restoration critics thought of language as "getting more precise and vivid as it got more general" (p. 185).

Contrast with this a typical Popean account of ironic fate:

> In the worst inn's worst room, with mat half-hung,
> The floors of plaister, and the walls of dung,
> On once a flock-bed, but repair'd with straw,
> With tape-ty'd curtains, never meant to draw,
> The George and Garter dangling from that bed
> Where tawdry yellow strove with dirty red,
> Great Villiers lies—alas! how chang'd from him,
> That life of pleasure, and that soul of whim!

The final line could well be by Johnson, but hardly the first lines, of which Aldous Huxley has remarked, "A floor of dung would have seemed almost normal, acceptable. But *walls*—Ah, no, no!"[25]

Or, finally, consider the couplet which Johnson told Mrs. Thrale was his own favorite in his works:

> Th' incumber'd oar scarce leaves the dreaded coast
> Through purple billows and a floating host.
>   [*Vanity of Human Wishes*, ll. 239-40]

Apart from whatever private associations these lines may have had, Johnson must surely have been proud of the intellectualization of horror, in precisely the opposite mode from the Gothic program of specifying everything as vividly as possible, as in the "ropy slime" described in Blair's *Grave*. The oar is encumbered, but one is not at first told how. It moves through "purple billows," a nice Latinism that suggests decorative painting but also the possibility of something dreadful, water covered with blood (which in poetic usage was often purple). And finally the encumbrance is explained, "a floating host"—not thousands of individual dead bodies, as in Dryden's version of the original in Juvenal's tenth satire: "In a poor Skiff he pass'd the bloody Main,/Choak'd with the slaughter'd Bodies of his Train"—but rather a collective body, weltering on the waves which its blood discolors like an oil slick. Johnson presents a general image which the reader is to make vivid by the force of his own imagination, very much as in the *Rambler* he presents truths generalized

[25]*Epistle to Bathurst*, ll. 299-306; Huxley, *Texts and Pretexts* (London, 1933), p. 221.

from his experience which the reader should confirm by testing them against specific experiences of his own

In theory, then, Johnson's idea of generality is conventional enough, but in practice he demands it with emotional urgency. The theory has analogues in Aristotle and Beattie and Reynolds and Blake and Austen; the practice implies a sustained *level* of generality that Mrs. Thrale thought unique and is exceptionally abstract in comparison with Dryden or Pope. We may now return to the question, What does Johnson do with generality when he is talking about specific literary works? The answer is that no single conclusion is necessary or possible: we should listen to what he has to say in each case, and we cannot predict in advance that an obsession with the grandeur of generality will determine or vitiate what he says.

Consider, first of all, an example where the theory does seem to get in the way, the note on Edgar's Dover Cliff speech in *King Lear*:

The description is certainly not mean, but I am far from thinking it wrought to the utmost excellence of poetry. He that looks from a precipice finds himself assailed by one great and dreadful image of irresistible destruction. But this overwhelming idea is dissipated and enfeebled from the instant that the mind can restore itself to the observation of particulars, and diffuse its attention to distinct objects. The enumeration of the choughs and crows, the samphire-man and the fishers, counteracts the great effect of the prospect, as it peoples the desert of intermediate vacuity, and stops the mind in the rapidity of its descent through emptiness and horrour. [Yale *Works*, VIII, 695]

It has been suggested that this note, the tenor of which was repeated in a conversation with Garrick (*Life*, II, 87), expresses mainly a specific objection to the analytical "enumeration" of detail that destroys the intuitive force of an image.[26] It is also true that Johnson is here attempting, rather self-consciously perhaps, to take account of the Burkean sublime. But the note is offered as commentary on a famous passage in a famous play, and we ought not to forget that it has that purpose.

[26] See Lionel Basney, "'Lucidus Ordo': Johnson and Generality," *Eighteenth-Century Studies*, 5 (1971), 39-57.

Now, if we recollect the passage in question, what do we find?

> How fearful
> And dizzy 'tis to cast one's eyes so low!
> The crows and choughs that wing the midway air
> Show scarce so gross as beetles; half way down
> Hangs one that gathers sampire, dreadful trade!
> Methinks he seems no bigger than his head.
> The fishermen that walk upon the beach
> Appear like mice, and yond tall anchoring bark
> Diminish'd to her cock, her cock a buoy
> Almost too small for sight. The murmuring surge,
> That on th' unnumber'd idle pebble chafes,
> Cannot be heard so high. I'll look no more,
> Lest my brain turn, and the deficient sight
> Topple down headlong.
>
> [*King Lear* IV.vi.11-24]

One's first reaction is of renewed wonder at how excellent Shakespeare is, and then of disappointment that Johnson can respond to these lines as he does. The conclusion seems inescapable that, theory or no theory, he distorts the real effect of the passage, in which imagining the tiny figures below and straining to hear the inaudible surf *increases* our sense of "vacuity" and of the danger of "irresistible destruction." Also Johnson treats the passage as if it occurred in a narrative poem; he ignores the ironies implicit in the fact that an actor is describing this purely imaginary scene to a blind man who, when he does try to leap into the void, merely falls on the ground—which, of course, is not actually the ground, but the stage in a theater. When all is said and done, Johnson does demand generalized description here of a quite un-Shakespearean kind, of the sort exemplified in the passage in Congreve's *Mourning Bride* which he said was better than any in Shakespeare.[27]

But for a very different kind of example, consider Johnson's treatment (alluded to earlier) of passages in the metaphysical poets that fall short of the grandeur of generality. Johnson's point is not just that these writers like particulars but that they insist on pursuing thoughts "to their last ramifications," so that

---

[27]See the *Life*, II, 85, and the *Life of Congreve*, II, 229-30.

the reader forgets the tenor in examining the ingenuity of the vehicle. "The force of metaphors is lost when the mind by the mention of particulars is turned more upon the original than the secondary sense, more upon that from which the illustration is drawn than that to which it is applied" (*Life of Cowley*, I, 45). Johnson then offers "a very eminent example" in Cowley's ode *The Muse.*

> Let the *postilion* Nature mount, and let
> The *coachman* Art be set;
> And let the airy *footmen*, running all beside,
> Make a long row of goodly pride,
> Figures, conceits, raptures, and sentences,
> In a well-worded dress,
> And innocent loves, and pleasant truths, and useful lies,
> In all their gaudy *liveries*.

Far from reminding one of the condensed brilliance of Donne, these lines do indeed contain, as Johnson says, a tediously "scrupulous enumeration," a term that seemed misapplied to Shakespeare's lines but is wholly appropriate here. The metaphor is labored, and it is reductive: the idea of the coach and footmen is not so witty that it deserves to be spun out at such length.

Johnson next gives a second example, followed by a counterexample:

In the same ode, celebrating the power of the Muse, he gives her prescience or, in poetical language, the foresight of events hatching in futurity; but having once an egg in his mind he cannot forbear to shew us that he knows what an egg contains:

> Thou into the close nests of Time dost peep,
>   And there with piercing eye
> Through the firm shell and the thick white dost spy
>   Years to come a-forming lie,
> Close in their sacred fecundine asleep.

The same thought is more generally, and therefore more poetically, expressed by Casimir, a writer who has many of the beauties and faults of Cowley:

> Omnibus mundi Dominator horis
> Aptat urgendas per inane pennas,
> Pars adhuc nido latet, et futuros
>   Crescit in annos. [p. 46]

(The Polish poet's lines may be translated, "The ruler of the world in all seasons makes ready wings to be urged through the void; some are still concealed in the nest, and others are growing for future years.") One need not agree with Johnson's final evaluation of these examples, but it is at least reasonable, and the "firm shell" and "thick white" might not be very eagerly defended by modern admirers of the line of wit. Coleridge, comparing Casimir and Cowley as Latin poets, arrived at a distinction similar to Johnson's. Though Casimir shares in the subjectivity of the moderns, "his *style* and *diction* are really classical: while Cowley, who resembles Casimir in many respects, compleatly barbarizes *his* Latinity, and even his metre, by the heterogeneous nature of his thoughts" (*Biographia*, Ch. 24, II, 209 *n.*). Cowley never knows when to stop; just as he follows out an image until it becomes grotesque, so he muddles his would-be classical Latin with inappropriate language that expresses the heterogeneity of his ideas.

Principles are important, then, in Johnson's criticism, but the criticism itself may be disappointing (the Dover Cliff speech) or persuasive (the passages in Cowley) even when precisely the same principle is being invoked. The reason is that Johnson's criticism exists to illuminate works of literature, not to corroborate a system of aesthetics. C. B. Tinker, who has been attacked for his counsel against seeking a Johnsonian system, was careful to explain: "Nor is this an argument for that romantic and belated type of criticism known as 'impressionism.' Johnson had more to express than mere likes and dislikes. To conceive of his opinions as casual is to forget his scholarship and his long experience with literature as a force in men's lives."[28] Throughout his career Johnson tried to follow an ideal of openness and escape from systems of every kind, knowing that any system tends to falsify the complexity of reality. There is a close analogy with his friend Edmund Burke, whose early book on the sublime and beautiful shares some of the aggressive logic of the more theoretical *Rambler* papers, but who wrote at the end of his life, "Circumstances (which with some gentlemen pass for nothing)

[28]*Essays in Retrospect* (New Haven, 1948), p. 30. Tinker is put forward as a bad example at the beginning of Keast's "Theoretical Foundations."

give in reality to every political principle its distinguishing colour, and discriminating effect."[29] Modern attempts to make Burke a systematic political theorist have had the same ambiguous results as the theoretical study of Johnson's criticism.

It follows from this line of reasoning that the attempt to locate Johnson in the history of criticism, like the attempt to deduce his own special theory, is not the most useful way of coming at his achievement as a critic. If one must define his general position, it is essentially neoclassical. But Johnson differs from most neoclassical critics in two crucial respects. First, he doubted the formalist dream of reducing literature to order and, as we shall later see, was deeply suspicious of genre. In consequence he tended to take seriously the uniqueness of specific literary works, rather than measuring them against conventional standards. Second, he constantly emphasized the power of original genius, thus departing from an aesthetics that tended to stress limitation and exclusion, achieving order and unity by leaving things out.[30]

In his profound skepticism about theoretical systems, Johnson is massively individual, opposed not only to earlier neoclassical writers but to his Romantic successors as well. Coleridge deeply believed that "the end and purpose of all reason" was "unity and system" (*Biographia*, Ch. 12, I, 187). Like Johnson in the *Rambler* period, he sought to base his aesthetics on the nature of the human mind, but unlike Johnson he hoped to penetrate to the mysterious unconscious, rather than accepting a commonsense version of faculty psychology. "A system, the first principle of which it is to render the mind intuitive of the *spiritual* in man (i.e. of that which lies *on the other side* of our natural consciousness) must needs have a greater obscurity for those, who have never disciplined and strengthened this ulterior consciousness" (p. 168).

Coleridge's famous distinction between imagination and fancy, in Chapter 13 of the *Biographia*, is offered as a universal test against which all poetry can be measured. Johnson's treatment of wit in the *Life of Cowley* has a very different purpose. He

[29]*Reflections on the Revolution in France*, ed. Conor Cruise O'Brien (Harmondsworth, Penguin Books, 1968), p. 90.
[30]See Walter Jackson Bate, *The Burden of the Past and the English Poet* (Cambridge, Mass., 1970), esp. pp. 20-21.

examines in turn a famous but inadequate definition of Pope's, a "more noble and adequate conception" based on the ideas of familiarity and novelty, and a "more rigorous and philosophical" definition of wit as *discordia concors*. Each of the last two definitions has its uses, the one general, the other technical. But after all has been said, the criticism is yet to do. Wit is neither good nor bad in itself, and the poems that exhibit it must be examined individually. Johnson would have been astonished at twentieth-century theories (building on Coleridge's doctrine of the union of opposites) that transform the definition of wit into the central principle of all poetry and make the metaphysical mode a paradigm.

So also Johnson answers the claim that Pope was not really a poet, not by defining poetry so as to include Pope, but by describing Pope's poetry as persuasively as he is able.

After all this it is surely superfluous to answer the question that has once been asked, Whether Pope was a poet? otherwise than by asking in return, If Pope be not a poet, where is poetry to be found? To circumscribe poetry by a definition will only shew the narrowness of the definer, though a definition which shall exclude Pope will not easily be made. Let us look round upon the present time, and back upon the past; let us enquire to whom the voice of mankind has decreed the wreath of poetry; let their productions be examined and their claims stated, and the pretensions of Pope will be no more disputed. [*Life of Pope*, III, 251]

Johnson would have approved Wordsworth's opinion that "no perverseness equals that which is supported by system." [31] And it is notable that Coleridge himself found it necessary to present his theory of the imagination in the context of a loosely organized intellectual autobiography, rather than in the work of formal aesthetics he always dreamed of writing.

In preference to any of Coleridge's definitions, Johnson would probably have liked Arnold's in his essay on Wordsworth: "Poetry is nothing less than the most perfect speech of man, that in which he comes nearest to being able to utter the truth." As in his treatment of generality, so in his criticism at large, Johnson's

[31]*Essay Supplementary to the Preface* (1815), *Prose Works*, ed. W. J. B. Owen and Jane W. Smith (Oxford, 1974), III, 66.

concern is in the largest sense moral; he sees literature, in Tinker's words, as a force in men's lives. His finest criticism occurs in the *Lives of the Poets*, where it is profoundly intertwined with moral reflection and openly depends upon its author's lifetime of earned experience. Johnson does not convey the sense of impersonal oracular truth to which many modern critics aspire, but offers wisdom about poetry and life that proceeds from a highly individual intelligence. The wisdom succeeds as wisdom, rather than collapsing into private preoccupations, because of Johnson's great gift for generalizing his own experience into public truth. In one sense we meet Johnson at every point in his writings, but in another sense his purpose is to help us to see beyond him, and beyond ourselves. Like George Orwell, he cuts through jargon and cant of every kind, and like Orwell he offers personal experience as an instance of universal experience, not as the confessional display of introspective egotism.

We have seen that Johnson's criticism is strong in large part because it resists the temptations of formal system. As we go on to examine it in detail, it is well to recognize that it is profoundly unspecialized: it treats poems as poems, but it draws continually on what is richest in the whole body of Johnson's moral writing. The *Prayers and Meditations* are Johnson's most personal writings, and are often eloquent. "Since the Communion of last Easter I have led a life so dissipated and useless, and my terrours and perplexities have so much encreased, that I am under great depression and discouragement, yet I purpose to present myself before God tomorrow with humble hope that he will not break the bruised reed" (Easter Eve 1761, Yale *Works* I, 73). But after a time this sort of thing grows wearisome. The endless litany of self-reproach, while fundamental to Johnson's emotional life, remains focused upon Johnson and does not spur the reader's mind into continued thought. The most interesting of the meditations are those that most resemble the *Rambler*, looking outward from Johnson's experience to generalize, with wry humor and deep understanding, on the experience of all men. "Every Man naturally persuades himself that he can keep his resolutions, nor is he convinced of his imbecillity but by length of time, and frequency of experiment. This opinion of our own constancy is so prevalent, that we always despise him who suffers his general and settled purpose to be overpowered by an occasional desire. They therefore whom frequent failures have made desperate cease to form resolutions, and they who are become cunning do not tell them" (1 June 1770, p. 133). Johnson achieves his effect here by a post-Augustan "open irony," which implies, as Ian Watt has well said, sympathy with other men rather than superiority to them. [32]

Many writers are most eloquent and impressive when they are most private and confessional. Johnson's mode is not the only one. But his real achievement deserves to be admired, in criticism as much as in moral analysis: the successful generalization of deeply felt experience into universal truth. To quote Watt again, "Johnson could be as personal as he pleased because he could be as impersonal as he pleased; he could introduce his own experience and his own mixed and fallible human nature into his public prose without any violation of neoclassical decorum, because his perspective on himself and on the world was broad enough and impersonal enough to avoid any deflection of our attention from the subject to the personality involved in it" (p. 110).

Even in purely private moments, even under the greatest psychological pressure, Johnson expressed his meaning best when he expressed it thus. When Mrs. Thrale went off with Signor Piozzi, Johnson's grief and sense of abandonment were intense. His letter to her begins, "What you have done, however I may lament it, I have no pretence to resent, as it has not been injurious to me. I therefore breathe out one sigh more of tenderness perhaps useless, but at least sincere" (Letters, III, 177). The rhetoric is scarcely convincing. Johnson does resent it, and feels he has a right to resent it. The sincere (though useless) sigh of tenderness would be more at home in A Sentimental Journey than here. But he then applies himself, with his usual magnificent honesty, to the fact that the past is forever lost. He thanks Mrs. Thrale in a splendid phrase for soothing "twenty years of a life radically wretched." He gives her good advice about where to

[32]"The Ironic Voice," in The Augustan Age, ed. Watt (New York, 1968), pp. 101-14.

live. And he then rises to a nobility of utterance that one could not anticipate after the wounded tone of the first paragraph:

When Queen Mary took the resolution of sheltering herself in England, the Archbishop of St. Andrew's attempting to dissuade her, attended on her journey and when they came to the irremeable stream that separated the two kingdoms, walked by her side into the water, in the middle of which he seized her bridle, and with earnestness proportioned to her danger and his own affection, pressed her to return. The Queen went forward.————If the parallel reaches thus far, may it go no further. The tears stand in my eyes.

"The tears stand in my eyes" is profoundly moving not only for its simplicity but also because it follows the historical anecdote. Johnson's experience is not unique. He assimilates it to a crucial moment in the life of a queen who has always captured men's imaginations (and alludes to Virgil's "irremeabilis unda"). As her devoted archbishop failed then, so must Johnson fail now; but his failure is thereby given dignity and shape. It is no longer the petulance of a cranky old man whose protectress has chosen to make a life of her own. Yet Johnson does not deny that feeling; the anecdote serves to enrich it, not conceal it.

In the rest of this book I shall have occasion to examine Johnson's idiosyncrasies and lapses, but I want always to return to this central fact of his criticism, the breadth of its humanity and moral wisdom. His finest criticism is offered in the *Lives of the Poets* at the end of his career, not in the theoretical *Rambler*s at its beginning. And its most vital and important principle, as we shall now go on to see, is not the abstract theory of generality or any other theory of that kind, but the active ideal of agreement between the critic and the common reader.

2 The Common Reader

My DISCUSSION THUS FAR has necessarily been partly negative, since I have tried to show that some influential approaches to Johnson's criticism tend to ask questions of a limited kind and to get answers that, although valid, ignore large areas of his best work. I now wish to explore his idea of the common reader, which has largely been dismissed as a convenient fiction by which he bolsters his own predetermined opinions. I shall argue that although it is a fuzzy and sometimes inconsistent notion— certainly not a "concept" formulated and upheld throughout a career of half a century—it can be usefully understood in two distinct aspects: as the test of time that proves the lasting value of literary works, and as a way of reading that depends upon fidelity to the unprejudiced common reader in every man. My discussion must take a somewhat circuitous course, because Johnson's ideas on the topic are complicated and subject to change as they are called forth in different contexts. I want to show, indeed, that his want of clarity here is a virtue, liberating him from the potentially restrictive implications of some of his other assumptions.

Near the end of the *Life of Gray* occurs the famous remark "In the character of his *Elegy* I rejoice to concur with the common reader; for by the common sense of readers uncorrupted with literary prejudices, after all the refinements of subtilty and the dogmatism of learning, must be finally decided all claim to poetical honours" (*Lives*, III, 441). Yet this strenuously democratic pronouncement directly follows a discussion of Gray that Johnson's contemporaries regarded as captious and ungenerous; he rejoices to concur here with readers whose judgment he has been continually rejecting. It is easy to suppose that the term represents nothing more than Johnson's own sense that readers ought to agree with his opinions, and a willingness to commend them occasionally when they seem to do so. According to Mrs. Thrale, he measured everyone else's notions by his own and refused to believe that thousands of people could like a book that he disliked (*Miscellanies*, I, 320).

In William R. Keast's view the common reader is simply another term for the generalized "audience" of literature and represents "the reasonable man, no other traits being involved than rationality and common experience of the world." But if he is so generalized, how is he to be known? René Wellek concludes that the common reader is only a cover for Johnson's own dogmatically held assumptions: "The common reader is surely not the average man nor the common man in any sense of low social status, but the universal man in the neoclassical sense which put such hope in the uniformity of human nature.... [Johnson] does not analyze the reader's response or the nature of the audience or the process by which an author established his fame.... The theory of the 'common reader' is merely a time-honored device to identify the critic with the audience, his voice with the verdict of the ages."[1]

It is certainly true that Johnson made no effort (as Mrs. Thrale confirms) to ascertain popular taste. He wrote in *Adventurer* 138, "A few, a very few, commonly constitute the taste of the time; the judgment which they have once pronounced, some are too lazy to discuss, and some too timorous to contradict" (II, 496). The audience of course is not irrelevant, and Dryden "might have observed, that what is good only because it pleases cannot be pronounced good till it has been found to please" (*Life of Dryden*, I, 340). But the converse is not true, that what pleases is therefore good. Johnson elsewhere regrets that Dryden "wrote, and professed to write, merely for the people; and when he pleased others, he contented himself" (*Life of Pope*, III, 220). As it happens, Dryden himself had made a similar point. [2] In the *Lives of the Poets* Johnson tends to approve the popular opinion of rela-

---

[1] Keast, "Theoretical Foundations," pp. 402, 403; Wellek, *A History of Modern Criticism, 1750-1950*, Vol. I, *The Later Eighteenth Century* (New Haven, 1955), p. 95.
[2] "To please the people ought to be the poet's aim, because plays are made for their delight; but it does not follow that they are always pleased with good plays, or that the plays which please them are always good" (*A Defence of An Essay of Dramatic Poesy* [1668], in *Of Dramatic Poesy and Other Critical Essays*, I, 120).

tively minor authors. "Of Roscommon's works the judgement of the publick seems to be right"; of Otway's *Orphan* "the publick seems to judge rightly of the faults and excellencies" (*Lives*, I, 239, 246). In the presence of greater writers, however, "the publick" is less sure of itself. The *Dunciad* caused confusion at first, but by the time of the variorum edition "the criticks had now declared their approbation of the plan, and the common reader began to like it without fear" (*Life of Pope*, III, 150).

The same difficulties appear, almost in the form of paradox, when Johnson talks about Milton. Defending the personal digressions in *Paradise Lost*, he maintains that "since the end of poetry is pleasure, that cannot be unpoetical with which all are pleased." Yet only a few pages earlier he contradicts this doctrine by claiming, "Surely no man could have fancied that he read *Lycidas* with pleasure had he not known its author" (*Life of Milton*, I, 175, 165). Readers can be deluded into thinking they like what they really don't, or at least wouldn't if they responded honestly to their own instincts. Milton had become an author, Johnson says in another place, "with whom readers of every class think it necessary to be pleased" (*Life of Addison*, II, 147). One such reader is his parrot-critic Dick Minim: "Milton is the only writer whose books Minim can read for ever without weariness" (*Idler* 61). It is Johnson secure in his judgments, rather than the common reader influenced by received opinion, who is able to say that "*Paradise Lost* is one of the books which the reader admires and lays down, and forgets to take up again. None ever wished it longer than it is" (*Life of Milton*, I, 183).

It follows that when Johnson objected to Prior's *Henry and Emma* as "a dull and tedious dialogue," he would not have been impressed by the reviewer who retorted, "Were the question to be asked, which of Prior's poems has been most generally read? we are of opinion, it would be determined in favour of Henry and Emma. What every one reads can hardly be thought tedious and dull." [3] Johnson would not have been impressed because the affection of readers does not *in itself* prove poetic excellence, though excellence is impossible without it. The reasons for popular appreciation of various works are of course not uni-

[3] Edmund Cartwright in the *Monthly Review*, 65 (1781), 354.

form. The perfunctory *Life of Pomfret* ends, "He pleases many, and he who pleases many must have some species of merit" (*Lives*, I, 302). But that species of merit is sufficiently indicated in the remark a little earlier that Pomfret "has been always the favourite of that class of readers, who without vanity or criticism seek only their own amusement." People may be amused in many ways; Pomfret pleases an unprejudiced but also a very unambitious class of readers. He is insignificant and harmless, and can be dealt with gently; a contemporary reader described the two-page *Life of Pomfret* as "a neat laconism." [4]

But there is more to the idea of the common reader than this. Partly, to be sure, it means simply the test of time or verdict of the ages, based, as Johnson says in the *Preface to Shakespeare*, on the repeated comparisons of works that result at last in "length of duration and continuation of esteem" (*Preface*, p. 60). But it also has a meaning, related to the first but by no means identical, that is concerned not with verdict but with process, with what happens to an individual when he reads. As Johnson observes in the *Life of Waller*, "From poetry the reader justly expects, and from good poetry always obtains, the enlargement of his comprehension and elevation of his fancy" (*Lives*, I, 292). The common reader is important not just in the act of judging—serving as an elector in the verdict of the ages—but also in responding to literature and being changed by it. And the critic, though better qualified than the average reader to think reasonably about beauties and faults, is inhibited by what the French call professional deformation from an unprejudiced and intuitive literary response. His criticism therefore will have little value if it is not founded on his own experience of reading: that is, on the common reader that exists in himself.

To clarify this argument it will be useful to consider the assumptions of some other critics who are commonly considered neoclassical. In their view the reader must educate himself to like what he ought to like. Thus Rymer derides those who "value themselves upon their *experience*": "I may write by the *Book* (say they) what I have a mind, but they *know* what will *please*. These are a kind of *Stage-quacks* and *Empericks* in Poetry, who have got a

---

[4]Robert Potter in the *Gentleman's Magazine*, 51 (1781), 467.

Receit to *please.*" Or in Shaftesbury's stunning formulation: "A French or Flemish style [in painting] is highly liked by me at first sight, and I pursue my liking. But what ensues? Do I not for ever forfeit my good relish? How is it possible I should thus come to taste the beauties of an Italian master, or of a hand happily formed on nature and the ancients? 'Tis not by wantonness and humour that I shall attain my end and arrive at the enjoyment I propose. The art itself is severe, the rules rigid." In order to enjoy what we know a priori to be the highest form of art, we must deliberately prejudice our taste in its favor. If we should brazenly persist in liking the Flemish painters, that would automatically prove our incompetence, since our liking is only relevant when we like what we ought to like. Reynolds, who goes so far as to call taste "a power of judging right from wrong," concludes that "we will not allow a man, who shall prefer the inferior style, to say it is his taste; taste here has nothing, or at least ought to have nothing to do with the question. He wants not taste, but sense, and soundness of judgment."[5]

Such a view is not wholly remote from Johnson's. He told Boswell that "difference of taste was, in truth, difference of skill" (*Life*, II, 191), and defended Dryden's right to preside magisterially over younger writers, for "he who excels has a right to teach, and he whose judgement is incontestable may, without usurpation, examine and decide" (*Life of Dryden*, I, 396). What distinguishes Johnson from Shaftesbury and Reynolds is his insistence that the critic must finally defer to a greater authority. It was a commonplace that criticism is judicial, but Johnson is unusual in elaborating the metaphor and placing it in subordination to a higher court of last appeal. "There is always an appeal open from criticism to nature," he writes in the *Preface to Shakespeare* (p. 67); and at greater length in *Rambler* 23, "There always lies an appeal from domestick criticism to a higher judicature, and the publick, which is never corrupted, nor often deceived, is to pass the last sentence upon literary claims" (III, 128).

By way of analogy, it is helpful here to consider a fundamental

[5]Rymer, *The Tragedies of the Last Age* (1677), *The Critical Works of Thomas Rymer*, ed. Curt A. Zimansky (New Haven, 1956), p. 19; Anthony Ashley Cooper, 3d earl of Shaftesbury, *Advice to an Author*, III.iii, in *Characteristics*, ed. J. M. Robertson (London, 1900), I, 219; Reynolds, *Discourses*, No. 7, pp. 93, 105.

contrast between English and French law. The French system assumes that an absolute truth exists and that the business of the court is to ascertain it. The English tradition determines nothing more than the apparent truth from the evidence available; it works from a mass of precedent rather than a simplified code, and is always prepared to reopen a case if new evidence is brought forward or to accept the ruling of a higher court that the evidence ought to have been interpreted differently. The only reason this process is not endless is that for practical purposes an ending must be made somewhere, and consequently there must be a court of last resort. But when the analogy is applied to literature, the process not only can but must be endless. Each generation is a new "higher judicature," free in its turn to reverse the evaluations of its predecessors. It is useless to wish that this were not so. To apply an observation that Johnson made in a larger context, "Of things that terminate in human life the world is the proper judge: to despise its sentence, if it were possible, is not just; and if it were just is not possible" (*Life of Pope*, III, 210).

We have already seen in Johnson's comments on Milton that this position involves him in difficulties. What I want to emphasize is that they are honorable difficulties, reflecting an unusual willingness to recognize facts of experience that are not easily assimilated into critical system. Johnson's position may be illuminated if we compare it for a moment with Hume's. In his essay "Of the Standard of Taste" Hume declares that by arduous discipline a few exceptional critics have qualified themselves to pass judgment in accordance with "the true standard of taste and beauty." As an empiricist he is obliged to believe that excellence in literature is located in "what has been universally found to please in all countries and all ages."

But though all the general rules of art are founded only on experience, and on the observation of the common sentiments of human nature, we must not imagine, that, on every occasion, the feelings of men will be conformable to these rules. Those finer emotions of the mind are of a very tender and delicate nature. . . . A perfect serenity of mind, a recollection of thought, a due attention to the object; if any of these circumstances be wanting, our experiment will be fallacious, and we shall be unable to judge of the catholic and universal beauty. [6]

[6]*Of the Standard of Taste and Other Essays*, pp. 17, 7, 8.

Hume of course recognizes that people in different historical periods, or of different ages and temperaments, vary in their preferences. As Johnson more memorably put it: "Our tastes greatly alter. The lad does not care for the child's rattle, and the old man does not care for the young man's whore" (*Life*, II, 14). But Hume's point is that the deeper and presumably uniform responses are inhibited from a true expression of themselves in all but a few thoughtful and highly cultivated individuals.

Johnson may seem to tend toward just such a view in his dismissal of those who mistake their own opinion of *Lycidas*: "Surely no man could have fancied that he read *Lycidas* with pleasure, had he not known its author." Or, to take another example, a reviewer influenced by the trend toward sensibility saw the *Preface to Shakespeare* as neoclassical in the narrowest sense: "We cannot help thinking that Mr. Johnson has run into the vulgar practice, by estimating the merits of Shakespeare according to the rules of the French academy, and the *little* English writers who adopted them, as the criterions of *taste*. . . . Of all our sensations, *taste* is the most variable and uncertain: Shakespeare is to be tried by a more sure criterion, that of *feeling*, which is the same in all ages and all climates." [7] Its other defects apart, this critique fails to take account of an important distinction in Johnson's criticism. Unlike Hume, Johnson does not believe that evaluation necessarily depends on a peculiar delicacy of taste or, for that matter, on a searching enumeration of parts. Good *criticism* certainly does imply these; as he observed in his review of Warton's *Essay on the Genius and Writings of Pope*, "Barely to say, that one performance is not so good as another, is to criticise with little exactness" (1825 *Works*, VI, 39). But a general statement of *value* need not depend on the kind of critical penetration that only a few can attain. "You *may* abuse a tragedy," Johnson told Boswell, "though you cannot write one. You may scold a carpenter who has made you a bad table, though you cannot make a table" (*Life*, I, 409). According to Hawkins, Johnson disliked "the cant of the Shaftesburian school," with their pretension to "tastes and perceptions which are not common to all men." [8]

For Johnson literary merit depends on two qualities, the power to delight and truth to nature. Any reasonably unprejudiced reader is perfectly well qualified to perceive these, though he might not be able to *explain* them as well as a critic could. The principle is the same as the general moral one stated in *Rambler* 52: "The common voice of the multitude uninstructed by precept, and unprejudiced by authority,...in questions that relate to the heart of man, is, in my opinion, more decisive than the learning of Lipsius." As so often in his criticism, Johnson sees systematic theory as needlessly confining; his procedure is to consider the effect before he asks the cause, in contrast to the kind of criticism that passes on the legitimacy of the cause before it will allow the effect. A good example of the latter is furnished by Hume's notorious remark in "Of the Standard of Taste": "Whoever would assert an equality of genius and elegance between Ogilby and Milton, or Bunyan and Addison, would be thought to defend no less an extravagance, than if he had maintained a mole-hill to be as high as Teneriffe, or a pond as extensive as the ocean" (p. 7). The unlucky choice of Bunyan is not offered at random, but as an illustration of the kind of critical certainty that "common sense" allows us to rely on. Johnson, on the other hand, told Boswell that *Pilgrim's Progress* "has great merit, both for invention, imagination, and the conduct of the story; and it has had the best evidence of its merit, the general and continued approbation of mankind" (*Life*, II, 238). The common reader could not explain the reasons why *Pilgrim's Progress* continues to give pleasure, but his admiration suggests what is in fact true, that these reasons do exist, and that a critic who was willing to look for them could find them.

The critic, then, should take seriously the unforced response of the public, though he may have to disagree with it, and must try to be true to the unforced response that ought to take place in his own mind. It is easy to propose a theoretical basis for this position: in a phenomenological sense a literary work can hardly

[8]Sir John Hawkins, *The Life of Samuel Johnson, LL. D.*, ed. and abr. Bertram H. Davis (New York, 1961), pp. 108-9.

be said to exist or have meaning unless we take account of the act of reading, its presence and "life" in the mind of the reader (whether the critic himself, an ideal reader postulated by him, or a generalized audience whose response the critic either guesses at or tries to establish by investigation). Furthermore, few works can have been written without regard to their effect upon potential readers, so that the reader's response is not only theoretically an aspect of the work's existence but is a necessary factor in the author's composition: he wants to interest his reader, perhaps teach him, perhaps astonish or appall him. This is of course an important theme in the *Lives of the Poets*.

I have suggested that, in contrast to Hume, Johnson is willing to grant that the common reader is a fairly good witness to the value of a work. While he is not always comfortable with this idea (as we shall see shortly), he does hold fast to the position that the common reader has the unanswerable last word on whether a work is interesting or not; and more than most critics he recognizes how important this really is. As he says in a noble passage in the *Life of Dryden*, "Works of imagination excel by their allurement and delight; by their power of attracting and detaining the attention. That book is good in vain which the reader throws away. He only is the master who keeps the mind in pleasing captivity; whose pages are perused with eagerness, and in hope of new pleasure are perused again; and whose conclusion is perceived with an eye of sorrow, such as the traveller casts upon departing day"(*Lives*, I, 454). Like many of Johnson's most deeply felt passages, this one has resonances throughout his criticism. "The power of attracting and detaining the attention" is mentioned in many places: *Comus* needs brisker dialogue "to invite attention and detain it"; Homer taught epic poets "all the stratagems that surprise and enchain attention" (*Life of Milton*, I, 169, 194); livelier dialogue in *Hudibras* would have increased its "power of engaging the attention" (*Life of Butler*, I, 211). The phrase "pleasing captivity" is borrowed from Isaac Watts, who describes how orators "lead the Senses and Passions of their Hearers in a pleasing and powerful Captivity." [9] This power is a

[9]*Logick: or, the Right Use of Reason in the Enquiry after Truth* (1725), IV.i, p. 518. Johnson's interest in Watts's *Logic* has often been documented.

necessary, though not a sufficient, element of every successful work. Prior's *Solomon* is a failure because despite its many excellences "it wanted that without which all others are of small avail, the power of engaging attention and alluring curiosity" (*Life of Prior*, II, 206). Milton, on the other hand, despite his alleged faults of language, does place the reader in "captivity": "Such is the power of his poetry that his call is obeyed without resistance, the reader feels himself in captivity to a higher and a nobler mind, and criticism sinks in admiration" (*Life of Milton*, I, 190). The foundation of Shakespeare's greatness is that he "has perhaps excelled all but Homer in securing the first purpose of a writer, by exciting restless and unquenchable curiosity, and compelling him that reads his work to read it through" (*Preface*, p. 83).

This may seem too obvious to deserve discussion, but I think it is not; most criticism, whatever the features it most values in literature, generally neglects to say much about whether it is interesting. There is a salutary warning in C. S. Lewis's remarks about highly "literary" people in whose homes "the only real literary experience . . .may be occurring in a back bedroom where a small boy is reading *Treasure Island* under the bedclothes by the light of an electric torch."[10] Lewis's statement, to be sure, is characteristically contentious in the way it is presented. Johnson's is more solemn and convincing; he appeals to the best in every reader, even the repellent parents in Lewis's vision of the child driven to furtive measures in order to enjoy literature after his enforced bedtime (while the parents stay up late and drive themselves to read the Prose Eddas in the original prose). Johnson's breadth of understanding may also be illustrated by comparison with Coleridge: "The reader should be carried forward, not merely or chiefly by the mechanical impulse of curiosity, or by a restless desire to arrive at the final solution; but by the pleasureable activity of mind excited by the attractions of the journey itself" (*Biographia*, Ch. 14, II, 11). This distinction is too restrictive, for as Johnson recognizes, both elements are involved. The reader does hurry onward because he wants to reach the end—in the common phrase, to discover how it comes

[10]*An Experiment in Criticism* (Cambridge, 1965), p. 8.

out—while he enjoys the activity itself so much that he is sorry
when it is over. Johnson's metaphor of the traveler is a little odd,
for in actuality a traveler does want to stop, to rest at last after a
long day's journey. What Johnson does is to vary the image and
imagine a traveler far from any destination but deprived of the
life-giving light of day.

At this point two questions must be asked: What does Johnson
mean by this idea of literary pleasure? and, How far can it be
extended as a definition of literary value? The first question has
been well answered by Hagstrum: Johnson "seems to have conceived of pleasure as being something like a particular visual
perception—sudden, authentic, complete in itself, and immediate in its effect."[11] As he puts it in the *Life of Cowley*, "Whatever professes to benefit by pleasing must please at once. The
pleasures of the mind imply something sudden and unexpected;
that which elevates must always surprise. What is perceived by
slow degrees may gratify us with the consciousness of improvement, but will never strike with the sense of pleasure" (*Lives*, I,
59). The effect is intuitive, but not irrational: those effects are
pleasing which strike home to the mind. Reynolds declares that
"a picture should please at first sight," and goes on to say,
"Whatever pleases has in it what is analogous to the mind, and is
therefore, in the highest and best sense of the word, natural"
(*Discourses*, No. 7, pp. 101, 102).

This conception of pleasure is radically different from the
ineffable mystery evoked by late Victorian writers who liked to
repeat that the wind bloweth where it listeth. Pleasure is not
excited at random, but by the communication of minds. Congreve felt very early, Johnson says, "that force of imagination,
and possessed that copiousness of sentiment, by which intellectual pleasure can be given" (*Life of Congreve*, II, 213). Arnold calls
Wordsworth's best poetry *inevitable*, borrowing the term from
Wordsworth himself, and would agree with Johnson that in-
evitability is achieved by genius and labor, not by luck. "[Cowley]
has indeed many noble lines, such as the feeble care of Waller
never could produce. The bulk of his thoughts sometimes swelled his verse to unexpected and inevitable grandeur, but his

[11]*Samuel Johnson's Literary Criticism*, p. 78.

excellence of this kind is merely fortuitous; he sinks willingly down to his general carelessness, and avoids with very little care either meanness or asperity" (*Life of Cowley*, I, 59-60). Cowley sometimes achieved "inevitable grandeur," as Waller could not, because his mind was greater than Waller's, but if he had shared Waller's "care" he could have achieved it more often. And although Johnson maintains that pleasure must be immediate, he distinguishes clearly between temporary pleasure and pleasure that grows with repeated readings. Edward Young "plays, indeed, only on the surface of life; he never penetrates the recesses of the mind, and therefore the whole power of his poetry is exhausted by a single perusal: his conceits please only when they surprise" (*Life of Young*, III, 394). The real master is the one whose works not only please at first sight—though they must do that—but "in hope of new pleasure are perused again."

The second question remains to be answered: how far can this idea of pleasure be extended as a definition of literary value? Johnson's position as sketched so far is remarkable for what it attempts to include, but it is not completely adequate, as he is often obliged to recognize. First of all, the reader's sense of interest and pleasure, though essential, is certainly not the whole story. Writers like Pomfret provide rather depressing forms of pleasure, and the concessions of the *de gustibus* formula cannot be indefinitely extended. In the second place, the critic is bound to rely on his own sense of literary value. What if he has done his best to be receptive to a work admired by the public and still feels profoundly that it is despicable? Johnson after all writes criticism from a position of authority, and the *Lives of the Poets*, not to mention his more dogmatic earlier criticism, represent an attempt to influence and redefine taste.

The first point is the more easily dealt with, though it has caused trouble for scholars who assume that to adopt the *de gustibus* line at all is to adopt it completely, abdicating any right to argue about value. " 'De gustibus non est disputandum,' " Johnson says in the *Life of Congreve*: "Men may be convinced, but they cannot be pleased, against their will" (II, 217). René Wellek quotes the passage with evident distaste, having taken care earlier to denounce critical relativism that "leads only to barren skepticism, to the old and vicious maxim of *De gustibus*

non est disputandum."[12] But it does no harm to notice the
context: in a dedication to *The Double Dealer* Congreve tried to
compel readers to like an unpopular work, and Johnson is only
saying that "these apologies are always useless." To make his
point he actually quotes ironically from Congreve's own
epilogue to *The Way of the World*: "And sure he must have
more than mortal skill/Who pleases any one against his will";
Congreve in turn was alluding to Dryden's preface to *Absalom
and Achitophel.*[13] You may *convince* someone that a poet is
better (or worse) than he had thought, but it is much harder to
compel delight. And without delight, as we have seen Johnson
saying over and over again, other qualities are useless.

The second point, however, needs to be taken more seriously.
There are many kinds of pleasure, some of which the critic can
only wonder at, and others which he may feel even in himself
and yet have qualms about, a paradox that Orwell exploits in his
analogy between Kipling's verse and a taste for cheap sweets
carried into middle life.[14] At times Johnson offers the solution
that really good writing will appeal to every kind of reader, from
the humblest common reader to the sternest critic. In Shakespeare "the ignorant feel his representations to be just, and the
learned see that they are compleat" (*Preface*, p. 90). A note to *2
Henry VI* reiterates the point: "These are beauties that rise out of
nature and of truth; the superficial reader cannot miss them, the
profound can image nothing beyond them" (Yale *Works*, VIII,
591). But when this happy concurrence is absent Johnson is not
inclined to take sides against the learned. In some very interesting notes of his conversation made by William Windham in 1784,
the ignorant / learned formula recurs only after the statement
that bad writing will always have admirers:

Opinion that there were three ways in which writing may be unnatural:
by being bombastic and above nature; affected and beside it, fringing
every event with ornaments which nature did not afford; or weak and

[12]*History of Modern Criticism*, I, 95, 26.
[13]"There's a sweetness in good Verse, which Tickles even while it Hurts:
And, no man can be heartily angry with him, who pleases him against his will"
("To the Reader," prefixed to *Absalom and Achitophel*, 1681).
[14]"Rudyard Kipling," in *George Orwell: A Collection of Essays* (New York, 1954),
p. 135.

below nature. That neither of the first would please long. That the third might indeed please a good while, or at least many; because imbecility, and consequently a love of imbecility, might be found in many.

Baretti had told him of some Italian author, who said that a good work must be that with which the vulgar were pleased, and of which the learned could tell why it pleased—that it must be able to employ the learned, and detain the idle. Chevy Chase pleased the vulgar, but did not satisfy the learned; it did not fill a mind capable of thinking strongly. The merit of Shakespeare was such as the ignorant could take in, and the learned add nothing to.[15]

In these remarks, which sound as if they have been accurately reported, Johnson manages to fall into the same error that Hume did in his denigration of Bunyan. Johnson shows no respect for the praise that Sidney and Addison conferred upon *Chevy Chase*; apparently they were simply giving in to unworthy feelings, for as he had already stated in print, the poem exhibits "chill and lifeless imbecility" (*Life of Addison*, II, 148)—the same word that Windham recorded.

Johnson's formula here is a very imperfect solution, not only because there are so few Shakespeares to whom it will apply, but also because the criterion of pleasure, though important, is far from an adequate response to Shakespeare or any other great writer. The power to give pleasure may be present in works of which all or part deserves the censure of the critic. Just after the passage on "pleasing captivity" in the *Life of Dryden*, Johnson says with deliberate paradox, "By his proportion of this pre-domination I will consent that Dryden should be tried; of this, which, in opposition to reason, makes Ariosto the darling and the pride of Italy; of this, which, in defiance of criticism, continues Shakespeare the sovereign of the drama" (I, 454).

It is easy to retort that "reason" and "criticism" are simply defined too narrowly here. But it is possible to think of cases where we would agree with Johnson that criticism can be inadequate even though not demonstrably mistaken. This I think

---

[15]From *The Diary of the Right Hon. William Windham*, reprinted in G. B. Hill's edition of Johnson's *Letters* (Oxford, 1892), II, 440, Appendix D. Johnson's three categories of bombast, affectation, and imbecility are taken from Dennis's criticism of Addison on *Chevy Chase*, quoted in the *Life of Addison*, II, 147.

is the reason for his long quotations from Dennis on Addison's
Cato. As Johnson shows, Dennis was entirely right—*Cato* is, as he
claimed, severely damaged by servile adherence to narrow
dramatic rules—but his criticism is vitiated in two ways. The first
is his own dog-in-the-manager role as failed playwright who
"could not sit quiet at a successful play; but was eager to tell
friends and enemies that they had misplaced their admirations"
(*Life of Addison*, II, 102). We may think we respond only to the
truth or falsity of a critic's statements, but we are influenced also
by his rhetoric and apparent reasons for saying what he does.
And there is a more fundamental reason for the failure of
Dennis's attack: accurate though it be, *Cato* continued (at least in
Johnson's time) to give pleasure to many readers. "His dislike
was not merely capricious. He found and shewed many faults: he
shewed them indeed with anger, but he found them with acute-
ness, such as ought to rescue his criticism from oblivion; though,
at last, it will have no other life than it derives from the work
which it endeavours to oppress.... As we love better to be
pleased than to be taught, *Cato* is read, and the critick is neglected" (pp. 133, 144). This then is the function of the "test of
time" that Johnson derives from traditional sources like Cicero
and Boileau. [16] If works continue to give pleasure long after their
own era, as those of Shakespeare do (*Preface*, p. 61), then the
strictures of criticism fade in significance: evidently there were
other merits than those the critics had discerned, and the faults
they detected, though real, are in some way canceled out.

This is a conclusion rather than a solution, agreeing to leave
unexplained what criticism turns out to have explained in vain.
It accounts for much of the strangely contradictory praise and
blame in the *Preface to Shakespeare*. But it is not quite fair to
charge, as Emerson Marks does, that Johnson is simply begging

---

[16]"What Cicero says of philosophy is true likewise of wit and humour, that
'time effaces the fictions of opinion, and confirms the determinations of Nature' " (*Life of Butler*, I, 214, quoting *De Natura Deorum* II.ii. 5). "Boileau justly
remarks, that the books which have stood the test of time, and been admired
through all the changes which the mind of man has suffered from the various
revolutions of knowledge, and the prevalence of contrary customs, have a
better claim to our regard than any modern can boast, because the long
continuance of their reputation proves that they are adequate to our faculties,
and agreeable to nature" (*Rambler* 92, IV, 122, quoting Boileau's *Réflexion*
VII).

the question here by evading the proper responsibilities of a theory of value. [17] Johnson knows very well that the test of time is not, and cannot be, a theory of value. It is simply a *test* of value. If a work survives by continuing to give pleasure to readers of all kinds and in all eras, then it must have some important value even if we cannot be sure what it is. The *Preface* and the *Lives* are full of attempts to explain these questions more precisely, and while the answers are not always convincing, Johnson sees at least that the questions must be asked. His most notable failures, indeed, occur when he refuses to concede that a work like *Lycidas* has survived the test of time.

Taste was a special problem for empirical philosophy because it involved the metaphorical extension of a physical faculty to a mental operation, and because that operation was surrounded by implications of value. It is much harder to defend the proposition "X is beautiful" than the proposition "X seems seems beautiful *to me.*" On the level of physical description, one can argue, as Hume does in "Of the Standard of Taste," that most healthy people are able to agree. "A man in a fever would not insist on his palate as able to decide concerning flavors" (p. 9). But healthy people who can distinguish between sweet and sour may still disagree about what tastes good. The usual application of the *de gustibus* principle is to dismiss differing value judgments as merely whimsical—"There's no accounting for tastes." Johnson wishes to use the principle positively, not negatively, to defend our *right* to know what we like. The problem of course is still with us, except for that minority of heroic critics like Northrop Frye who seek to describe literature objectively and to exclude statements of value from the science of criticism. The essential point about Johnson's test of time is that it is positive, not negative: it tells us which works have been actively admired, not just which ones have been forgotten. The "length of duration and continuation of esteem" does not represent the lump sum of a majority

[17]"We have been told that among his major contributions to theory is the test of time. The final criterion of worth, he is fond of repeating, is how long a literary work continues to be read and admired. But this is no more than a truism that evades the question of literary excellence by posing it anew. What causes one work to appeal through the ages and another to be forgotten is the very problem any respectable theory of value seeks to solve" (*The Poetics of Reason* [New York, 1968], p. 114).

vote, the referendum of history, but rather an accumulating series of individual judgments that are active (good or bad), not passive (sweet or sour). Each reader must be his own common reader, trusting his immediate, but not unreflecting, response to what he reads. A successful work will continue to give pleasure to such common readers after its local allusions and accidental attractions have become obscure, and in so doing will stand the test of time. Feebler works will soon lose their temporary charms, like those of Mallet, which are "such as a writer, bustling in the world, shewing himself in publick, and emerging occasionally from time to time into notice, might keep alive by his personal influence; but which, conveying little information and giving no great pleasure, must soon give way, as the succession of things produces new topics of conversation and other modes of amusement" (*Life of Mallet*, III, 410).

No doubt there are still deeper difficulties in the notion of the test of time, if one is prepared to believe that many excellent works, which once impressed intelligent and sensitive readers, have simply *not* survived. But at any rate we can recognize that Johnson appreciates the difference between the critic and the common reader, and he certainly does not recommend that we submit blindly to the taste of the ignorant and, as he sometimes calls them, the imbecilic. The critic ought always to argue as eloquently as he can for the values he perceives in literary works; the *Lives of the Poets* are intended to help ordinary readers to think more clearly about dozens of authors. But to accomplish that end, the critic must listen to the testimony of the common reader within himself. For as I have tried to show, Johnson has in mind not only the verdict of "the publick" but also an openness to literature, with the possibility of surrender and "captivity," without which no critical analysis can be valuable. "Whether your submission is permanent or must be withdrawn," R. P. Blackmur writes, "will be determined by the judgment of all the standards and all the interests you can bring to bear. These will differ with the work in hand. But the act of submission must be made before you can tell; it is an act of imagination, not of will; and it is the enabling act of criticism." [18] The critic is far from immune to the

[18]"The Enabling Act of Criticism," *American Issues*, II (Philadelphia, 1941), rpt. in R. W. Stallman, ed., *Critiques and Essays in Criticism* (New York, 1949), p. 417.

impulse that led the first readers of Gray's odes "to be shewn beauties which they could not see" (*Life of Gray*, III, 426). As A. C. Bradley observed in his great study of Shakespeare, "Many a man will declare that he feels in reading a tragedy what he never really felt, while he fails to recognise what he actually did feel." [19] In many of the *Ramblers* Johnson discusses the tendency of the human mind to seek "commodious" explanations in all areas of life (*Rambler* 155). Criticism has the worthy task of finding reasons for what interests us in literature, but our very eagerness for those reasons should make us cautious about finding them too easily.

In a way, therefore, the common reader is indeed Johnson himself, not as a disguise under which to impose his own opinions, but rather as an attempt to be faithful to the freshness and immediacy of his response to literary works. He would have been delighted by Eliot's judgment of Akenside's *Pleasures of the Imagination*: "I have put myself through the mechanical operation of reading this poem through, yet I cannot say that I have read it; for, as Johnson foretold, 'attention deserted the mind' [and settled in the ear]." [20] Eliot is very far from being the common man, but as a well-meaning and disappointed reader of Akenside he is a representative of the common reader.

At the start of this discussion we noticed that Johnson concurred with the common reader in admiring Gray's *Elegy* but sternly contradicted the common reader's approval of the odes. By now it should be apparent that he is perfectly consistent here; he may be sarcastic and unfair in analyzing the odes, but his irritation makes perfect sense in the light of his assumptions about the common reader. When they were published "the readers of poetry were at first content to gaze in mute amazement," but the odes found "champions" to praise them, "and in a short time many were content to be shewn beauties which they could not see" (*Life of Gray*, III, 426). The crucial phrase is not "content to be shewn," but rather "which they could not see." Any new genius reinvents his art to some degree, and readers may need help in understanding him. Johnson says of Thomson's *Winter*, "The poem, which, being of a new kind, few would venture at

---

[19]*Shakespearean Tragedy* (London, 1905), p. 25.
[20]T. S. Eliot, "Johnson as Critic and Poet," *On Poetry and Poets* (London, 1957), p. 173. Eliot is quoting the *Life of Akenside*, III, 417.

first to like, by degrees gained upon the publick" (*Life of Thomson*, III, 285). It gained on them because familiarity helped them to see beauties which it really possessed. In Johnson's opinion, a very different conversion explains the popularity of Gray: "My process has now brought me to the 'Wonderful Wonder of Wonders,' the two Sister Odes; by which, though either vulgar ignorance or common sense at first universally rejected them, many have been since persuaded to think themselves delighted. I am one of those that are willing to be pleased, and therefore would gladly find the meaning of the first stanza of *The Progress of Poetry*" (p. 436). Johnson really *is* willing to be pleased. Common sense at first rebelled against the odes, because Gray had taken care, as his epigraph from Pindar indicates, to make them unintelligible to common sense: "vocal to the intelligent alone." But Johnson does not despise Gray's powers: he laments the misuse of a strong intelligence. Gray's letters, Johnson shrewdly observes, show "that his mind had a large grasp; that his curiosity was unlimited, and his judgement cultivated" (p. 432). Even in the odes, therefore, "to say that he has no beauties would be unjust: a man like him, of great learning and great industry, could not but produce something valuable. When he pleases least, it can only be said that a good design was ill directed" (p. 441). This is not the perfunctory praise that it is usually treated as being. The *Elegy* is not a lucky and inexplicable accident; it is the one masterpiece of a true poet whose perverted theory—as Johnson sees it—prevented him from writing great poems. "Had Gray written often thus it had been vain to blame, and useless to praise him" (p. 442).

As we go forward through Johnson's criticism, we shall see the immense value of his idea of the common reader. As systematic theory it may be weak, though more consistent theories are strong partly because of what they leave out. In practice, however, it helps to explain how so opinionated a critic can offer such a range of striking and valuable observations on particular authors and works: they derive from the active response that precedes any theory. This concern for what happens in reading is what enables Johnson to go beyond the potential limitations of his didactic aesthetic, since he feels obliged to emphasize the pleasure which, whether or not it may lead to moral knowledge, is experienced as an end in itself. In Shakespeare, for example, Johnson is deeply alarmed at the suspension of moral judgment that is possible when we are thoroughly captivated by an author, and he would have found matters simpler if he could have rejected the unforced response of the common reader in all of us, or at least refused to take it seriously. It is greatly to his honor as a critic that he would not do so, and we can learn from his example.

3 *Style and Criticism*

JUST AS JOHNSON liked to talk of reducing criticism to science and method, so we ourselves may assume that a critic's argument is the main thing we learn from reading him and that we adopt or reject that argument on more or less logical grounds. To some extent such assumptions are justified, but they tend to ignore the way in which rhetoric works upon us. A critic persuades us in the manner of a politician or classical orator rather than of a physicist. Logical argument is only one of his means, and often not the most important. We are impressed by the sense of his powers that the critic conveys; we are impressed by the sense of our own powers that we feel him stimulating; we are impressed by the vision of an author or work that he conjures up, and we desire that it be true. Every great critic has relied upon persuasion, whether at the theoretical extreme (Aristotle's "catharsis" is as much a compelling metaphor as a definable entity) or at the emotive (Arnold's moral stance and tone of cultural authority have had more influence than his arguments *qua* arguments).

In this chapter I shall attempt to describe how Johnson's critical performance rests upon the energy and persuasive eloquence of his style. To do so, I am obliged to adopt a polemical stance, for it is widely felt that Johnson's style is ponderous, rigid, and hence unsuited to subtlety of critical perception. This view, which is as old as Walpole and Blair, has been rendered doubly formidable by receiving support from an eminent Johnsonian in the standard work on the subject, William K. Wimsatt's *The Prose Style of Samuel Johnson*. Accordingly I shall begin by trying to meet the theoretical case against Johnson, in order to show that those features of his style most often condemned or parodied do not reflect the critical limitations that have often been alleged.

The central theme of Wimsatt's study is that style is inseparable from meaning. But the meaning itself may be discouragingly earthbound, as he suggests in his only partly reassuring explanation for the peculiarities of Johnson's style: "What is sometimes called cumbrousness or pompousness in Johnson is but the exaggeration into more rigid lines of an expressive principle that lies in the very warp of all verbal discourse." [1] This shows that Johnson's style has affinities with those of other men, but does not deny that it is exaggerated and rigid, like the weight lifter who has swelled his normal muscles into a grotesque parody of the human form and can no longer walk with ease.

The issue here is more crucial than it seemed to eighteenth-century critics of Johnson's style, for whom language was only the dress of thought and his style therefore an unfortunate encrustation on his ideas. For the modern critic the style embodies and determines the ideas, so that a rigid style reflects rigid thought. In just this way Wimsatt describes with obvious approval Hazlitt's "rush and flood and profusion" and concurs with Hazlitt's dislike of the balanced antitheses of the *Preface to Shakespeare*. "The danger of the antithetic mode, like that of the other kinds of meaning we have considered, is that it may assert itself at the cost of other meaning more relevant and satisfactory. . . . We may call this a fault of *style*—just as Hazlitt attributes it to 'the very structure of his style'—because it arises from a habit of meaning. It may be called an exploitation of medium. It is cultivating expressive forms for their own sake" (pp. 48-49).

I should not care to defend the specific points in the *Preface* that Hazlitt attacks, but two qualifications can be urged against the Hazlitt-Wimsatt position in its general application. The first is that Johnson's "habit of meaning," if it necessarily misses some aspects of truth, is peculiarly suited to perceiving others. It is not obvious that Hazlitt, for all his rush and profusion, is a greater critic than Johnson. And, second, we should recognize that Johnson, like other great writers, compels us to come to terms with a style that is highly idiosyncratic and is read more sympathetically as we read it longer. There is a close analogy with Milton, against whom three hundred years of rebuke have been expended in vain. If one lists the most obvious features of Milton's verse, it must seem hopelessly Latinate and cumbrous, just as Johnson's prose must; yet does either Milton or Johnson really

---

[1]*The Prose Style of Samuel Johnson* (New Haven, 1941), p. 14.

convey a sense of rigidity for its own sake? Is rigidity even a useful term?

I do not claim that Johnson is never cumbrous, never rigid. At its worst his style doubtless gives the impression merely of habitual mannerism, but no writer should be judged by his worst. More usually—particularly in the *Lives of the Poets*—he achieves a very different effect, the nature of which can be defined by another objection of Hazlitt's. "All his periods," Hazlitt complains, "are cast in the same mould, are of the same size and shape, and consequently have little fitness to the variety of things he professes to treat of"; and again, "The structure of his sentences . . .is a species of rhyming in prose, where one clause answers to another in measure and quantity, like the tagging of syllables at the end of a verse; the close of the period follows as mechanically as the oscillation of a pendulum, the sense is balanced with the sound; each sentence, revolving round its centre of gravity, is contained within itself like a couplet, and each paragraph forms itself into a stanza." [2] Hazlitt is thus the first critic to make the acute point that Johnson's prose bears a close analogy to the heroic couplet. His assumption that this is a bad thing must depend on the assumption that the couplet itself is vicious (distorting the sense by mechanical devices) or else on the assumption that what is good in poetry is bad in prose. Not many critics today will argue that the couplet is incapable of variety and interest, so we will abandon that possibility, though Hazlitt may intend it. The second alternative requires more comment.

Though the boundaries between poetry and prose are not so obvious as they once were, the belief persists that they draw upon different resources and imitate each other at some peril. In certain respects this is manifestly true. All of us, for example, in revising our own prose, tend to employ "elegant variation" by altering a word that appears too frequently in a passage, even if doing so involves a good deal of effort. Likewise we avoid irrelevant repetition of sounds, like the "jingle" discussed by Wimsatt (pp. 13-14). As Northrop Frye observes, "Verse, in contrast to prose, employs a number of special devices to mark its repeti-

---

[2]*Lectures on the English Comic Writers* (Oxford, 1907), pp. 131, 132. These and related passages are quoted by Wimsatt, p. 32.

tion, such as rhyme and alliteration. . . . In normal prose, on the other hand, no such features appear at all, unless by accident. In prose the emphasis falls on the syntactical relations of words, hence the prose writer seeks variety of sound, and the sharp clash of rhyme or alliteration in prose is rejected by the ear at once." [3]

But true though this is for the modern plain style, we should be wary of extending its implications too widely. We may feel that euphuistic prose or prose that resembles blank verse are somehow "too close" to poetry (though in specific cases we may not feel that at all). But the larger syntactical patterns in Johnson's prose, though Hazlitt rightly sees their resemblance to the couplet in verse, are not at all a violation of prose logic. They are, of course, very different from Hazlitt's kind of prose logic, but they are not used with the metronomic inflexibility that he describes. In his chapter on parallelism Wimsatt sees its use in Johnson as a means of emphasis (as opposed to "range"), "a purpose which we all must feel when we double words, but which we may feel is obtained at considerable cost of meaning when the words used mean nearly the same" (p. 22). At times this probably does turn out to be true, but more usually Johnson is doing something very like Sir Thomas Browne, who has always been thought to have influenced him: we get a sense of fecundity of mind that can constantly elaborate fresh ideas and language, but is nonetheless disciplined enough to move within stable boundaries. Quite possibly its ordered rhythms represent a willed conquest of inner anxiety, [4] but in any event it conveys a sense of confidence and ease. It is remote also from Burke's onrushing flow of metaphors and gorgeous rhetoric. Rather, it gives the impression of hiding nothing and disguising nothing, moving

[3] *The Well-Tempered Critic* (Bloomington, Ind., 1963), pp. 56-57.
[4] See Walter Jackson Bate, *The Achievement of Samuel Johnson*, pp. 170-76. George Irwin, discussing Johnson's grief at the time of his mother's death, adds that "at the same time as Johnson in these stricken letters was telling Lucy [his stepdaughter, Lucy Porter] that he lacked the composure to determine anything, he was writing *Idler*, No. 41, a calm dissertation upon the death of a friend, full of philosophic and religious comfort, adult feeling, and majestic Johnsonian periods" (*Samuel Johnson: A Personality in Conflict* [Auckland and Oxford, 1971], p. 111).

forward with great energy of mind but spelling out for the reader all possible qualifications and corollaries.

The best defense of the artificiality of Johnson's style is implied in his own comment on Clarendon's: "His diction is indeed neither exact in itself, nor suited to the purpose of history. It is the effusion of a mind crouded with ideas, and desirous of imparting them; and therefore always accumulating words, and involving one clause and sentence in another. But there is in his negligence a rude inartificial majesty, which, without the nicety of laboured elegance, swells the mind by its plenitude and diffusion" (*Rambler* 122, IV, 289). Johnson's mind, like Clarendon's, is full of ideas and fills that of the reader, but Clarendon's defect is that he is *inartificial*: his majesty is occluded by the awkward entanglement of his clauses.

It may be that in compensating for this danger, Johnson encounters the opposite one. As Wimsatt says, his fondness for antitheses gives his writing an "abrupt, sectional character." "It is put together with tight logic, it is eminently coherent and articulate, but it does not flow. Or, Johnson is like a man who marches a short length in one direction, hitting to right and left as he goes, hammers three times at the end, then turns at right angles or back again and repeats" (pp. 46-47). One can easily accept the first part of this description—"coherent and articulate" reflects just the qualities Johnson seems to have sought—but the mechanical image of the hammering man is altogether unfair unless Hazlittian flow is the only acceptable mode of discourse. Johnson's prose does move in discrete units, but it moves forward; the best of the *Lives of the Poets* develop with a cumulative richness that is far from mechanical and has little to do with "tight logic"—rather, with an associative power that gathers up each new piece of evidence into an ever-enlarging whole. And if each paragraph (Johnson's basic unit) is full of antithetical tensions, it is nonetheless conceived as a unity. The effect is much like that of Gibbon, who wrote, "It has always been my practise to cast a long paragraph in a single mould, to try it by my ear, to deposit it in my memory; but to suspend the action of the pen, till I had given the last polish to my work." [5] Johnson himself

[5]*Memoirs of My Life*, ed. Georges A. Bonnard (London, 1966), p. 159.

describes the dilemma of the writer who will not force a facile
parallelism unless the mot juste, the appropriate meaning, can
be achieved. "It is one of the common distresses of a writer, to be
within a word of a happy period, to want only a single epithet to
give amplification its full force, to require only a correspondent
term in order to finish a paragraph with elegance and make one
of its members answer to the other: but these deficiencies cannot
always be supplied; and after long study and vexation, the passage is turned anew, and the web unwoven that was so nearly
finished" (*Adventurer* 138).

This is not to say that Johnson is always felicitous. It is easy to
compile long lists of passages in which his parallelism or antitheses are objectionable, though of course they look worse in lists
than in context. Walpole called his triads of phrases "triple
tautology," and Coleridge said that "the antithesis of Johnson is
rarely more than verbal." [6] Such attacks are sometimes well
founded, and it is furthermore clear that these devices are so
habitual in Johnson as to channel the movement of his thought
in directions that are not always useful. Having written that the
metaphysical poets "had no regard to that uniformity of sentiment, which enables us to conceive and to excite the agitation or
perception of other minds," Johnson decides that "agitation or
perception" is unsatisfactory, and alters the phrase; but the new
phrase, though it has a new meaning, must still be a doublet, and
he inserts "the pains and the pleasure of other minds." [7]

Yet it is instructive to look at the passage in its larger context.

As they were wholly employed on something unexpected and surprising, they had no regard to that uniformity of sentiment which enables
us to conceive and to excite the pains and the pleasure of other minds:
they never enquired what on any occasion they should have said or
done, but wrote rather as beholders than partakers of human nature;
as beings looking upon good and evil, impassive and at leisure; as
Epicurean deities making remarks on the actions of men and the
vicissitudes of life, without interest and without emotion. Their court-

---

[6] Walpole to the Countess of Upper Ossory, 1 Feb. 1779; *The Yale Edition of
Horace Walpole's Correspondence*, ed. W. S. Lewis (New Haven, 1937-), XXXIII,
88. Coleridge, *Table Talk* (Oxford, 1917), p. 255 (3 July 1833).
[7] *Life of Cowley*, I, 20; the original reading is given by Boswell (*Life*, IV, 39).

ship was void of fondness and their lamentation of sorrow. Their wish was only to say what they hoped had been never said before.

In this passage there are at least a dozen examples of parallelism and antithesis, more perhaps than the most tone-deaf parodist of Johnson would venture to attempt in so short a space, but they do not give the impression of jerky progress and ironbound logic. Rather, the sense is of immense care and discrimination, of setting the metaphysicals against all the potentialities of human life that are excluded from their poems. The orderly progression of distinctions serves to suggest that hardly anything human is *not* alien to these writers, who can make love without fondness and lament without sorrow. And what carries the paragraph forward is the running metaphor that controls and organizes the repeated parallels: "rather as beholders than partakers of human nature . . .as beings looking upon good and evil, impassive and at leisure . . .as Epicurean deities." The dehumanization is progressive, from "beholders" through "beings" to "Epicurean deities" (representing an intellectual abstraction against which Johnson often vented his wrath). But of course they were really men, not disembodied wraiths, and there has to be a reason for this behavior. The reason is given in a simple sentence that emerges after all the weighty deliberateness: "Their wish was only to say what they hoped had been never said before."

The parallelisms here justify their existence by the use—as much moral as critical—to which they are put. To say that Johnson sometimes overuses such devices is only part of a fair assessment, which must include the recognition that they often permit him to express his meaning with great effectiveness. The point is well made by Robert Burrowes, the first (and one of the best) of careful students of his style, who is not afraid to name Johnson's defects, but sees his virtues clearly too.

For antithesis indeed he was most eminently qualified; none has exceeded him in nicety of discernment, and no author's vocabulary has ever equalled his in a copious assortment of forcible and definite expressions. Thus, in his comparison of Blackmore's attack on the dramatic writers with Collier's, "Blackmore's censure," he says, "was cold and general, Collier's was personal and ardent: Blackmore taught his readers to dislike, what Collier incited them to abhor." But it is useless to multiply instances of that which all must have perceived, since all his contrasts and comparisons possess the same high degree of accuracy and perfection. From the same cause may be inferred the excellence of his parallel sentences, where praise-worthy qualities are separated from their concomitant faults, or kindred effects are dis-united: as where he calls Goldsmith "a man who had the art of being minute without tediousness, and general without confusion; whose language was copious without exuberance, exact without constraint, and easy without weakness." [8]

Johnson's greatest talent lies in the exposition of the complexity of things. In the *Rambler* and everywhere else in his writings, the piling up of clauses reflects neither an uncontrollable garru-lousness nor a passion for nonexistent order (like the obsession with the quincunx that he mocks in Browne), but rather a convic-tion that reality is always more complex than it appears at first glance.

Apart from these syntactical features, which need to be consid-ered in context rather than as entities in themselves, Johnson has most offended readers with his predilection for big words and abstractions (generally combined in the form of big abstract words). Let us begin with the polysyllables. There is not much value in Boswell's defense, "Mr. Johnson has gigantic thoughts, and therefore he must be allowed gigantic words." [9] We some-times wish for the assistance of the aunt who counseled Bellaria to read the *Rambler* "and often cried out, when she saw me look confused, 'If there is any word that you do not understand, child, I will explain it'" (*Rambler* 191). Here it is a question of audience, of choosing words that will be familiar to one's readers; yet we allow poets to press their readers beyond familiar bounds, and Johnson may be forgiven for doing so too. He never coins terms like Coleridge's *coadunative* and *esemplastic*, and many of his hard

[8]"Essay on the Stile of Doctor Samuel Johnson," *Transactions of the Royal Irish Academy* (Dublin, 1787), rpt. in James T. Boulton, ed., *Johnson: The Critical Heritage* (London, 1971), pp. 339-40. Wimsatt rightly says that Burrowes's essay "in some respects is as penetrating as anything since written" (*Prose Style*, p. 59n). Burrowes quotes here from the *Life of Blackmore* (II, 241) and the *Life of Parnell* (II, 49).

[9]*Private Papers of James Boswell*, ed. Geoffrey Scott and F. A. Pottle (New York, 1936), VIII, 174.

words have become easy with the passage of time. Who today would object to *multifarious*, *transcendental*, *disruption*, *sensory*, *panoply*, *emitted*, or *veracious*? Yet all were complained of by eighteenth-century readers of Johnson. [10]

So far as criticism is concerned, what matters about this diction is not its girth but its use. Wimsatt has shown in detail that it often reflects "philosophic" language and embodies implied metaphor.[11] But many of Johnson's polysyllables are not technical or metaphorical; they are just big. The question then is whether this is a defect. We may start with a brief example: "He that runs against Time, has an antagonist not subject to casualties" (*Life of Pope*, III, 117). Walpole called this sentence a "piece of bombast nonsense," yet many readers have remembered it with pleasure. [12] The Latinate amplitude of the second clause balances the simplicity of the first, and helps to enforce the idea of the vastness of time. Whatever the sentence is, it is certainly not bombast nonsense. Walpole's disdain rests on the assumption that big words are bad, as in Orwell's famous pronouncement in "Politics and the English Language," "Never use a long word where a short one will do." The example of Orwell, indeed, suggests that Johnson's prose is illustrative of the politics of style. James T. Boulton has shown that in his political pamphlets both style and ideas appeal to the values of a conservative, classically educated culture. [13] But it can only be through prejudice that an admirer of the modern (and perhaps democratic) plain style will denounce polysyllables on a priori grounds. And Johnson's precision of language is at the furthest possible extreme from the debased officialese that Orwell exposes so well.

Johnson's big words often achieve effects that small ones could

[10]The first two are mentioned in a review of *Rasselas* by Owen Ruffhead in the *Monthly Review*, 20 (1759), 428—he calls them "hard compounds, which it is difficult to pronounce with composed features." The next three are mentioned by Burrowes, who says that "they may be found, perhaps, in the works of former writers, but they make no part of the English language" (p. 331). Boswell cites the last two from the *Lives of the Poets* but remarks that "custom would make them seem as easy as any others" (*Life*, IV, 39).

[11]*Philosophic Words: A Study of Style and Meaning in the Rambler and Dictionary of Samuel Johnson* (New Haven, 1948).

[12]Walpole to William Mason, 14 April 1781, *Correspondence*, XXIX, 130.

[13]*The Language of Politics in the Age of Wilkes and Burke* (London, 1963), Chs. 3 and 4.

not. Swift, he says, "washed himself with oriental scrupulosity," a fine expression that has been deservedly praised and is even better in the context of the simple diction that surrounds it: "The person of Swift had not many recommendations. He had a kind of muddy complexion, which, though he washed himself with oriental scrupulosity, did not look clear. He had a countenance sour and severe, which he seldom softened by any appearance of gaiety. He stubbornly resisted any tendency to laughter" (*Life of Swift*, III, 55-56). Or, again, Addison is described as wandering behind the scenes during the first night of *Cato* "with restless and unappeasable solicitude" (*Life of Addison*, II, 101).

Very often the big words will follow upon short ones with a deliberately amusing effect, as in the splendid sentence "Nothing is less exhilarating than the ludicrousness of Denham." "He appears to have had, in common with almost all mankind, the ambition of being upon proper occasions *a merry fellow*, and in common with most of them to have been by nature or by early habits debarred from it. Nothing is less exhilarating than the ludicrousness of Denham. He does not fail for want of efforts: he is familiar, he is gross; but he is never merry" (*Life of Denham*, I, 75-76).

At times this alternation of simple and Latinate diction seems intended to embody a critical point, as when Johnson comments on Cowley's *Olympic Ode*, "The connection is supplied with great perspicuity, and the thoughts, which to a reader of less skill seem thrown together by chance, are concatenated without any abruption" (*Life of Cowley*, I, 43). The careless (and probably ignorant) reader sees only a series of thoughts that have been "thrown together." The skillful (and probably learned) reader sees thoughts that have been "concatenated without any abruption." The magnitude of the diction is a compliment to the qualified reader of Cowley. "Abruption," incidentally, may not have seemed to Johnson a serious departure from ordinary English usage. When he repeats the distinction he uses a more familiar form, saying of Young that "his style is sometimes concatenated and sometimes abrupt" (*Life of Young*, III, 393).

Johnson's virtuosity enhances the effect of his criticism in two ways: by impressing us with the mental resources of a man so versatile in language, and by keeping up our interest with pacing and control. As Frye observes, "What distinguishes, not simply the epigram, but profundity itself from platitude is very frequently rhetorical wit."[14] Johnson draws on an extraordinarily acute sense of the weight and range of language, whether he uses big words or little: for instance, in his playfulness about Milton's obsession with a "lagging race of frosty grovellers" (*Life of Milton*, I, 138) or his account of the lady to whom Waller addressed passionate verses until she "drove him away" (*Life of Waller*, I, 253). Similarly, in conversation, where his gifts have been more clearly recognized, he can use the simplest language memorably—"Babies do not want to hear about babies" (*Miscellanies*, I, 156)—or can use his favorite antitheses to make a penetrating observation, as in the remark about the violinist: "Difficult do you call it, Sir? I wish it were impossible" (*Miscellanies*, II, 308). The statement is perfectly logical—if something becomes too difficult, it *is* impossible—but it contradicts all our assumptions about art, in which hard equals good, as in "the fascination of what's difficult" that tormented Yeats.

Any close study of a writer's style runs the risk of exaggerating those aspects which, being "characteristic" of the author, are most convenient for analysis or most useful for the specialized task of determining the attribution of anonymous works. What Johnson's admirers enjoy most in his prose cannot be reduced to definition, and depends on his fine sense of pace and rhythm. Here, for instance, is a passage wholly without polyllables that is unmistakably Johnsonian: "I eat meat seldom, and take physick often, and fancy that I grow light and airy. A man that does not begin to grow light and airy at seventy, is certainly losing time, if he intends ever to be light and airy" (*Letters*, II, 316). Whenever we have access to Johnson's revisions, we see him striving to give his prose greater life and strength. Sometimes this means adopting simpler words. "All future votaries of solitude" becomes "all that may hereafter pant for solitude." Or, again, "Socrates was rather of opinion that what we had to learn was, how to obtain and communicate happiness" becomes ". . . to do good and avoid

[14]Northrop Frye, *Anatomy of Criticism* (Princeton, 1957), p 329. Earlier Frye remarks, "A style founded on simple native words can be the most artificial of all styles. Samuel Johnson at his most bumbling is still colloquial and conversational compared to a William Morris romance" (p. 270).

evil." At other times grander language is required. The splendid sentence "The stream of time, which is continually washing the dissoluble fabricks of other poets, passes without injury by the adamant of Shakespeare" originally contained the phrase "is continually shattering the frail cement of other poets."[15]

Another of Johnson's alleged defects is his fondness for abstractions. Donald J. Greene has effectively disposed of the idea that Johnson is incapable of sensory imagery, but we can go further and say that even when his abstractions really *are* abstract, containing not even buried metaphors, they may still be as lively and striking as the metaphors of other men. Anna Seward (who detested Johnson but thought well of his essays) wrote in 1789, "Johnson's best prose, so justly admired, strikes me as highly poetic, from his habit of using abstract expressions, which at once elevate his language, and compress his sense."[16]

Consider the sort of thing that Wimsatt singles out for censure:

"That vehemence of desire which presses through right and wrong to its gratification, or that anxious inquietude which is justly chargeable with distrust of heaven." An abstraction of an abstraction pressing through right and wrong to another abstraction. . . . In *The False Alarm*, "Lampoon itself would disdain to speak ill. . ." The danger of constant abstraction, besides its leading to occasional violation of idiom, is, like the danger of other types of meaning we have considered, that of irrelevant meaning. A series of metaphysical substantives engrafted into a discourse, standing out like shadows from every concrete substantive or rising like ghosts in the level road of verbs and adjectives, is a series of meanings that may point in many wrong directions. Abstraction is the conjuring into substantiality of qualities which in the physical world have not this dignity." [*Prose Style*, pp. 58-59]

I have quoted this argument at length because it corresponds to a widespread attitude and is defended only on a priori grounds:

[15]The first two quotations are from the *Life of Cowley*, I, 16, and the *Life of Milton*, I, 100; the original readings are given by Boswell in the *Life*, IV, 38, 44. The final quotation is from the *Preface* in the Yale *Works*, VII, 70; a photograph of the revised proof sheet appears facing that page, and a transcription of the original version on p. 113*n*.

[16]Greene, " 'Pictures to the Mind': Johnson and Imagery," in *Johnson, Boswell, and Their Circle* (Oxford, 1965), 137-58; Anna Seward to Erasmus Darwin, 29 May 1789, *Letters* (Edinburgh, 1811), II, 267.

real ("concrete") things are more dignified than abstract ones. But why should this be so, except in Laputa where people must carry about every object of which they speak? *Vehemence, presses through*, and *anxious inquietude* are all strong and interesting words, though I would not claim the sentence as Johnson's finest; how would rewriting it more concretely be an improvement?

Here the abstraction is only used to gain concentration, but in the second example it has a clear rhetorical effect. It is not Johnson who disdains to speak ill, or even satirists who do; "lampoon itself" disdains. The very spirit of abuse finds Wilkes not worth bothering about, for as Johnson goes on, "Lampoon itself would disdain to speak ill of him of whom no man speaks well." Wilkes is safe from satirical invective because he is below it. A similar example is familiar from the *Life of Gray*: "Criticism disdains to chase a school-boy to his common-places" (III, 436). Although neither Johnson nor criticism will stoop to look at Gray, the diction sufficiently conveys what the two of them would say if they did so: "disdains" is expressive, "chase" is deliberately belittling, and the immensely learned Gray is reduced to an uncritical "school-boy." No wonder the *Life of Gray* enraged the poet's admirers. This is brilliant critical innuendo.

What Johnson is doing here is familiar enough in rhetoric as the convention of refusing to say what you are in fact saying. The show of open-minded honesty masks the insertion of the knife. One of the best examples in Johnson's writings occurs in the characterization of Junius in *Thoughts on the Late Transactions respecting Falkland's Islands*: "Let us abstract from his wit the vivacity of insolence, and withdraw from his efficacy the sympathetick favour of plebeian malignity; I do not say that we shall leave him nothing; the cause that I defend, scorns the help of falsehood; but if we leave him only his merit, what will be his praise?" (1825 *Works*, VI, 205). The political pamphlets of 1770s helped Johnson to hone these techniques, which are also apparent in the letters to Chesterfield and Macpherson and in some of his conversational sallies. The point is important because much of the critical rhetoric in the *Lives* is not dissimilar to the political rhetoric of the pamphlets. The weakness of Swift's plain style, in Johnson's opinion, is its neglect of persuasion. "For purposes merely didactick, when something is to be told that was not known before, it is the best mode, but against that inattention by which known truths are suffered to lie neglected it makes no provision; it instructs, but does not persuade" (*Life of Swift*, III, 52). Rhetoric in Johnson's hands is never used except in the service of what he considers rationally defensible. It accompanies and enriches argument. He thought Wilkes and Junius wicked and Gray's mythologizing puerile; his departure from measured reasoning to say so, though exasperating to Patriots and Gray enthusiasts, is not at all an abdication of intellectual responsibility. Of course if he is wrong about Junius or Gray the invective will not show us why, but the *Falkland's Islands* tract and the *Life of Gray* contain plenty of conventional argument for that purpose. Johnson's is a highly personal style that urges the reader into complicity with the writer. If we can share his views we can enjoy his treatment of Junius and Gray.

These considerations lead us to a recurring feature in the *Lives of the Poets* that has bothered many readers, and in any given instance may bother them rightly. This is Johnson's habitual tendency to damn with faint praise, in particular when he defines what a poet is by reminding us what he is not. Consider this paragraph in the *Life of Swift*, which is filled with insidious qualifiers:

In his other works is found an equable tenour of easy language, which rather trickles than flows. His delight was in simplicity. That he has in his works no metaphor, as has been said, is not true; but his few metaphors seem to be received rather by necessity than choice. He studied purity; and though perhaps all his structures are not exact, yet it is not often that solecisms can be found: and whoever depends on his authority may generally conclude himself safe. His sentences are never too much dilated or contracted; and it will not be easy to find any embarrassment in the complication of his clauses, any inconsequence in his connections, or abruptness in his transitions. [III, 51-52]

The passage continues for two more paragraphs, dealing out more of the same apparently even-handed analysis. Taken simply as description, it seems accurate enough: it leaves a good deal out, but does not seriously distort what it includes. Yet it is full of negative implications, beginning with the paradoxical notion of a style that can be easy and yet fail to flow. Swift is defended against the charge that he has no metaphors, *but* the only ones he has were somehow forced upon him "rather by necessity than choice." He studied purity, though "perhaps" not always successfully, and anyone trusting his authority will "generally" be safe. Johnson's sense of irritation appears especially clearly in the implication that he would find more faults in Swift if he could, and perhaps that he could indeed find them if he really tried: "yet it is not often that solecisms can be found"; "it will not be easy to find any embarrassment."

The *Life of Swift* is particularly full of such devices; Johnson can even conduct a positive-and-negative antithesis in such a way that *both* elements turn out to be negative: "When distinctions came to be made the part which gave least pleasure was that which describes the Flying Island, and that which gave most disgust must be the history of the Houyhnhnms" (p. 38). He had written similarly in the *Journey to the Western Islands*: "Inch Keith is nothing more than a rock covered with a thin layer of earth, not wholly bare of grass, and very fertile of thistles" (Yale *Works*, IX, 3).

Still, in the *Life of Swift* we know how to allow for Johnson's hostility. In other places the concealed negative may be harder to interpret or even to detect. His revisions show that an interchangeability of positive and negative forms was a habit of mind that could be exercised without obvious rhetorical intent.[17] At times he can use the mode for wholly complimentary purposes, as in the account of Goldsmith which we have already seen quoted by Burrowes. Here Johnson is simply using the "though deep, yet clear, though gentle, yet not dull" framework of Denham's famous lines, which he praised for the way in which "the particulars of resemblance are so perspicaciously collected, and every mode of excellence separated from its adjacent fault by so nice a line of limitation" (*Life of Denham*, I, 79). The framework

---

[17]"His images are sometimes confused" is altered to " . . .are not always distinct" (*Life of Waller*, I, 286); "Every sheet enabled him to write the next with less trouble" becomes " . . .with more facility" (*Life of Pope*, III, 142; readings in the *Life*, IV, 40, 52). I do not suggest that these alterations have no effect on the meaning, only that they do not change the implications of value (negative for Waller, positive for Pope).

itself is neutral; it takes on its evaluative aspect by the context and the kinds of words that are chosen.

When Johnson wishes he can be unequivocal in his praise (Goldsmith) or open in his blame (Swift), but he is also capable of being very tricky indeed, as in the account of Addison's style:

> His prose is the model of the middle style; on grave subjects not formal, on light occasions not groveling; pure without scrupulosity, and exact without apparent elaboration; always equable, and always easy, without glowing words or pointed sentences. Addison never deviates from his track to snatch a grace; he seeks no ambitious ornaments, and tries no hazardous innovations. His page is always luminous, but never blazes in unexpected splendour. [*Life of Addison*, II, 149]

The passage rises to the unreserved praise of the conclusion, "Whoever wishes to attain an English style, familiar but not coarse, and elegant but not ostentatious, must give his days and nights to the volumes of Addison" (p. 150). No one would choose to be coarse and ostentatious; the categories here exclude only defects. But in the earlier remarks this is not so clear, and one's interpretation will depend largely on factors external to the passage. If an equable, luminous style is one's own ideal, then this is unqualified praise. But if one shares Johnson's admiration for "the heroes in literature" (*Rambler* 137), one will expect poets and moralists to attempt at least as much as the scholars to whom he there refers. Addison will not take risks ("tries no hazardous innovations"). There is an analogy with "the dilatory caution of Pope" and the contrast that explains Johnson's greater love for Dryden: "If of Dryden's fire the blaze is brighter, of Pope's the heat is more regular and constant" (*Life of Pope*, III, 223). Addison is luminous "but never blazes in unexpected splendour." It follows that the passage about Addison's prose is potentially disparaging, but only for a reader who brings a prior evaluation of his own to the qualities Johnson describes. Boswell quotes it as being wholly favorable (*Life*, I, 224-25); Mrs. Thrale believed she had got Johnson to admit "he never did like [Addison's style] though he always thought fit to praise it" (*Miscellanies*, I, 283). One sort of reader may feel that the passage contains only praise, while another may detect covert blame in the distinctions that tell what Addison is not as well as what he is.

We have been looking at some of the more equivocal possibilities of Johnson's style; let us close with three examples from the *Lives* (none of them formal set pieces) that illustrate how flexible and judicious it can be. The first is concerned with the Pindaric fashion that prevailed in the time of Cowley:

This lax and lawless versification so much concealed the deficiencies of the barren and flattered the laziness of the idle, that it immediately overspread our books of poetry; all the boys and girls caught the pleasing fashion, and they that could do nothing else could write like Pindar. The rights of antiquity were invaded, and disorder tried to break into the Latin: a poem on the Sheldonian Theatre, in which all kinds of verse are shaken together, is unhappily inserted in the *Musae Anglicanae*. Pindarism prevailed above half a century, but at last died gradually away, and other imitations supply its place. [*Life of Cowley*, I, 48]

The vigor of the passage derives from the central idea of Pindarism as an active force, almost like the contagious Bacchic frenzy, or like a disease that "overspreads" the nation and attacks especially the weakest people (the barren and the idle). This active role is nicely balanced, in Johnson's ironic language, by the real facts: the force that tries to break into Latin verse is in truth nothing more impressive than a preference for mindless poetry whose parts can be "shaken together" at random. At length the plague passes away, as mysteriously as it came, "and other imitations supply its place." The barren and idle will always want some excuse to avoid striving for the highest standards; the boys and girls who once believed that they wrote like Pindar must now find some other reason not to write like themselves.

The next example is a fragment of literary biography:

He was not yet deterred from heroick poetry; there was another monarch of this island (for he did not fetch his heroes from foreign countries) whom he considered as worthy of the epick muse, and he dignified Alfred (1723) with twelve books. But the opinion of the nation was now settled; a hero introduced by Blackmore was not likely to find either respect or kindness. *Alfred* took his place by *Eliza* in silence and darkness: benevolence was ashamed to favour, and malice was weary of insulting. Of his four epick poems the first had such reputation and popularity as enraged the criticks; the second was at least known enough to be ridiculed; the two last had neither friends nor enemies. [*Life of Blackmore*, II, 249-50]

This paragraph is remarkable for conciseness and accuracy of statement. There is a brief hint of *ubi sunt* pathos in the "silence and darkness" that have enveloped the twelve books of Blackmorean verse; immediately afterward comes a very Johnsonian parallelism made up of abstractions whose effect seems perfect. As the multiplied individuals who might have bought Blackmore's book have been united into "the nation" that refuses to, so now they are generalized still further, like the lampoon that disdained to ridicule Wilkes. No patrons can encourage Blackmore since benevolence itself is now "ashamed" to notice him; no critics can attack him (as they did his earlier efforts) because malice itself has grown exhausted in the endless labor of deriding him. The parallel clauses of the conclusion emphasize the pathetic decline of a poetic career in which it is at least better to be mocked than ignored. Blackmore is reduced to one of the tiny figures of the *Dunciad*, scribbling on in vain with insectlike diligence; and Johnson's balanced clauses, like Pope's couplets, present him to our view in a more ordered perspective than he himself could ever achieve.

My final example is a brief paragraph in the *Life of Savage*, composed of a single sentence: "He was still· in his usual Exigences, having no certain Support but the Pension allowed him by the Queen, which though it might have kept an exact Oeconomist from Want, was very far from being sufficient for Mr. *Savage*, who had never been accustomed to dismiss any of his Appetites without the Gratification which they solicited, and whom nothing but Want of Money withheld from partaking of every Pleasure that fell within his View" (*Savage*, p. 87). This slowly evolving sentence exhibits an interesting alternation of active and passive senses as Johnson surveys a central feature of Savage's character. Savage appears as an agent who was not accustomed to *dismiss* his appetites; yet they are represented as *soliciting* a gratification which he permits before he does dismiss them. So we have a sort of psychomachia in which Savage believes he is acting (dismissing his appetites when he is ready to do so) but really is being acted upon. The final clause starts out as passive, Savage now appearing as *whom*, as a subject whom an external force *withholds*. But that force is a privation, "Want of Money," not a positive thing, and what it withholds him from is activity: "*partaking* of every Pleasure that fell within his View ," like the tireless sybarites of *Vathek*. I do not mean to make too much of these perfectly ordinary syntactical effects, only to point out how neatly they reinforce the image of Savage that is built up in the *Life* as a whole, a strangely passive man who drifts through life, living from moment to moment, while deceiving himself and sometimes his friends with the rhetoric and mental assumptions of a man of action. As evidence, incidentally, that Johnson appreciates the possibilities of these effects, there is his comment on Rochester's *On Nothing*: "*Nothing* must be considered as having not only a negative but a kind of positive signification; as I need not fear thieves, I have *nothing*; and *nothing* is a very powerful protector. In the first part of the sentence it is taken negatively; in the second it is taken positively, as an agent" (*Life of Rochester*, I, 225).

Johnson's style should be seen, then, not as a collection of curious mannerisms, but as a medium perfectly suited to the ever-widening relations between narrative, moral assessment, and criticism that he likes to develop. It is not a flowing style on the order of Hazlitt's. In the terms of seventeenth-century rhetoric it is Ciceronian as opposed to Attic. Though it may lack the close logical progression of the Ciceronian mode, still it is closer to oratorical rhetoric than to the subtle windings of the style that sought, in Morris Croll's words, to express "the secret experiences of arduous and solitary minds."[18] But both Attic and Ciceronian styles resemble each other in one respect; they place great importance on the connectedness of thought, in contrast to the later prose of which Coleridge said, "In your modern books, for the most part, the sentences in a page have the same connexion with each other that marbles have in a bag: they touch without adhering."[19]

"In Johnson's prose," James Sutherland writes, "the foreseen triumphs continually over the fortuitous."[20] This is accurate enough so long as we recognize its ex post facto quality. Johnson foresees the outcome of each sentence, each paragraph; but the

[18]"'Attic Prose' in the Seventeenth Century," *Studies in Philology*, 18 (1921), 122.
[19]*Table Talk*, p. 242 (15 May 1833).
[20]"Some Aspects of Eighteenth-Century Prose," *Essays on the Eighteenth Century, Presented to David Nichol Smith* (Oxford, 1945), p. 103.

reader does not, and the desire to see the clausal relationships work themselves out is one of the impelling forces that carries him forward. Sir Joshua Reynolds, knowing nothing yet of Johnson, began to read the *Life of Savage* while he was leaning against a chimneypiece, and read on till he had finished the book and his arm had gone numb (*Life*, I, 165). In the *Gentleman's Magazine* in 1781 Robert Potter said of the *Lives*, "By adopting a style familiar and nearly colloquial, Dr. Johnson rather talks than writes to his reader;. . .he directs him on a new-made road to knowledge as if present, informs him of the characters, circumstances, and incidents of the inhabitants as he passes along, and stops with him now and then for refreshment, becoming his friend as well as fellow-traveller." Another correspondent indignantly retorted that to call Johnson's style colloquial was highly paradoxical, yet there is great justice in the description.[21] Johnson does not attempt the colloquial style of Addison or Swift, but he has developed an *equivalent* for it, in which his many peculiarities, rather than inhibiting our interest as we read, strike us as the expression of an uncommon energy of mind, and encourage us to think with responsive energy.

[21]*Gentleman's Magazine*, 51 (1781), 564, and 52 (1782), 21. Potter ("W. B.") had been offering a long series of comments on specific passages in the *Lives*.

4 Pastoral and Epic: The Implications of Genre

AMONG THE DISTINGUISHING CHARACTERISTICS of Johnson's criticism, one of the most striking is its relative neglect of genre, in contrast either to his neoclassical predecessors or to most modern literary theorists. This indifference is at least partly accounted for by Johnson's emphasis on the entirety of a writer's work, suppressing generic considerations in a unitary interpretation that can work in either of two directions. On the one hand he may seek to define the qualities of a writer's genius that manifest themselves in any of his works: "Pope had likewise genius, a mind active, ambitious, and adventurous, always investigating, always aspiring; in its widest searches still longing to go forward, in its highest flights still wishing to be higher" (*Life of Pope*, III, 217). Or on the other hand he may dwell upon the complexity of the real world to be imitated: "Shakespeare's plays are not in the rigorous and critical sense either tragedies or comedies, but compositions of a distinct kind; exhibiting the real state of sublunary nature, which partakes of good and evil, joy and sorrow, mingled with endless variety of proportion and innumerable modes of combination" (*Preface*, p. 66).

Despite this antigeneric orientation, however, Johnson's specific opinions are influenced to a surprising degree by his reaction to existing theories of genre, and a submerged theoretical argument underlies some of his best-known critical discussions. In this chapter I shall examine two such topics, pastoral and epic. Johnson's dislike of pastoral is notorious, but we can understand it better if we realize that his attitude developed in direct response to contemporary theory. And if the theory of pastoral gave him his chief weapon for attacking Milton's *Lycidas*, the theory of epic provides him with a very interesting approach to the virtues as well as the limitations of *Paradise Lost*. A study of Johnson's response to critical tradition, moreover, will help to illuminate his conception of the relation between poems and reality and between readers and poems.

Pastoral

Johnson has long served as a convenient lay figure for scholars recommending pastoral poetry to readers who may find themselves put off by it. Frank Kermode, for example, intends his influential anthology for general readers "who experience discomfort when confronted with literary shepherds, nymphs, mazers, sheep-hooks, and the rest of the properties of pastoral poetry," much as Johnson says that "an intelligent reader acquainted with the scenes of real life sickens at the mention of the *crook*, the *pipe*, the *sheep*, and the *kids*" (*Life of Shenstone*, III, 356). Kermode begins his discussion by quoting Johnson on *Lycidas*, and concludes that "the old poetry, and everything that gave it its peculiar richness, had been largely forgotten by the time Johnson expressed his rational objections to *Lycidas*." Johnson in turn has had his defenders, who have not cared much for Walter Jackson Bate's concessive opinion that the *Lycidas* passage is one of his "few quaint misfires" and have striven instead to show the consistency of his position. "Johnson was true to his norms," Warren Fleischauer concludes in a valuable study of Johnson's moral and aesthetic presuppositions, "and therefore not false to *Lycidas*."[1]

Whether such a defense would placate the poem's admirers may be doubted, but Fleischauer has succeeded in showing that Johnson's chief objections to *Lycidas* are directed not so much against pastoral as against Milton's use of pastoral *form* in an inappropriate context, and that his real animus depends upon a series of other assumptions about syntactical "harshness," elegiac sincerity, and Christianized mythology. For these reasons the *Lycidas* passage is not a rewarding source of information about Johnson's most thoughtful opinion of pastoral. "Easy,

[1]Kermode, *English Pastoral Poetry* (London, 1952), pp. 6, 13, 42; Bate, *Achievement of Samuel Johnson*, p. 219; Fleischauer, "Johnson, *Lycidas*, and the Norms of Criticism," in *Johnsonian Studies*, ed. Magdi Wahba (Cairo, 1962), p. 256. For two recent attempts to order Johnson's pastoral criticism, see Richard Kelly, "Johnson among the Sheep," *Studies in English Literature*, 8 (1968), 475-85, and Oliver F. Sigworth, "Johnson's *Lycidas*: The End of Renaissance Criticism," *Eighteenth Century Studies*, 1 (1967), 159-68, followed by an exchange with Victor J. Milne in Vol. 2 (1969), 300-302.

vulgar, and therefore disgusting" (*Life of Milton*, I, 163) is one of those phrases that have passed into common recollection, like "nasty, brutish, and short." Johnson uses it with conscious polemical intention to rebuke Milton for choosing a form beneath his highest abilities, and does not imply a considered and dispassionate view of the genre.

If we turn to Johnson's more fully developed ideas about pastoral, particularly as expressed in *Ramblers* 36 and 37, we will see the issue in a wider and more interesting context: not as the cranky dismissal of a single masterpiece, but as a shrewdly calculated contribution to an ongoing theoretical debate, with important implications for the poetry of the future rather than the past. That debate, familiar from J. E. Congleton's survey,[2] tended to organize itself around a neoclassical and a rationalist school, the former taking Virgil's *Eclogues* as its model and approving the myth of the Golden Age, the latter preferring Theocritus and Spenser and deducing the nature of pastoral from actual rustic life and the nature of the human mind rather than from classical precedent. Fontenelle, the leading rationalist theorist, was a disciple of Descartes, and his *Discours sur la nature de l'églogue* reflected a general commitment to the moderns in preference to the ancients. In the early eighteenth century a revival of the debate produced a moderate amount of excitement in England, as Thomas Tickell elaborated the rationalist view and praised the Spenserian rusticity of Ambrose Philips, while Pope offered an eclectic theory that placed heavy emphasis on the neoclassical arguments of René Rapin.

In such an account Johnson will emerge, as he does in Congleton's book, as a member of the rationalist school whose preference for Virgil is explained merely as personal taste. But Johnson's position is more complicated than that, for reasons that will become clear if we realize that both theoretical schools shared a scarcely examined genetic assumption that the origin of pastoral could and should determine what it continued to be (just as, more recently, people have tried to define tragedy by locating its origin in harvest rituals and goat dances). Pope therefore thought it important to show that Fontenelle's rational

_____

[2]*Theories of Pastoral Poetry in England, 1684-1798* (Gainesville, Fla., 1952).

principles were identical with Rapin's classical rules. The rationalists argued that a study of nature will *not* give us Virgil, who, in Scaliger's words, does not seem "to have been taught by nature, but to have vied with it, or even better to have given it laws. . . . We have not been able to get from nature a single pattern such as the *ideas* of Virgil can furnish us." But to answer the rationalists, Pope wants to argue that nature, suitably idealized, really is as Virgil describes it, or at least must have been so in the historically real Golden Age. "As the keeping of flocks," Pope explains, "seems to have been the first employment of mankind, the most ancient sort of poetry was probably pastoral. . . . Pastoral is an image of what they call the Golden age. So that we are not to describe our shepherds as shepherds at this day really are, but as they may be conceiv'd then to have been; when the best of men follow'd the employment."[3]

When Johnson came to write on pastoral in the *Rambler*, some forty years after the debate between Pope and Tickell, his intention was clearly to break out of an impacted critical tradition by going back to fundamental questions. Just as *Rambler* 125 recommends that literary kinds be defined "by their effects upon the mind," so *Rambler* 36 begins by naming the psychological reason that has made pastoral poetry popular: "It exhibits a life, to which we have been always accustomed to associate peace, and leisure, and innocence" (III, 195). True though this statement may be, it implies a further assumption common to most earlier theorists, that unrest and vice must be excluded from the genre. Such a definition of pastoral is too narrow to admit Sidney's *Arcadia*, which, Johnson elsewhere says, confounds "the pastoral with the feudal times, the days of innocence, quiet and security, with those of turbulence, violence and adventure" (*Preface*, p. 72).

As the remark about the *Arcadia* suggests, Johnson cannot quite stay clear of the trap of geneticism that entangled his predecessors. The energetic beginning of the next paragraph in

[3]J. C. Scaliger, *Ars Poetica* (1561), in *Select Translations from Scaliger's Poetics*, trans. F. M. Padelford (New York, 1905), p. 52; Pope, *Discourse on Pastoral Poetry*, in The Twickenham Edition of the Poems of Alexander Pope (hereafter cited as Twickenham Ed., *Poems*), Vol. I, *Pastoral Poetry and An Essay on Criticism*, ed. E. Audra and Aubrey Williams (London, 1961), pp. 23, 25.

Rambler 36 seems an attempt to fight clear of it: "It has been
maintained by some, who love to talk of what they do not know,
that pastoral is the most ancient poetry." But Johnson goes on to
accept this conjecture as reasonable and to drive home its implications in a most unflattering way. As he sees it, ontogeny re-
capitulates phylogeny, as the embryo repeats the history of its
species: the poems that served for the first men are likewise
associated with childhood today. "We are therefore delighted
with rural pictures, because we know the original at an age when
our curiosity can be very little awakened by descriptions of courts
which we never beheld, or representations of passion which we
never felt" (p. 196). By an adroit use of the genetic assumption
Johnson is able to suggest that pastoral chiefly interests those
who have not yet seen life and those of mature age who wish to
relive their immaturity. In the same way, Scaliger had begun his
survey with pastoral in order to "follow the suggestion of nature,
which derives the more complex from the simpler," and, like
Johnson, regarded it as "the mildest, the most naive, and the
most inept" of genres. It was a rare critic who saw that pastoral is
really a highly sophisticated form that seeks, as William Empson
has said, to put "the complex into the simple." To recognize this,
it was necessary to break free of geneticism as Puttenham did,
denying "that the *Eglogue* should be the first and most auncient
form of artificiall Poesie, being perswaded that the Poet deuised
the *Eglogue* long after the other *dramatick* poems, not of purpose
to counterfait or represent the rusticall manner of loues and
communication, but under the vaile of homely persons and in
rude speeches to insinuate and glaunce at greater matters."[4]

     Thus Johnson's procedure allows him to assume the puerility
of pastoral, with its revived appeal in second childhood when
"we recur to it in old age as a port of rest." And another assumption is quickly introduced, that poetry of this kind can only be
conventional, adopted by apprentice poets who can write nothing else and imitated from each other rather than from life,
"transmitting the same images in the same combination from
one to another, till he that reads the title of a poem, may guess at

[4]Scaliger, *Select Translations*, p. 20; Empson, *Some Versions of Pastoral* (London, 1935), p. 23; Puttenham, *Arte of English Poesie* (1589), in *Elizabethan Critical
Essays*, ed. G. Gregory Smith (Oxford, 1904), II, 40.

the whole series of the composition" (p. 197). Johnson is following here an established tradition that the young poet should
begin with pastoral,[5] but it was not usual to imply that *only* the
young could have any use for it. Whenever one meets pastoral in
Johnson's criticism, these connotations of childishness and con-
ventionality are present. The comedy Cowley wrote at school "is
of the pastoral kind, which requires no acquaintance with the
living world" (*Life of Cowley*, I, 4). Pope began in the same way
since "it seems natural for a young poet to initiate himself by
Pastorals, which, not professing to imitate real life, require no
experience, and, exhibiting only the simple operations of un-
mingled passions, admit no subtle reasoning or deep inquiry"
(*Life of Pope*, III, 224).

From this it is only a step to the idea that the audience for
pastoral must be as puerile as its authors: "There is something in
the poetical Arcadia so remote from known reality and speculative possibility, that we can never support its representation
through a long work. A Pastoral of an hundred lines may be
endured; but who will hear of sheep and goats, and myrtle
bowers and purling rivulets, through five acts? Such scenes
please barbarians in the dawn of literature, and children in the
dawn of life; but will be for the most part thrown away as men
grow wise, and nations grow learned" (*Life of Gay*, II, 284-85). In
reading Johnson's survey of Renaissance pastoral in the *Life of
Ambrose Philips* (III, 316-18), one gets the impression of a dead
genre artificially revived by bookish men and then kept tenu-
ously alive by shallow imitators. *Rambler* 121, which deals with
the dangers of imitation, mentions that "at one period, all the
poets followed sheep, and every event produced a pastoral," and
adds that any fashion will become popular "by which idleness is
favoured, and imbecillity assisted" (IV, 284).

These passages from Johnson's criticism confirm the two
half-buried assumptions with which *Rambler* 36 begins: that pastoral (or at least modern pastoral) must be mild and weak, and
that its antiquity makes it appropriate only for barbarians, chil-

[5]See Congleton, p. 16. Spenser's annotator E. K. thought that pastoral was
well suited to beginners, "being both so base for the matter, and homely for the
manner" (*Poetical Works of Edmund Spenser*, ed. J. C. Smith and Ernest de
Selincourt [London, 1932], p. 417).

dren, and trivial poets who would rather copy than invent. The rest of the paper follows inevitably: "The range of pastoral is indeed narrow. . . . Not only the images of rural life, but the occasions on which they can be properly produced, are few and general" (pp. 197, 198). A rather long discussion is devoted to the piscatory eclogues of Sannazarius, to show the absurd expedients of a poet trying to enlarge the narrow bounds of pastoral ("the indignation of a fisher that his oysters are refused, and Mycon's accepted") and the tendency of pastoral poets to be out of touch with reality ("this defect Sannazarius was hindered from perceiving, by writing in a learned language").

In the following paper, *Rambler* 37, Johnson proposes "to enquire after some more distinct and exact idea of this kind of writing" than previous critics have afforded, but the apparently commonsense observations of *Rambler* 36 have effectively predetermined what he will find. He can afford to say at this point, "If we search the writings of Virgil, for the true definition of a pastoral, it will be found 'a poem in which any action or passion is represented by its effects upon a country life' " (p. 201). This definition is very close to that of Fontenelle: "the imitation of the Action of a Sheapard, or of one taken under that Character."[6] But the difference between them is important, as may be seen by glancing at the full definition in Johnson's *Dictionary* (1755): "A poem in which any action or passion is represented by its effects upon a country life; or according to the common practice in which speakers take upon them the character of shepherds; an idyl; a bucolick." As a lexicographer Johnson has to include the second definition in which speakers *take upon them* the character of shepherds. By implication they need not be actual shepherds, and this definition is much closer to Virgil's practice than the one advanced in *Rambler* 37 and repeated in the first part of the *Dictionary* definition.

Though claiming the authority of Virgil, Johnson has covertly imposed the assumptions of *Rambler* 36, in which nothing is essential to pastoral save rusticity and simplicity. He therefore goes on to reject the idea that the persons in a pastoral must be

---

[6]"A Treatise de Carmine Pastorali," *Idylliums of Theocritus*, trans. Thomas Creech (1684), p. 19.

shepherds, since the form "admits of all ranks of persons, because persons of all ranks inhabit the country" (p. 203). This
apparently liberalizing assertion is in fact part of a skillful effort
to rule out most of what happens in existing pastorals, including
Virgil's. As Johnson cheerfully admits, he has made "no mention
of the golden age" (p. 201), and he goes on to denounce as well
the sort of thing that Milton does in *Lycidas*: "It is therefore
improper to give the title of a pastoral to verses, in which the
speakers, after the slight mention of their flocks, fall to com-
plaints of errors in the church, and corruptions in the government, or to lamentations of the death of some illustrious person,
whom when once the poet has called a shepherd, he has no
longer any labour upon his hands, but can make the clouds
weep, and lilies wither, and the sheep hang their heads, without
art or learning, genius or study" (pp. 204-5).

   By now it is clear what a subversive use Johnson has made of
critical tradition, even while he avoids a clean break with it. If he
had begun as he seems to do, by asking why people actually like
existing pastorals, he could not have been so contemptuous of
Lycidas. Instead he begins by defining what a pastoral poem must
be and is then able to conclude that *Lycidas* is an unacceptable
one. The same procedure appears in *Adventurer* 92, written three
years later, in which he examines the *Eclogues* of Virgil. We have
independent evidence that he enjoyed these poems, but his
narrow definition of pastoral (implied here but not openly
stated) allows him to disqualify eight out of the ten as being at
least partly unsuccessful. Only the first and tenth remain un-
blemished, and these turn out to be admirable because in deriv-
ing them from real events, Virgil has surmounted the artificiality
in which pastoral has always gloried. "It may be observed, that
these two poems were produced by events that really happened;
and may, therefore, be of use to prove, that we can always feel
more than we can imagine, and that the most artful fiction must
give way to truth" (II, 424).

   It should be noted that Johnson does not refer to "events that
really happened" in a naive sense. The first *Eclogue* grows out of
the suffering of farmers who lost their lands after the civil wars,
but Johnson is equally interested in the positive satisfactions of
Tityrus, made doubly attractive because they are named by the

unhappy exile Meliboeus: "The description of Virgil's happiness in his little farm, combines almost all the images of rural pleasure: and he, therefore, that can read it with indifference, has no sense of pastoral poetry" (p. 423). What appeals to Johnson is the sense of real simplicity, all the more moving since it is mediated through sophisticated verse. The poem perfectly satisfies his prescription for pastoral: a great poet is responding to real life in the real country. More surprising is Johnson's esteem for the tenth *Eclogue*, which might have been expected to arouse his dislike of amatory pastoral as several of the others do. Here again it is the reality of the emotions that matters. "The complaint of Gallus disappointed in his love, is full of such sentiments as disappointed love naturally produces; his wishes are wild, his resentment is tender, and his purposes are inconstant." Gallus speaks, as Johnson goes on to say, "in the genuine language of despair." And he observes that Gallus knows his pastoral imaginings to be purely visionary, retaining his actual existence as a soldier. "Desirous to be any thing but what he is, he wishes himself one of the shepherds" (pp. 420-21). It is the poet, again, who must mediate his despair, as the final address to the muses makes clear.

Virgil's crucial achievement is to be faithful at once to rural life and to the heightening that Johnson expects from verse. That he attained complete success only twice shows how difficult, how liable to failure, the pastoral mode must be for any lesser poet. In Johnson's opinion most verse that attempts poetic heightening loses itself in fantasy and artificiality, while most verse about rural reality is rustic in the worst sense. That is to say, he agrees with the rationalists, as Congleton calls them, in believing that country life can be the only proper subject for pastoral, but unlike them he has little use for descriptions of ordinary country life. The early reviewers of Johnson's *Lives* were not being irrelevant when they argued that his strictures must come from a man who disliked the country. His friends were agreed that he had little taste for its usual pleasures; what is more to the point, he believed that art should be about human beings and had small sympathy for human beings in their rustic aspect. That is why it is most misleading to classify him with Fontenelle and Tickell and the other rationalists.

The rationalists as a rule preferred Theocritus to Virgil, regarding him as simpler and more natural; poets like Philips followed Spenser in trying to suggest artlessness with the clumsy rustic dialect that Pope ridicules in *Guardian* 40. To cite a typical late expression of this view, a reviewer in 1770 says that Thomas Warton "very judiciously proves the superiority of Theocritus over Virgil, by shewing, that the Greek poet copied real manners, and actual scenes of pastoral life, which have been misapplied, misrepresented, and distorted, in Virgil's imitations."[7] From everything that has been said so far about Johnson's definition of pastoral and his discussion of Virgil, one might expect him to join in the preference for Theocritus. He was no admirer of imitation, and indeed preferred Homer to Virgil in the epic. Yet here this is not the case. He told Bennet Langton that in Theocritus "the manners painted are coarse and gross,"[8] and the discussion in *Adventurer* 92, though more diplomatic ("Theocritus united elegance with simplicity") makes it clear that Virgil is better because he is less a writer of pastorals: "Virgil, however, taking advantage of another language, ventured to copy or to rival the Sicilian Bard: he has written with greater splendour of diction, and elevation of sentiment; but as the magnificence of his performances was more, the simplicity was less; and, perhaps, where he excels Theocritus, he sometimes obtains his superiority by deviating from the pastoral character, and performing what Theocritus never attempted" (II, 418). And the rusticity that might be excused in Theocritus, since the low connotations of his diction are lost in the mists of a dead language, is merely stupid in the moderns. Pope quotes a couplet from Spenser in *Guardian* 40—"Diggon Davey, I bid hur God-day/Or Diggon hur is, or I mis-say"—and comments archly that "one shepherd bids the other good-morrow in an unusual and elegant manner." Johnson, quoting the same lines, says more bluntly that "Spenser begins one of his pastorals with studied barbarity" (*Rambler* 37, III, 203).

Johnson's dislike of Theocritus, then, is not the accidental

---

[7]Review of Warton's edition of Theocritus, *Critical Review*, 29 (1770), 277.
[8]*Life*, IV, 2. Johnson must be thinking of Theocritus' use of homosexual themes, but his language suggests a broader application. On Homer and Virgil, see the *Life*, III, 193*n*, and IV, 218-19.

result of his fondness for Virgil, but indicates a serious disagreement with the rationalists. And as we have seen, his affection for the *Eclogues* is sufficiently qualified to make him a very
dubious neoclassicist. The much-imitated fifth *Eclogue*, for instance, which lies behind Pope's fourth *Pastoral*, is dismissed in
exactly the same terms as *Lycidas*: "Whoever shall read it with
impartiality, will find that most of the images are of the
mythological kind, and therefore easily invented; and that there
are few sentiments of rational praise, or natural lamentation"
(*Adventurer* 92). Johnson's contempt for the myth of the Golden
Age makes him hostile to the very thing that the neoclassical
theorists most admired in Virgil. His reasons for this attitude are
not very plainly stated in the papers on pastoral, but are made
clear in a later *Rambler*:

The poets have numbered among the felicities of the golden age, an
exemption from the change of seasons, and a perpetuity of spring; but
I am not certain that in this state of imaginary happiness they have
made sufficient provision for that insatiable demand of new gratifications, which seems particularly to characterize the nature of man. . . . It
is therefore not unlikely that however the fancy may be amused with
the description of regions in which no wind is heard but the gentle
zephir, and no scenes are displayed, but vallies enamelled with unfad-
ing flowers, and woods waving their perennial verdure, we should soon
grow weary of uniformity, find our thoughts languish for want of other
subjects, call on Heaven for our wonted round of seasons, and think
ourselves liberally recompensed for the inconveniencies of summer
and winter, by new perceptions of the calmness and mildness of the
intermediate variations. [*Rambler* 80, IV, 56-57]

Johnson will not concede that just because man *is* insatiable, a
changeless Golden Age is a profoundly attractive ideal. He wants
to think of pastoral as literally true. Much the same thing happens in *Rasselas*, where he skillfully deflates the Englishman's
perennial fascination with Arabia and Abyssinia and makes fun
of Nekayah's fantasies of playing the shepherdess.

   Still, Johnson prefers Virgil to Theocritus, for he realizes that
the rationalists are only deceiving themselves in their claim that
pastoral is about real life in the country. The inherent contradiction in their position can be illustrated in Tickell's *Guardian*

essays, the first of which begins by admitting the imaginary nature of the world it creates:

Pastoral poetry, not only amuses the fancy the most delightfully, but is likewise more indebted to it than any other sort whatsoever. It transports us into a kind of fairyland, where our ears are soothed with the melody of birds, bleating flocks, and purling streams; our eyes inchanted with flowery meadows and springing greens; we are laid under cool shades, and entertained with all the sweets and freshness of nature. It is a dream, it is a vision, which we wish may be real, and we believe that it is true.

Yet in a later paper we find Tickell defending Spenser's (and Philips's) use of humble British superstitions as follows: "The reason why such changes from the ancients should be introduced is very obvious; namely, that poetry being imitation, and that imitation being the best which deceives the most easily, it follows that we must take up the customs which are most familiar or universally known, since no man can be deceived or delighted with the imitation of what he is ignorant of."[9] This combination of fantasy and realism, with the connecting link of "deceit" that Johnson always opposed (like "delusion" in the drama) suggests how unsatisfactory the compromises of the rationalists must have looked to him.

There were plenty of writers besides Johnson who argued that pastoral should be about real life in the real country.[10] They assumed, however, that faithful description would produce good poetry; Johnson did not. In his eagerness to demolish the positions of both theoretical camps he virtually succeeded in doing away with pastoral altogether. If it is too elegant or allegorical it is not like life. If, on the other hand, it is like life it is almost sure to be ugly and uninteresting. Johnson relishes the irony that Gay's attempt to parody Philips was welcomed by the public as a just imitation of nature.

[Pope] is supposed to have incited Gay to write *The Shepherd's Week* to shew, that if it be necessary to copy nature with minuteness, rural life must be exhibited such as grossness and ignorance have made it. . . .

[9]*Guardians* 22 (6 Apr. 1713) and 30 (15 Apr. 1713).
[10]For a full survey see Congleton's Ch. 6, "The Emergence of Romanticism."

But the effect of reality and truth became conspicuous, even when the intention was to shew them groveling and degraded. These Pastorals became popular, and were read with delight, as just representations of rural manners and occupations, by those who had no interest in the rivalry of the poets, nor knowledge of the critical dispute. [*Life of Gay*, II, 269]

But images of a "groveling and degraded" truth, though better than mere fiction, are only a little better. Johnson was accustomed to use the term *pastoral* sarcastically in reference to actual rural life; in the *Journey to the Western Islands* he says that a hut at Loch Ness was owned by people who "possessed such property as a pastoral poet might exalt into riches," and relates that an old woman there, "with the true pastoral hospitality, . . .asked us to sit down and drink whisky" (Yale *Works*, IX, 32-33). Regardless of Gay's accidental success, "the poet's art is selection, and he ought to shew the beauties without the grossness of the country life" (*Life of Shenstone*, III, 356). From this it is only a short distance to the assertion that the pastoral poet is obliged to falsify the truth and invent fantasy worlds of no relevance to human life. Of Philip's poems Johnson writes with evident irony, "That they exhibit a mode of life which does not exist, nor ever existed, is not to be objected; the supposition of such a state is allowed to Pastoral (*Life of Philips*, III, 324).

However grave may be the limitations in Johnson's theory, our assessment of it can gain in sympathy if we reflect that like most other great critics—like Dryden, Coleridge, or Eliot—he looks toward the future as well as the past. The realist school, not the neoclassical, commanded the future, and Johnson was far from eccentric in opposing the artificiality of classical pastoral. As a writer in the year of *Lyrical Ballads* observed, pastoral had really been kept artificially alive by the prestige of Theocritus and Virgil in the system of classical education, not by its intrinsic interest. "In most of our dissertations on pastoral poetry, after due encomium on the merits of the Sicilian bard, few authors save Virgil, Spenser, Pope, Gay, and Philips are noticed, all except the second, translators, imitators, or parodists rather than original writers in the branch of poetry. If rural life no longer presents us with shepherds singing and piping for a bowl or a crook, why persist, in violation of all probability, to introduce such characters? If pastoral cannot exist without them, let us cease to compose it."[11]

One may add that only a very active will to admire could find much to enjoy in Spenser's "Doric" language—"Diggon Davey, I bid hur God-day"—and that Spenser was consciously artificial in what was later taken to be his naturalism, regarding the real peasants in Ireland with abhorrence. A successful "Doric" style had to come from more immediate sources, like the Scottish poetry that Johnson avoided knowing, of which the great master was to be Robert Burns.[12] Johnson's support of the young Crabbe is significant: against Goldsmith's sentimentalized (though impressive) rural ideal, he prefers Crabbe's gloomy picture of the narrowness and brutality of country life.

The examples of Burns and Crabbe point to the fullest explanation for Johnson's attitude toward pastoral, which needs to be seen as an expression of his fundamental honesty. His dislike of Renaissance literary conventions, though it results in unfairness to poets like Milton for whom they possessed imaginative life, is altogether appropriate with regard to the pale and exhausted conventions available to poets in his own time. It is not irrelevant that pastoral had become a senescent form that insulted the reader's intelligence whenever he opened a magazine or poetical miscellany.[13] Johnson may have been theoretically mistaken in believing that pastoral must be about real country life, but this belief was wholly appropriate as the eighteenth century drew to a close, and indeed was prophetic of what was to come. Wordsworth as well as Burns would soon reinvigorate the pas-

---

[11] Nathan Drake, "On Pastoral Poetry," *Literary Hours* (1798), p. 224.

[12] When Boswell waxed enthusiastic about a pastoral by Ramsay Johnson said, "You shall retain your superiority by my not knowing it" (*Life*, II, 220). Burns wrote in 1792, "In the sentiment & style of our Scotish airs, there is a pastoral simplicity, a something that one may call, the Doric style & dialect of vocal music, to which a dash of our native tongue & manners is particularly, nay peculiarly apposite" (*Letters*, ed. J. D. Ferguson [Oxford, 1931], II, 126).

[13] Many reviewers expressed disgust similar to Johnson's, as in this account of a volume of elegies by Gray's friend William Mason: "He then proceeds to describe the place of his friend's retreat, talks about *Sylvan wonders, Vertumnus* and *Pomona, huddling* brooks (which by the bye is a vile phrase) *cool* caves, and *whispering* vales, and ends with an invocation to the *genius of the wood*, with which, as there is nothing very excellent in it, we shall not trouble our readers" (*Critical Review*, 14 [1763], 449).

toral vision by locating it in a countryside that was no longer conventional scenic backdrop, but an actual place of life and work. The deepest lesson of Johnson's criticism of pastoral is that he hated the restrictions of arbitrary theory, especially when used to underwrite a moribund genre, and was prepared to rethink its theoretical basis in ways that point forward rather than back.

Epic

Johnson has left no extended discussion of epic, but his analysis of *Paradise Lost*, his longest treatment of any literary work, derives structure and coherence from his response to Addison and earlier neoclassical theorists. "These little pieces," Johnson begins, "may be dispatched without much anxiety"—*Lycidas* has been only a distraction—but "I am now to examine *Paradise Lost*, a poem which, considered with respect to design, may claim the first place, and with respect to performance the second, among the productions of the human mind" (*Life of Milton*, I, 170). In conception it is greater even than the *Iliad*, but in performance cannot quite deserve the first place for the very reason that the design is so exalted. As we shall see, Milton has chosen precisely the genre in which his aspiring genius could best express itself, but in doing so has aspired too high, dared too greatly.

Johnson's approach allows him to make direct connections between Milton's intellectual powers and the literary genre in which they are revealed. "The characteristick quality of his poem is sublimity," which shows that Milton perfectly understood the genre in which he ought to work: "He seems to have been well acquainted with his own genius, and to know what it was that Nature had bestowed upon him more bountifully than upon others; the power of displaying the vast, illuminating the splendid, enforcing the awful, darkening the gloomy, and aggravating the dreadful: he therefore chose a subject on which too much could not be said, on which he might tire his fancy without the censure of extravagance" (p. 177). But Milton did not abandon himself to misty obscurity, like the would-be sublime ode writers

whom Johnson detested, for the epic had always been considered the form in which sublimity was most properly expressed.
In the "epic kind," Dryden wrote, "all things must be grave,
majestical, and sublime"; by the same token *Paradise Lost* was
"undoubtedly one of the greatest, most noble, and most sublime
poems which either this age or nation has produced."[14]

After his brief introduction Johnson offers a condensed account of the many skills that the epic poet must master, and then
proceeds to analyze the poem under a set of traditional
categories derived from Addison, who got them from Le Bossu,
who claimed to have gotten them from Aristotle.[15] Nothing
could be more conventional than this decision to follow Addison
and Le Bossu, but it is important to realize that it *is* a decision.
John Dennis, who celebrated the sublime in Milton before Addison did, preferred to emphasize the poet's originality: "That
great Man had a desire to give the World something like an Epick
Poem; but he resolv'd at the same time to break thro' the Rules of
Aristotle." In a less rhapsodic way Voltaire introduced a commonsense discussion of *Paradise Lost* in very Johnsonian terms: "We
have in every Art more Rules than Examples, for Men are more
fond of teaching, than able to perform. . . . The greatest Part of
the Criticks have fetch'd the Rules of *Epick* Poetry from the
Books of *Homer*, according to the Custom, or rather, to the
Weakness of Men, who mistake commonly the Beginning of an
Art, for the Principles of the Art itself, and are apt to believe, that
every Thing must be by its own Nature, what it was, when
contriv'd at first."[16]

It has lately been noticed that Johnson's comments on *Paradise*

---

[14]Dryden, Preface to the *Aeneis* (1697) and Preface to *The State of Innocence*
(1677), in *Of Dramatic Poesy and Other Critical Essays*, II, 224; I, 196.

[15]Most English writers adopted Bossu's categories; see H. T. Swedenberg,
Jr., *The Theory of the Epic in England, 1650-1800* (Berkeley, 1944), p. 51 and
passim. Swedenberg regrets that Johnson "had nothing new to offer" in epic
theory (p. 125).

[16]Dennis, *The Grounds of Criticism in Poetry* (1704), in *Critical Works*, ed. E. N.
Hooker (Baltimore, 1939-43), I, 333; Voltaire, *An Essay upon the Civil Wars of
France . . . And also upon the Epick Poetry of the European Nations from Homer down to
Milton* (1727), pp. 37, 38. Voltaire's essay was originally published in English.

Lost are often occasioned by those of earlier writers.[17] But one
can go further and say that his critique, at least in its positive half,
is essentially a restatement of Addison's. Each critic surveys the
poem under the four main heads of fable, characters, sentiments, and language (though Johnson defers the last of these to
the end of the *Life*), together with various subtopics like "the
probable and the marvelous" and "the machinery." Each critic
follows this survey with an examination of defects. What is more,
Johnson directly echoes or paraphrases Addison on many
points, including the central one that in exploiting the sublime
"*Milton* seems to have known, perfectly well, wherein his
Strength lay, and has therefore chosen a Subject entirely conformable to those Talents, of which he was Master" (*Spectator*
315). Why should he not address *Paradise Lost* freshly and on its
own terms, as Voltaire had claimed to do?

In answering this question, we are impelled to see what is
distinctive and even subversive in Johnson's approach. He follows Addison and Le Bossu because he considers their terms
appropriate, but Addison's method—Johnson seems to have
believed—should have led him to a more serious exposure of
faults in the poem than he was willing to face. Milton's genius
impelled him to "break thro' the Rules of *Aristotle*," but in deciding to write an epic in the first place, he had committed himself to
those rules; and the soaring genius described by Dennis is precisely the cause of the defects that the common reader perceives
even if Addison does not.

Thus Johnson approaches *Paradise Lost* much as he approached the pastoral, with the difference that he greatly admires *Paradise Lost*. Underlying his argument is a largely invisible
debate with previous critics, especially Addison, in which
Johnson accepts their categories and then shows that they fail to
pursue the logical consequences. In the positive part of his
survey, however, Johnson is glad to concur with his great predecessor. "An instructor like Addison was now wanting [after

---

[17]See Vereen M. Bell, "Johnson's Milton Criticism in Context," *English
Studies*, 49 (1968), 127-32. Paul K. Alkon suggests that Johnson gave an
idiosyncratic meaning to the conventional term *admiration* and intended the
reader to notice his implied disagreement with earlier critics of *Paradise Lost*
("Johnson's Conception of Admiration," *Philological Quarterly*, 48 [1969], 59-
81).

Dryden], whose remarks being superficial, might be easily understood, and being just might prepare the mind for more attainments" (*Life of Addison*, II, 146). While Addison has not said everything that could be said, he has said most of the important things and has performed the invaluable service of making Milton "an universal favourite." Johnson's survey of *Paradise Lost* must be far briefer than Addison's eighteen *Spectator* papers, and at many points takes the form of simple restatement. Thus on Raphael (p. 173) Johnson echoes *Spectator* 273; on Satan (p. 173), *Spectator* 303; and on Milton's use of "episodes" (in the technical sense, p. 175), *Spectator* 267. The highly condensed account of the subject of the poem (pp. 171-72) is essentially a rewriting, with more parallelism and more abstractions, of a paragraph in *Spectator* 267. One reviewer of the *Lives*, indeed, pointed this out for the purpose of condemning Johnson's Latinate style.[18]

But Johnson's relation to Addison goes deeper than these correspondences. The earlier critic had set out to show that *Paradise Lost* is not merely a great poem but more precisely a great epic poem, and therefore analyzed it by means of Bossu's categories. It is a good poem because it is a good epic. But in handling its "defects," which he does with evident embarrassment, Addison sees no significance in Milton's choice of subject and form. Each "defect" is presented simply as a lapse from the proper epic mode, a relatively minor flaw that the poet might well have avoided.[19] Johnson's treatment of defects is much more discursive and concentrates on the crucial charge that "the want of human interest is always felt" (p. 183), which exposes a concealed weakness in Addison's adoption of the Bossuvian mode. For if *Paradise Lost* is an epic and should be judged as one, then it betrays an insoluble dilemma. In choosing to vie with Homer, Milton avoided Virgilian imitativeness by attempting a subject of superhuman grandeur. "With respect to design" (p.

[18] A brief notice in the *Westminster Magazine, or the Pantheon of Taste*, 7 (1779), 265.

[19] In *Spectator* 297 Addison approaches Milton's faults with much hesitation, ranges them carefully under his four heads—faults in the fable, characters, sentiments, and language—and does not represent them as central to Milton's conception of his poem. The one inescapable difficulty, that the story ends unhappily, is obviously inherent in the subject, but Addison believes that Milton has done his best "to cure [this imperfection] by several Expedients."

170) his poem deserves the first place among the productions of the human mind. But in attempting the one subject that could rival Homer, he cut himself off from the material on which Homer's greatness is based. As Dennis saw, Milton circumvented the limitations of Homeric precedent by conceiving an epic of a new kind, taking his theme from Scripture. Moreover, he did not draw his fable from Hebrew history, a procedure that Johnson and others believed to be fatally damaging to such works as Cowley's *Davideis*, since it committed the poet to a literal transcription of revealed truth.[20] The alternative was to dwell upon the great mythic events that precede the Fall, for which the Biblical evidence (even though understood as literally true) is briefer and more poetic. Here the dangers of "invention" are particularly great; no reader would sympathize more than Johnson with Marvell's relief, in the lines prefixed to the poem, that Milton had managed not to "ruin (for I saw him strong) / The sacred truths to fable and old song."

Johnson's admiration is thus wholehearted when he describes the success with which Milton has embodied his religious theme:

To convey this moral there must be a *fable*, a narration artfully constructed so as to excite curiosity and surprise expectation. In this part of his work Milton must be confessed to have equalled every other poet. He has involved in his account of the Fall of Man the events which preceded, and those that were to follow it: he has interwoven the whole system of theology with such propriety that every part appears to be necessary, and scarcely any recital is wished shorter for the sake of quickening the progress of the main action. [P. 171]

As opposed to all other epics, the foundation here is eternal truth, in whose presence the categories of Aristotle collapse: "The probable therefore is marvellous, and the marvellous is probable" (p. 174).

In principle, then, nothing could possibly command the reader's attention more strongly than *Paradise Lost*. Milton has

---

[20]"Sacred History," Johnson says of the *Davideis*, "has been always read with submissive reverence, and an imagination over-awed and controlled. We have been accustomed to acquiesce in the nakedness and simplicity of the authentick narrative.... All amplification is frivolous and vain" (*Life of Cowley*, I, 49). Rymer expressed a similar view of the *Davideis* in his *Preface to Rapin* in 1674 (*Critical Works*, p. 8). On analogous grounds Dennis explained the weakness of the last two books of *Paradise Lost* (*The Grounds of Criticism in Poetry*, *Critical Works*, I, 351).

brilliantly escaped the usual pitfalls awaiting the post-Homeric poet. "It is justly remarked by Addison that this poem has, by the nature of its subject, the advantage above all others, that it is universally and perpetually interesting" (p. 174). This assertion is often described as contradicting the later one that we lay the poem down and forget to take it up again. But Johnson is speaking here of Milton's *subject*, not of the poem as a whole; furthermore, "interesting" means "involving our deepest concerns," not "fascinating." Addison says of Milton's Adam and Eve, "We have an actual Interest in every thing they do, and no less than our utmost Happiness is concerned, and lies at Stake in all their Behaviour" (*Spectator* 273). Johnson goes on to expound a view of religious poetry (repeated in the *Lives* of Cowley and Waller) in which known truths "are too important to be new" and too solemn to admit of ornament: "the good and evil of Eternity are too ponderous for the wings of wit" (p. 182).

Milton's solution was to employ his imagination upon what Johnson calls "a new train of intermediate images," ramifying the few "radical positions" of Scripture "with pregnancy and vigour of mind peculiar to himself" (pp. 182-83). In so doing, he was able to indulge precisely that talent for sublimity that Johnson sees as his distinguishing characteristic. "Milton's delight was to sport in the wide regions of possibility; reality was a scene too narrow for his mind. He sent his faculties out upon discovery, into worlds where only imagination can travel, and delighted to form new modes of existence, and furnish sentiment and action to superior beings, to trace the counsels of hell, or accompany the choirs of heaven" (pp. 177-78). This is praise of a very specialized kind. For nothing is more native to Johnson's mind than a distrust of unbounded imagination; Shakespeare's peculiar excellence is his fidelity to actual sublunary life. As Hagstrum has shown, Johnson's praise of Milton's sublime sounds disturbingly similar to his suspicion of the sublime in other places. Moreover, he was unusual in separating the sublime from the pathetic.[21] From what has been said thus far it should be apparent why he separates them: in proportion as

[21]*Samuel Johnson's Literary Criticism*, Ch. 7. David B. Morris discusses the implications of Johnson's praise of Milton's dramatized sublime in *The Religious Sublime* (Lexington, Ky., 1972), pp. 214-21.

Milton achieves the sublime by inventing imaginary worlds, he leaves behind "the appearances of nature and the occurrences of life" (p. 177). Most of his characters are nonhuman or superhuman, and therefore inaccessible to ordinary human sympathies. "As human passions did not enter the world before the Fall, there is in the *Paradise Lost* little opportunity for the pathetick" (p. 180). In his essay on biography Johnson says, "We are all prompted by the same motives, all deceived by the same fallacies, all animated by hope, obstructed by danger, entangled by desire, and seduced by pleasure" (*Rambler* 60, III, 320). Each of these phrases could stand as a description of Eve and then Adam at the time of the Fall, and each is inappropriate to the prelapsarian state.

Homer and Shakespeare, unlike Milton, have managed to incorporate "the marvellous" with a convincing imitation of human life. Shakespeare, Johnson says in the *Preface*, "always makes us anxious for the event, and has perhaps excelled all but Homer in securing the first purpose of a writer, by exciting restless and unquenchable curiosity, and compelling him that reads his work to read it through" (p. 83). In wanting human interest Milton's epic lacks this crucial property of exciting curiosity. "*Paradise Lost* is one of the books which the reader admires and lays down, and forgets to take up again. None ever wished it longer than it is. Its perusal is a duty rather than a pleasure. We read Milton for instruction, retire harrassed and overburdened, and look elsewhere for recreation; we desert our master, and seek for companions" (pp. 183-84). No part of the *Life of Milton* has been more bitterly denounced by the poet's admirers, but it is not obvious that Johnson means to condemn. "It may be doubted," an early commentator remarked, "whether this is panegyric or satire."[22] For if Milton is too great for us, it may be we who are at fault: the great epics are not to be read with casual attention, and Milton's "fit audience though few" must approach the poem with humility and discipline. And curiosity is not necessarily a noble faculty; Swift calls it "that spur in the side, that bridle in the mouth, that ring in the nose, of a lazy and

---

[22]Robert Potter, *The Art of Criticism, as exemplified in Dr. Johnson's Lives of the Most Eminent English Poets* (1789), p. 13.

impatient and a grunting reader" (*Tale of a Tub*, section xi). The possibility that Johnson sympathizes with Milton is supported by the rueful admission in the final *Rambler*: "As it has been my principal design to inculcate wisdom or piety, I have allotted few papers to the idle sports of imagination. Some, perhaps, may be found, of which the highest excellence is harmless merriment; but scarcely any man is so steadily serious, as not to complain, that the severity of dictatorial instruction has been too seldom relieved, and that he is driven by the sternness of the Rambler's philosophy to more chearful and airy companions" (*Rambler* 208, V, 319).

However this may be, Johnson's treatment of the poem's "defects" depends upon the idea that Milton has overreached the bounds of human nature, and therefore represents something more important than the literalistic misreading it is often dismissed as being. "Another inconvenience of Milton's design," Johnson continues, "is that it requires the description of what cannot be described, the agency of spirits. He saw that immateriality supplied no images, and that he could not show angels acting but by instruments of action; he therefore invested them with form and matter" (p. 184). Johnson's sensible analysis of the incongruities of spirits in armor, which had been anticipated by Dennis,[23] derives its force from two considerations: the assumption that Milton has to make so much of these perplexing beings because his story does not supply him with human agents; and the recognition that the result, however it might be justified in theory, is generally unattractive to readers of the poem.

The same assumptions underlie Johnson's discussion of the allegory of Sin and Death, which Addison had admired while denying its appropriateness in an epic poem (*Spectators* 309, 357). It had been rather lamely defended by the distinguished

---

[23]"Most of the Machines then in *Paradise Lost*, have the appearance of something that is inconsistent and contradictory, for in them the Poet seems to confound Body and Mind, Spirit and Matter. . . . Now Form and Shape suppose Extension, and Extension implies Matter. Besides, he has given them solid Arms and Armour" ("Observations on the *Paradise Lost* of Milton," *Critical Works*, II, 228). Dennis goes on to say that the pagan gods "come incomparably nearer to humane Nature, than the Machines of the Christian Poetry, and are therefore more delightful to it" (p. 229). This closely corresponds to Johnson's demand for "human interest."

editor Bishop Newton in terms that precisely confirm Johnson's interpretation:

Milton may rather be justified for introducing such imaginary beings as Sin and Death, because a great part of his poem lies in the invisible world, and such fictitious beings may better have a place there; and the actions of Sin and Death are at least as probable as those ascribed to the good or evil Angels. Besides as Milton's subject necessarily admitted so few real persons, he was in a manner obliged to supply that defect by introducing imaginary ones: and the characters of Sin and Death are perfectly agreeable to the hints and sketches, which are given of them in Scripture.[24]

For Johnson that is exactly what has gone wrong: in his need to supply the defect of "want of human interest," Milton has expanded what Newton calls the "hints and sketches" of the Bible into an "unskilful allegory" (p. 186).

Finally, a similar common-reader response explains the complications of Johnson's remarks on Milton's language, remarks that had been partly set forth earlier in a series of *Rambler*s that express warm praise and yet betray a sense of dissatisfaction. Johnson casually dismisses some of the usual objections to Milton's puns and technical terms as being of trivial importance (p. 188). He is concerned rather to establish the essential nature of Milton's verse. It is eminent for "grace" and "melody," so that "from his book alone the Art of English Poetry might be learned" (p. 191). But since Milton's diction is "perverse and pedantick" and since his blank verse violates the fundamental need for rhyme in English poetry, Johnson's admiration is couched in terms of deliberate paradox.

Such is the power of his poetry that his call is obeyed without resistance, the reader feels himself in captivity to a higher and a nobler mind, and criticism sinks in admiration.... Of him, at last, may be said what Jonson says of Spenser, that "he wrote no language," but has formed what Butler calls "a Babylonish Dialect," in itself harsh and barbarous, but made by exalted genius and extensive learning the vehicle of so much instruction and so much pleasure that, like other lovers, we find grace in its deformity. [Pp. 190, 191]

[24]*Paradise Lost*, ed. Thomas Newton (1749), II, 231n.

Johnson's view has affinities with Pope's account of the *Vivida vis animi*, the "Poetical Fire" that appears in the greatest writers. Homer, Pope says, is like a fire that burns steadily and irresistibly; Shakespeare "strikes before we are aware, like an accidental Fire from Heaven"; Milton "glows like a Furnace kept up to an uncommon ardor by the Force of Art."[25] What seems natural and inevitable in Homer and Shakespeare is forced (though brilliant) in Milton. In his style, as in his mighty but nonhuman fable, Milton compels the reader to feel at all times the pressure of "art."

Here precisely is the point at which the modern critic parts company with Johnson. Today this potency of art is seen as defining Milton's greatness: he makes large demands on us, demands of a different order than those we expect in most narrative literature. Consequently Johnson's treatment of *Paradise Lost* as epic supplies a more telling critique of Addison than of *Paradise Lost*. Presumably the reason he did not follow Voltaire in rejecting traditional epic criticism is that Milton so obviously draws upon existing epics. Instead he attempted to show that *Paradise Lost* is at once too similar to Homeric epic, in adopting its "structure" (p. 194), and too unlike it, in escaping the bounds of human nature on which Homer's greatness is founded. This is described as a noble originality—"Of all the borrowers from Homer Milton is perhaps the least indebted" (p. 194)—and as a serious drawback, for the reasons we have seen. But it would have been better to throw out Addison's categories altogether instead of showing their logical implications and to recognize that *Paradise Lost* is not a Homeric epic at all, just as *Samson Agonistes* is not an Aristotelian tragedy. It draws upon other epics besides Homer's (Virgil, in Satan as the nation-founding Aeneas; Spenser, in the allegory of Sin and Death; Ariosto, in the war in Heaven) and it seeks to modify their values in a perspective of its own. Johnson is therefore right to assert that the poem does not succeed as Homeric epic, and wrong to suppose (with Addison) that it should. Distrusting genre, he

---

[25] Preface to the *Iliad*, in Twickenham Ed., *Poems*, Vol. VII, *The Iliad of Homer*, ed. Maynard Mack et al. (London, 1967), p. 5.

criticizes Milton for adhering too closely to genre and does not realize that the terms of analysis may be the wrong ones.

Johnson's supposed weakness on this subject is more a function of later critical attitudes than of his actual deficiencies. The attack comes from two directions: from scholars who have convinced themselves that eighteenth-century literature was distributed into rigidly distinct generic compartments, and from theorists who see the great genres as moving with a life of their own, like great cloudy constellations, above the specific works upon which they shed their influence. The shallowness of the former view is coming under increasing attack,[26] and the grandiose claims of the latter, which interprets genres almost as Platonic forms, remain so far from proven that Johnson may easily be forgiven for failing to corroborate them. On a less exalted level I have sought to show that his critique of *Paradise Lost*, like his theory of pastoral, represents something more than an idiosyncratic tendency to ignore genre and impose literal readings upon formally conventional works. He reveals (though elliptically) a penetrating scrutiny of contemporary theory. He clearly appreciates the fact of the persistence of genre: poets imitate poets as well as life. Wordsworth, after listing the mental powers that a poet needs, says that "the materials of Poetry, by these powers collected and produced, are cast, by means of various moulds, into divers forms"; and he goes on to list the traditional genres—epic, tragedy, various lyric forms, and so on. A poem has its own special shape, and a good poem is unique, but insofar as it does have form—especially if the poet chooses to write an elegy or ode or sonnet—then it can be seen as taking shape within what Wordsworth calls a "mould." Thus the greatest of the Romantic poets, far from insisting on a mysterious élan vital producing organic form, understood the force of genre in a very Johnsonian way.[27]

[26]For instance by Ralph Cohen, "On the Interrelations of Eighteenth-Century Literary Forms," in *New Approaches to Eighteenth-Century Literature*, ed. Philip Harth (New York, 1974), pp. 33-78.

[27]Preface to the 1815 *Poems, Prose Works*, III, 27. Coleridge takes the more familiar "Romantic" view of molds: "The form is mechanic when on any given material we impress a pre-determined form not necessarily arising out of the properties of the material, as when to a mass of wet clay we give whatever shape we wish it to retain when hardened. The organic form, on the other hand, is innate; it shapes as it develops itself from within" (notes for a lecture in 1808, in *Coleridge's Shakespearean Criticism*, ed. T. M. Raysor [London, 1960], II, 198).

The great poet will use a mold creatively, not passively. In deciding to adopt an existing mode, he is accepting a challenge, not finding a solution. Johnson may not *like* certain genres or even the idea of genre, but he shows a real understanding of its inner logic, the inescapable decisions imposed on the poet who chooses to work within it. The logic of pastoral, in Johnson's view, all but demands puerility. Even the great Virgil rarely overcomes its inherent limitations. Epic, at the other extreme, is a truly majestic genre, calling for mighty powers in the poet who would dedicate himself to it. Blackmore's incessant stream of epics could only be shallow: "He depended with great security on his own powers, and perhaps was for that reason less diligent in perusing books. . . . Nor does it appear that he saw beyond his own performances, or had ever elevated his views to that ideal perfection which every genius born to excel is condemned always to pursue, and never overtake" (*Life of Blackmore*, II, 253).

Milton, unlike Blackmore, had great powers and was prepared to develop them with arduous care. And having once aspired to the highest of genres, he understood that he must submit himself to Homer's discipline: epic existed, had its own essential nature, and could not be arbitrarily reinvented. But if a trivial genre will produce failure, as Johnson believes it does in *Lycidas*, it does not follow that a great genre must produce unqualified success in *Paradise Lost*. Johnson's strategy in analyzing the poem is to show it straining against the bounds of genre, solving its inherent problems in a manner that is brilliant but imposes the "want of human interest" that is its crucial flaw. Johnson's discussion here can help us to appreciate his remark on Shakespeare that I quoted at the outset. While Shakespeare's plays are not so radically ungeneric as Johnson claims, their generic nature develops from within, not from classical models or critical doctrine. Johnson sees it as no accident that Shakespeare and Homer excite "restless and unquenchable curiosity." In dramatizing the real state of sublunary nature, Shakespeare has escaped the restrictions of genre as understood by neoclassical critics (many of whom, of course, abused him for doing so). Homer, the founder of the greatest of genres, was able to handle it with the freedom of a creator. But once established it must impose a logic of its own, and become a bow of Ulysses that not even Virgil and Milton can draw with full success.

5 Shakespeare and Didacticism

A LEADING THEME of this book is that Johnson's best criticism combines literary with moral judgment. But his moral aesthetic, as has often been observed, tends toward a rigid didacticism that is disagreeable to most modern readers. That is particularly true of the *Preface to Shakespeare*, which has long been treated as Johnson's central critical statement, probably because it addresses a number of theoretical questions, concerns a great poet whom everyone knows, and is relatively short. I myself have offered a description of its limiting didacticism, though without fully explaining the reasons for its limitations.[1] I want now to take a new look at the *Preface*, with two ends in view: to explain as sympathetically as possible the basis for Johnson's didactic demands; and to argue that it is transitional rather than central in his critical writing, a work that poses problems which will be solved much more successfully in the *Lives of the Poets*.

Unfriendly readers have often pointed to inconsistencies in what Coleridge called the "strangely overrated, contradictory, and most illogical preface to Shakespeare."[2] But most, if not all, of these can probably be resolved, even if Johnson himself has not always been careful to resolve them. It seems likely that such readers have mainly been offended—though they may have explained their uneasiness on logical grounds—by the almost inexplicable severity that Johnson shows toward England's greatest writer. As the *Critical Review* observed, "Mr. Johnson, to preserve the character of impartiality, has often thrown the blemishes of his author in too odious a light . . . .[and] has been *immoderately* moderate." A decade later Maurice Morgann wrote with more asperity that Johnson seemed to consider Shake-

---

[1]*Samuel Johnson and the Tragic Sense* (Princeton, 1972), esp. pp. 224-33. My topic in that work led me to conclude that Johnson feared the emotional pressure and openness to evil of tragic drama. I put forward here a more general version of that conclusion.

[2]Samuel Taylor Coleridge, to Daniel Stuart, 13 May 1816, *Letters*, ed. Ernest Hartley Coleridge (New York, 1895), II, 664.

speare "as a sort of wild Proteus or madman, and accordingly knocks him down with the butt-end of his critical staff, as often as he exceeds that line of sober discretion, which this learned Editor appears to have chalked out for him."[3]

We must try to understand, therefore, how Johnson can assert that Shakespeare's "excellencies" are accompanied by "faults sufficient to obscure and overwhelm any other merit" (*Preface*, p. 71), and why he insists on the faults with such energy. It is true that most of his objections, though strongly expressed, are not outrageous when taken in context. Shakespeare does allow anachronisms; his plots are sometimes careless; and he exhibits all the features of language that Johnson, as author of the English dictionary, feels particularly qualified to identify as faults.[4] It is also true that Johnson conceives his role as magisterial: "Some initiation is however necessary; of all skill, part is infused by precept, and part is obtained by habit; I have therefore shewn so much as may enable the candidate of criticism to discover the rest" (p. 104). Still, something more must be involved besides Johnson's inveterate habit, as described by Reynolds, of "pointing out the bad as well as the good in every character" (*Life*, II, 306).

The explanation may be partly personal. Sir John Hawkins, weighing the tone of the *Preface*, concluded that Johnson criticizes Shakespeare's faults "with such a degree of asperity as critics discover when they are criticizing the works of a rival."[5] In *Rambler* 140 Johnson had anticipated the charge, lamenting that readers tend to impute "envy, captiousness, and malignity" to an impartial critic. But Hawkins is right to emphasize the "asperity" in the *Preface*, and he may be right to suggest a psychological

[3]*Critical Review*, 20 (1765), 329; Morgann, *An Essay on the Dramatic Character of Sir John Falstaff* (1777), in *Eighteenth Century Essays on Shakespeare*, ed. D. Nichol Smith (Oxford, 1963), p. 232.

[4]"Johnson has furnished a catalogue of defects," R. D. Stock concludes, "which is conventional, reasonable, and quite consistent with his earlier praise of Shakespeare; as such, it need occasion Johnson or his partisans no embarrassment, though at the same time it affords the historian of ideas with little that is exceptional or new" (*Samuel Johnson and Neoclassical Dramatic Theory* [Lincoln, Neb., 1973], p. 141. While rightly emphasizing that Johnson's negative opinions are not merely idiosyncratic, this sort of defense overlooks the hostility of *tone* that has disturbed many readers of the *Preface*.

[5]Hawkins, *Life*, p. 196.

explanation. As Johnson finally neared completion of the work that had cost him so many years and so much guilt for failing to complete it, he may have projected his dissatisfaction on the author who had attracted his interest in the first place. Foreseeing, perhaps, the objections that would be brought against an edition whose shortcomings he knew only too well, Johnson might easily give way to outbursts of truculence that would put Shakespeare firmly in his place, followed by compensatory passages of exaggerated praise.

I raise this possibility only to suggest that something is going on in the *Preface* beneath the surface of its ostensible argument. And however severe may be Johnson's censure of language or plot, his most serious anxiety is clearly aroused by moral considerations. No statement of these comes close to the amplitude of the discussions of tragicomedy and the unities, but they are not therefore insignificant, and indeed they disturb Johnson so much that he keeps bringing them up at moments when they may seem to contradict other aspects of his argument.

His first defect is that to which may be imputed most of the evil in books or in men. He sacrifices virtue to convenience, and is so much more careful to please than to instruct, that he seems to write without any moral purpose. From his writings indeed a system of social duty may be selected, for he that thinks reasonably must think morally; but his precepts and axioms drop casually from him; he makes no just distribution of good or evil, nor is always careful to shew in the virtuous a disapprobation of the wicked; he carries his persons indifferently through right and wrong, and at the close dismisses them without further care, and leaves their examples to operate by chance. This fault the barbarity of his age cannot extenuate; for it is always a writer's duty to make the world better, and justice is a virtue independant on time or place. [P. 71]

Johnson here contradicts the argument on which he has rested his defense of Shakespeare's tragicomedies and is about to rest his defense of the violation of the unities. Shakespeare's plays exhibit "the real state of sublunary nature, . . .this chaos of mingled purposes and casualties" (p. 66). Likewise they have as much unity as life itself affords: "He has not, indeed, an intrigue regularly perplexed and regularly unravelled; he does not endeavor to hide his design only to discover it, for this is seldom the order of real events, and Shakespeare is the poet of nature" (p. 75). But that argument, though strategically useful against narrow technical objections, is unacceptable to Johnson here.

Another passage that occurs unexpectedly later on, in the middle of the historical section, gives a clue to the partly suppressed moral argument that accounts for many anomalies in the *Preface*. Johnson begins by discussing the old romances that fascinated readers in the nation's "infancy" and made them eager for incredible adventures. "The mind, which has feasted on the luxurious wonders of fiction, has no taste of the insipidity of truth" (p. 82). Now, Shakespeare, as we have been told earlier, is more than any other writer the poet of real sublunary nature, "who caught his ideas from the living world, and exhibited only what he saw before him" (p. 63). But paradoxically enough, in order to hold the attention of his unsophisticated audience, Shakespeare has had to depict reality *as if it were romance*.

What is happening is that Johnson is drawing upon, without making plain, a deep suspicion of the relation between art and imagination which he had developed more fully in the *Rambler* and in *Rasselas*. We should therefore look backward from the *Preface* and consider the works in which its moral dilemma is explored more explicitly. Less than two weeks after beginning the *Rambler*, Johnson defined that dilemma in an aggressively paradoxical form. The newly invented novel, he says in *Rambler* 4, represents a real change from previous narratives, for "the works of fiction, with which the present generation seems more particularly delighted, are such as exhibit life in its true state, diversified only by accidents that daily happen in the world, and influenced by passions and qualities which are really to be found in conversing with mankind" (III, 19). Like Shakespeare, these novelists have combined the imaginative pleasures of romance with the accuracy of a true imitation of life. But in moral terms, Johnson goes on to say, it may be fortunate that the romances *were* unmistakably different from life. "If the world be promiscuously described, I cannot see of what use it can be to read the account; or why it may not be as safe to turn the eye immediately upon mankind, as upon a mirror which shows all that presents itself without discrimination" (p. 22).

As Hagstrum has shown, Johnson recognized that a mirror

could be either an unselective "looking-glass" or a selective pattern, exemplar, archetype.[6] But mimetic theory had never been anxious to face the potential contradictions here. Neoclassical critics constantly praised the moral lessons conveyed by art. But how accurately, in that case, can art really mirror life as we know it? In its idealizing and instructive capacity, can it not be charged with misrepresenting the actual world?

Critics who touched on this issue were often tempted to gloss over it. Thus Dryden makes much of Le Bossu's rule that the poet should begin with his moral—"that is, to lay down to yourself what that precept of morality shall be, which you would insinuate into the people." The term *insinuate* sounds rather like trickery, as in Sidney's analogy of art luring men into the presence of truth "as if they tooke a medicine of Cherries." In a later discussion of Bossu's precept Dryden freely applies the term *deceit*.

> The principal end of painting is to please, and the chief design of poetry is to instruct. . . . But if we consider the artists themselves on both sides, certainly their aims are the very same: they would both make sure of pleasing, and that in preference to instruction. Next, the means of this pleasure is by deceit. One imposes on the sight, and the other on the understanding. Fiction is of the essence of poetry, as well as of painting; there is a resemblance in one, of human bodies, things, and actions which are not real, and in the other, of a true story by a fiction. And as all stories are not proper subjects for an epic poem or a tragedy, so neither are they for a noble picture. The subjects both of the one, and of the other, ought to have nothing of immoral, low, or filthy in them.[7]

Poets, then, would rather please than instruct, and as Dryden says elsewhere, instruction that neglects to please is unreadable. But their means of pleasing is deception, the art of imposing on

---

[6]*Johnson's Literary Criticism*, p. 56, drawing on Johnson's definitions in the *Dictionary*. "How, then, does art instruct? It instructs by performing its essential function, that is, by imitating nature in its two large aspects. Art instructs by representing lifelike and particular reality, extensive in its range and various in its forms; and by representing, or at least implying, moral and psychological truth, which is general, rational, and normative" (p. 71).

[7]Dryden, *The Grounds of Criticism in Tragedy* (1679) and *A Parallel Betwixt Poetry and Painting* (1695), in *Of Dramatic Poesy and Other Critical Essays*, I, 248, and II, 186-87; Sidney, *An Apology for Poetry*, in *Elizabethan Critical Essays*, I, 173.

the understanding. Plato threw the poets out of his republic for that. What guarantee is left of the moral influence of art? Simply the integrity of the poet, who is to choose only those "stories" that are innocent of anything "immoral, low, or filthy." Dryden is offering a prescription here for epic poetry, which helps him to reach this high-minded solution. But what if the epic should descend, as Fielding's comic prose epic does, to the familiar materials of ordinary life? Will not the deceitful imitation tempt the reader to admire what he should not?

By resting his case on the poet's integrity and on the nobility proper to epic poetry, Dryden escapes (or evades) the potential contradiction in the union of mimesis and morality. Johnson insists on the contradiction. And he complicates the issue further by pursuing its implications in audience psychology. Aristotle's perplexing theory of catharsis seems to have been developed as an answer to Plato: art does differ from the truly real, and it does work on the emotions, but it helps us to understand reality and heals emotions rather than inflaming them. Later critics tended to dwell on the formalist scheme of the *Poetics* and to treat "the pleasures of tragedy" as a specialized phenomenon, not as an instance of the emotional aspect of art in general. But in the eighteenth century aestheticians gave increasing attention to the psychological aspect of art. And a central theme of their investigations was that the imagination tends to operate independently from reason.

Addison, popularizing Locke, emphasized the positive force of the image-forming faculty, which "has something in it like Creation; It bestows a kind of Existence, and draws up to the Reader's View, several Objects which are not to be found in Being" (*Spectator* 421). Johnson was always suspicious of this tendency of the mind to create unreal objects. All that is wanted to make Addison's formulation dangerous, in Johnsonian terms, is a recognition that it describes the diseased mind as much as—or more than—the healthy. Addison himself goes on to observe, "When the Brain is hurt by any Accident, or the Mind disordered by Dreams or Sickness, the Fancy is overrun with wild dismal Ideas, and terrified with a thousand hideous Monsters of its own framing." Addison's master Locke, in treating the association of ideas, had declared that "opposition to

reason . . .is really madness" and that scarcely any man is altogether free from it. Or in Dennis's words, "The warmer the
Imagination is, the more present the Things are to us of which
we draw the Images; and therefore, when once the Imagination
is so inflam'd, as to get the better of the Understanding, there is
no Difference between the Images, and the Things themselves;
as we see, for Example, in Fevers and Madmen."[8]

These considerations lead directly to Johnson's famous
analysis of insanity in the forty-fourth chapter of *Rasselas*, published nine years after *Rambler* 4, six years before the *Preface to
Shakespeare*. "Perhaps, if we speak with rigorous exactness,"
Imlac says, "no human mind is in its right state. There is no man
whose imagination does not sometimes predominate over his
reason. . . . All power of fancy over reason is a degree of insanity." For the present discussion what matters most is the close
relation between uncontrolled imagination (or fancy) and the
wish-fulfilling pleasures of art. "To indulge the power of fiction,
and send imagination out upon the wing, is often the sport of
those who delight too much in silent speculation. . . . By degrees
the reign of fancy is confirmed; she grows first imperious, and in
time despotick. Then fictions begin to operate as realities, false
opinions fasten upon the mind, and life passes in dreams of
rapture or of anguish." This account of the fictionalizing power
of fancy could easily be extended to art. "Fancy" as Johnson
describes it is no merely passive sequence of associations; it
releases and gives expression to frustrated desires, just as its
cognate "fantasy" does in the theories of Freud, who identified
in it both the source and the appeal of art. "In phantasy," Freud
writes, "man can continue to enjoy a freedom from the grip of
the external world, one which he has long relinquished in actuality. He has contrived to be alternately a pleasure-seeking animal
and a reasonable being; for the meagre satisfaction that he can
extract from reality leaves him starving."[9] Or as Johnson expresses it, "The mind, which has feasted on the luxurious wonders of
fiction, has no taste of the insipidity of truth" (*Preface*, p. 82). In
Rasselas he had used different language to suggest that if truth

[8] John Locke, *Essay concerning Human Understanding*, II.33.4; John Dennis,
The Advancement and Reformation of Modern Poetry, Critical Works, I, 218.

[9] Sigmund Freud, *A General Introduction to Psychoanalysis*, trans. Joan Riviere
(New York, 1938), pp. 324-25.

seems tasteless, it is because we are afraid to taste it: "The mind...feasts on the luscious falsehood whenever she is offended with the bitterness of truth" (Ch. 44).

In *Rambler* 4, to which we may now return, Johnson is not concerned with the inner life of the artist and the genesis of fiction. Instead he focuses on the response of readers, and says in a central statement, "If the power of example is so great, as to take possession of the memory by a kind of violence, and produce effects almost without the intervention of the will, care ought to be taken that, when the choice is unrestrained, the best examples only should be exhibited; and that which is likely to operate so strongly, should not be mischievous or uncertain in its effects" (III, 22). Art is received not with rational analysis—we remember the common reader—but with emotional rapture, in a kind of paralysis of the will. The finer the work of art, the closer it will come to penetrating what Johnson described, in his praise of *Clarissa*, as "the recesses of the human heart" (*Life*, II, 49). But therein lies the danger. For fancy or imagination is always struggling to break free of reason and to liberate forbidden impulses. In *Rambler* 8 Johnson urges the importance of "keeping reason a constant guard over imagination" in order to suppress the potential corruption of "pernicious and tyrannical appetites and wishes," and concludes, "He therefore that would govern his actions by the laws of virtue, must regulate his thoughts by those of reason; he must keep guilt from the recesses of his heart, and remember that the pleasures of fancy, and the emotions of desire, are more dangerous as they are more hidden" (III, 43, 46).

Art is a two-edged weapon that may tempt us to pay attention to truth, but may tempt us also to forget reality, to lose ourselves in dangerous fantasies in which our hopes can all be effortlessly fulfilled and our most dubious instincts gratified with impunity. "Poesy," in Bacon's statement, "was ever thought to have some participation of divinenesse, because it doth raise and erect the Minde, by submitting the shewes of things to the desires of the Mind; whereas reason doth buckle and bowe the Mind unto the Nature of things."[10] In Johnson's combination of empirical

[10]Francis Bacon, *The Advancement of Learning*, Bk. II, in *Critical Essays of the Seventeenth Century*, ed. J. E. Spingarn (Oxford, 1908), I, 6.

psychology and moral imperative, such a submission of reality to the desires of the mind is at least idle and probably dangerous. Similarly, Swift had ironically suggested, in the "Digression concerning Madness" in *A Tale of a Tub*, that the imagination "can build nobler scenes and produce more wonderful revolutions than fortune or nature will be at expense to furnish." This is the dubious happiness of being well deceived.

Without passing judgment on the ultimate validity of Johnson's position, we may recognize at least that it takes an impressive place in an ongoing debate whose implications have always troubled thoughtful people. Had he rested his aesthetic in the intellect, one might scoff at the claim that a reader cannot judge for himself what is good and bad. But his postulate is that art appeals to the imagination at an emotional level over which the intellect has only intermittent control. Shakespeare's failure to instruct is important because his plays are so much more imaginative than the works of other poets. Johnson is that rare being, a didactic critic who fully respects the power of art. For him it is not the pallid handmaiden of official truth but a highly independent force that can short-circuit the reason and the will, presenting a compelling image of life over which the intellectual censor has lost its crucial authority.

It is worth observing that Coleridge, who takes a very traditional view of pleasure and truth—"The communication of pleasure is the introductory means by which alone the poet must expect to moralize his readers" (*Biographia*, Ch. 22, II, 105)—comes extremely close to Johnson in fearing the dangers of mental association: "I will at least make the attempt to explain to myself the Origin of Moral Evil from the *streamy* Nature of Association, which Thinking = Reason, curbs & rudders, how this comes to be so difficult / Do not the bad Passions in Dreams throw light and shew of proof upon this Hypothesis?"[11] Like Johnson, Coleridge brooded upon the power of illness to liberate association in "the dreams, by which the blind fancy would fain interpret to the mind the painful sensations of distempered sleep" (*Biographia*, Ch. 1, I, 6). Wordsworth, in the 1815 *Preface*, argued that Coleridge's distinction between imagination and

[11]MS Notebook No. 16, quoted by Humphry House, *Coleridge* (London, 1962), pp. 44-45.

fancy was too rigid: "To aggregate and to associate, to evoke and to combine, belong as well to the Imagination as to the Fancy. . . . Fancy, as she is an active, is also, under her own laws and in her own spirit, a creative faculty." But Coleridge, like Johnson, had emotional reasons for handling the concepts as he did. As M. H. Abrams observes, he was able to retain the mechanist theory of association in Fancy, and his own organic theory of the creative Imagination, in a kind of "bifocal lens." Association would still be the ground upon which our thinking operates, just as we move by using (and resisting) gravity, but the active imagination would prevent its "streamy nature" from carrying him away in futile reverie.[12] (Hazlitt observed in *The Spirit of the Age*, "All his ideas indeed are like a river, flowing on for ever.")

While Coleridge could rehabilitate and protect imagination in this way, Johnson, for whom it was fully defined by Lockean association, could only regard it with doubt and anxiety. In *Rambler* 96 he recasts Addison's allegory of the battle between Falsehood and Truth (*Spectator* 63) by proposing that Truth cannot hope to be reverenced for herself and must actually *pretend to be falsehood* in order to insinuate her lessons: "The Muses wove in the loom of Pallas, a loose and changeable robe, like that in which Falsehood captivated her admirers; with this they invested Truth, and named her Fiction. She now went out again to conquer with more success; for when she demanded entrance of the Passions, they often mistook her for Falsehood, and delivered up their charge; but when she had once taken possession, she was soon disrobed by Reason, and shone out, in her original form, with native effulgence and resistless dignity" (IV, 152).

As always when Johnson handles this subject, there is a note of defiant paradox. If truth makes herself indistinguishable from falsehood, can reason always identify her? And what if fiction, here identified with falsehood, be more attractive in itself than the truth whose bitterness the mind rejects? Johnson's doubts

---

[12]Wordsworth, Preface to the 1815 *Poems, Prose Works*, III, 36, 37. Abrams, *The Mirror and the Lamp* (New York, 1953), p. 176. See also House, *Coleridge*, Ch. 6. The analogy of gravity is found in Ch. 7 of the *Biographia*—"In every voluntary movement we first counteract gravitation, in order to avail ourselves of it" (I, 85).

about Shakespeare are completely intelligible in this light: his power of compelling attention is the first requirement of a writer, but is morally dangerous. Because he mirrors reality so perfectly, he replaces reality. And what ought to be ugly in reality may not be so at all in fiction. Johnson exhibits here a radical distrust of the power of art. His position resembles that of Simone Weil in her observation "Imaginary evil is romantic and varied; real evil is gloomy, monotonous, barren, boring. Imaginary good is boring, real good is always new, marvellous, intoxicating. 'Imaginative literature,' therefore, is either boring or immoral or a mixture of both."[13]

It helps to understand Johnson's view if we see it not simply as a personal preoccupation but as a conscious hostility to the most profound movement of thought and feeling that was taking place in his lifetime. *Movement* is perhaps too strong a term for so diffuse and leaderless a phenomenon, to which no very precise definition can be given; still the terms *sentiment* and *sensibility* sufficiently describe an ever-growing current of feeling in the later eighteenth century. What seems to have been particularly offensive to Johnson in all versions of it, especially in the romanticized Rousseauism of which he patiently tried to cure Boswell, was the assumption that moral truth should be determined, and moral behavior impelled, by feeling rather than reason. While Johnson accepted the Lockean, empiricist account of reason, he continued to regard its *moral* function as the older humanists had done. Thus he held reason (despite its obvious limitations) to be the highest faculty and primary guide to ethical conduct, rather than replacing it with feeling as Hume and other empiricist thinkers were doing.[14]

The relation between "sentiment" and literature could only seem pernicious to a man holding Johnson's views about morals and art, which I take to be that the two are distinct but should mutually reinforce each other. In the simplest version of sentimentalism, following the Shaftesburyan equation of moral and aesthetic response, the good and the beautiful are apprehended intuitively and are virtually synonymous. To Johnson this must be dangerous; but even worse must be the inversion of the principle that could occur if Shaftesbury's confidence in the

[13]Quoted by W. H. Auden in the *New Yorker*, 1 Apr. 1972, p. 104.
[14]See Voitle, *Samuel Johnson the Moralist*, Chs. 1 and 2.

uniformity of human ethical responses were shaken, together with his assumption that the beautiful must correspond to what traditional morality regarded as good. Such an inversion could cast art free from the bounds of conventional morality: the marquis de Sade claimed that he was simply giving faithful expression to his natural impulses. Against the advocates of sensibility, for whom feeling is the guarantor of virtuous behavior, Johnson sees reason as the only possible defense against a chaos of inadmissible desires and fantasies. "Such, therefore, is the importance of keeping reason a constant guard over imagination, that we have otherwise no security for our own virtue, but may corrupt our hearts in the most recluse solitude, with more pernicious and tyrannical appetites and wishes, than the commerce of the world will generally produce" (*Rambler* 8). In just this way the young Rousseau indulged his unfocused sexual feelings by recalling and varying situations from his reading, "so that I would become one of the characters I imagined, and would always see myself in situations that were the most agreeable to my own taste. . . . This love of imaginary objects and this ability to occupy myself with them ended by disgusting me with everything that surrounded me, and caused that taste for solitude which has remained with me ever since."[15]

Similar preoccupations account for the stridency of Johnson's denunciations of Fielding. Though the philosophical difference between the two men was far smaller than Johnson indignantly supposed, it remains true that Fielding's principle of "good nature" has close affinities with sentimentalism. As Martin Price says, "Fielding discriminates carefully between moral laxity and moral obliviousness—or, as Coleridge puts it, between what a man does and what he is."[16] Like Aristotle in the *Ethics*, Johnson

[15]" . . . Tellement que je devinsse un des personnages que j'imaginois, que je me visse toujours dans les positions les plus agréables selon mon goût. . . . Cet amour des objets imaginaires et cette facilité de m'en occuper achevèrent de me dégoûter de tout ce qui m'entouroit, et déterminèrent ce goût pour la solitude qui m'est toujours resté depuis ce tems-là" (*Confessions*, Livre Premier, ed. A. van Bever [Paris, 1952], I, 56-57).
[16]*To the Palace of Wisdom: Studies in Order and Energy from Dryden to Blake* (New York, 1964), p. 308. Voitle has an interesting discussion of the similarities as well as differences between Johnson and Fielding (p. 131). It should be emphasized that in his nonfictional writings Fielding often adopts positions that are very close to Johnson's. In his "Essay on the Knowledge of the Characters of Men," for instance, he stresses the point that only actions can reveal character.

repudiates such a distinction and sees a man's actions not only as our chief means of insight into his true nature but also as the expression and definition of that nature. We are what we do. "Those faults," Johnson says with bitter self-knowledge, "which we cannot conceal from our own notice, are considered, however frequent, not as habitual corruptions, or settled practices, but as casual failures, and single lapses. . . . There are men who always confound the praise of goodness with the practice" (*Rambler* 28, III, 153-54).

In actual life Johnson is prepared to be lenient in enforcing this principle, as when he describes Richard Savage in very similar language: "The reigning Error of his Life was, that he mistook the Love for the Practice of Virtue, and was indeed not so much a good Man, as the Friend of Goodness" (*Savage*, p. 74). But Savage's immorality found no echo in his writings. "He never contributed deliberately to spread Corruption amongst Mankind," and his poems "may improve Mankind, when his Failings shall be forgotten" (pp. 74-75). Fielding's fault is in having introduced sentimental morality into a novel and—in Johnson's opinion—showing it triumphant. It goes without saying that this represents a misreading of *Tom Jones* ("I, indeed, never read 'Joseph Andrews' "—*Life*, II, 174) but it is a misreading, not a travesty. Johnson understands, as many Victorian critics could not, that the sexual theme in *Tom Jones* is part of a larger ethical argument.

Everyone knows that Johnson would have liked to sign the sentence for Rousseau's transportation, but the context of the remark is not always remembered: "JOHNSON . . .'I think him one of the worst of men; a rascal, who ought to be hunted out of society, as he has been. . . .' BOSWELL. 'I don't deny, Sir, but that his novel may, perhaps, do harm; but I cannot think his intention was bad.' JOHNSON. 'Sir, that will not do. We cannot prove any man's intention to be bad. You may shoot a man through the head, and say you intended to miss him; but the Judge will order you to be hanged' (*Life*, II, 11-12). This is exactly what Johnson abhors in *Tom Jones*, a novel that he believes to set a vicious example even while it proclaims the purity of its intentions. The phrase "hunted out" was anticipated in a *Rambler* that denounces the kind of writer "who tortures his fancy, and ransacks his memory, only that he may leave the world less virtuous than he found it."

What were their motives, or what their excuses, is below the dignity of reason to examine. If having extinguished in themselves the distinction of right and wrong, they were insensible of the mischief which they promoted, they deserved to be hunted down by the general compact, as no longer partaking of social nature; if influenced by the corruption of patrons, or readers, they sacrificed their own convictions to vanity or interest, they were to be abhorred with more acrimony than he that murders for pay; since they committed greater crimes without greater temptations. [*Rambler* 77, IV, 44]

Though this is a reasoned position, there is no denying that the voice is raised. Johnson's language would be strong not just for Fielding but even for the seediest Grub Street chronicler of scandal and obscenity. His hatred of *Tom Jones* reflects a serious limitation in his critical range; I have only wanted to show that it is not merely outrageous, but rests on an elaborated moral position as well as on the more familiar objections to Fielding's superficial characterization.

One may speculate further that the modern loathing of didacticism may be a temporary phenomenon. While a dislike of Johnson's moralizing can be found in late-Victorian writers,[17] it receives its dogmatic support from a modern poetics in which an immense gulf between art and life is taken as axiomatic. In this system the notion of language as the dress of thought—which Johnson and his contemporaries took for granted—is treated as anathema, and in accounts like René Wellek's affords a convenient way of merging Johnson's didacticism and his aesthetics into a single object of attack.[18] If we know that form and content are inseparable, we are able to reject Johnson's didacticism as Wellek does, by calling it a confusion of art with life, rather than having to confront and criticize Johnson's moral judgments in themselves. When the modern critic does wish to act as a

---

[17]The distinguished editor of Sophocles, Richard Jebb, told the ladies of Newnham College, Cambridge, in 1894, "The great fault of his school was that they judged poetry too much by its moral value and its logical coherence, and too little by its qualities as a work of art" ("Samuel Johnson," rpt. in *Essays and Addresses* [Cambridge, 1907], p. 499).

[18]*History of Modern Criticism*, I, Ch. 5, "Dr. Johnson."

moralist, the assumption of a form / content unity compels him
to make a dubious sort of case against works he dislikes, translat-
ing moral judgments into aesthetic ones. In the writings of F. R.
Leavis, for example, close verbal analysis is used to prove what is
really a moral case: writers who arouse Leavis's disapproval are
shown to write prose or verse that is "coarse" or "mechanical."
Instead of straightforward moral assertions, therefore, we often
get what looks like scrupulous examination of specific texts in
which the very movement of the language is said to exhibit
qualities that prove the writer's incompetence to tell us anything
important about life. For this reason Leavis is not quite fair in
saying that Johnson "cannot appreciate the ways in which not
only Shakespeare's drama but all works of art *act* their moral
judgments."[19] Johnson does objects to the amorality, as he conceives it, of Shakespeare's plays, but he does so openly and in
such a way that his aesthetic and moral judgments are clearly
distinct. For Leavis the richness and seriousness of the plays
prove by definition the presence of a profound moral vision. For
Johnson aesthetic and moral criteria are by no means identical,
and in Shakespeare he finds them seriously out of harmony with
each other.

But whatever theoretical defense may be offered for
Johnson's didacticism, it does often seem obtrusive and limiting
in the *Preface* (and notes) to Shakespeare. If, as I shall argue, it
seems less so in the *Lives*, the reason cannot simply be that
Johnson has mellowed in old age: many of his judgments,
whether of Milton, Swift, or Gray, have excited violent reaction
ever since their first publication. The fundamental reason is that
in the *Lives* he can found his moral analysis on biographical
reality and thereby escape the most awkward difficulty in his
approach in Shakespeare. For in the *Preface* he follows earlier
editors in seeking to define "Shakespeare" as an organizing
intelligence that can be perceived in the plays as a whole. This is
the intention of Dryden's famous character of Shakespeare ("the

[19]"Johnson as Critic," *Scrutiny*, 12 (1944), 197. For a discussion of this aspect
of Leavis (and Arnold) see John Casey, *The Language of Criticism* (Cambridge,
1966), pp. 184 ff. In such an aesthetic, as Casey says, "Johnson's notion of how
literature can be 'true', or how it can have 'moral purpose', suffers from being
excessively didactic and literal. Johnson so emphasizes content, that formal or
aesthetic qualities can be no more than ornamental" (p. 196).

largest and most comprehensive soul") with which Johnson closes the *Preface* and which he later describes as a permanently adequate account. "In a few lines is exhibited a character, so extensive in its comprehension and so curious in its limitations, that nothing can be added, diminished, or reformed" (*Life of Dryden*, I, 412). But to dwell on the general qualities of Shakespeare's mind is to minimize the individuality of the plays. Johnson of course sees some of the differences, particularly in the notes, but in the *Preface* he is mainly concerned to define Shakespeare's intellectual character in universal terms. And this the plays do not very readily yield: they are too rich, too various, for us to say anything except that their author had a rich and various mind.

In the *Lives of the Poets* Johnson will show great skill in relating moral and intellectual character to an author's works. But in the *Preface* he seems consciously disturbed by the impossibility to doing this with any success: Shakespeare is a *deus absconditus* hidden so completely behind the bulky folio that Johnson strikes out at him irritably and ineffectively. What he misses above all is a clear sense of a moral center in the plays, so that unlike the earlier preface-writers (though there are anticipations in the pamphlets of Rymer and Dennis) he dwells on moral faults as well as faults of structure and language. The two kinds of defects are indeed related, for Johnson sees the indistinct "Shakespeare" in the plays as insufficiently committed to the excellence that he admires in Milton or Pope. Here is a poet of unparalleled powers who is too careless to write or teach as well as he should.

Thus the *Preface* is a strangely complicated work, put forward as an objective survey of artistic achievement but riven by hostilities that depend in part on a powerful dislike of the amorality proper to art. In proportion as a writer is brilliant and compelling, Johnson may distrust and even fear his power over the imagination. Of course the final impressions of the *Preface* is positive; I have perhaps exaggerated its negative aspect in order to focus attention on it. But many readers, especially those more interested in Shakespeare than in Johnson, have felt that Johnson is unfair to Shakespeare. I would urge at least that although the *Preface* is full of interest, it is not as a whole representative of Johnson at his best. His sympathies and hostilities are more successfully engaged in the *Lives of the Poets*, where he can deal directly with the moral and critical issues that are appropriate in literary biography.

These matters will be more fully explored in the next chapter. Here, I want to conclude by showing that Johnson saw biography, even at the time of the *Rambler*, as a window to moral truth that might escape the dangers inherent in fiction. *Rambler* 60 begins, "All joy or sorrow for the happiness or calamities of others is produced by *an act of the imagination*, that realises the event *however fictitious*, or approximates it however remote, by placing us, for a time, in the condition of him whose fortune we contemplate; so that we feel, *while the deception lasts*, whatever motions would be excited by the same good or evil happening to ourselves" (III, 318-19). I have italicized those phrases that strongly recall Johnson's anxiety about the deceptions of the imagination. And he goes on to say that no kind of writing is more certain than biography to "enchain the heart by irresistible interest"—the terms in which he repeatedly describes the poet's power over his readers. What softens his language here, what redeems biography from the moral ambiguities of fiction, is the fact that it seeks to describe what is *literally true*.

The writer of fiction releases his imagination to sport in dangerous realms; the writer of biography applies his judgment to establish the true nature of events that really occurred.

There are many who think it an act of piety to hide the faults or failings of their friends, even when they can no longer suffer by their detection; we therefore see whole ranks of characters adorned with uniform panegyrick, and not to be known from one another, but by extrinsick and casual circumstances. "Let me remember," says Hale, "when I find myself inclined to pity a criminal, that there is likewise a pity due to the country." If we owe regard to the memory of the dead, there is yet more respect to be paid to knowledge, to virtue, and to truth. [*Rambler* 60, III, 323]

The analogy is surprising: the dead person appears as a criminal before the bar, and the biographer, by implication, is the stern judge whose allegiance is to knowledge, virtue, and truth.

A great advantage of biography, furthermore, is that the judicial biographer is free to comment directly on the meaning of his story, while the writer of fiction must generally let the story speak for itself—in Leavis's terms, act its moral judgments.[20] Johnson requires not only that a work of art be morally unexceptionable but also that it convey specific truths, or, as he likes to call them, "precepts." (The definition of "precept" in the *Dictionary* is: "A rule authoritatively given; a mandate; a commandment; a direction.") When Johnson says that Shakespeare's "precepts and axioms drop casually from him" (*Preface*, p. 71), that is exactly what he means. There is a discussion in *Rambler* 29 of an analogous defect in the ancient poets, whose "precepts are to be always considered as the sallies of a genius, intent rather upon giving pleasure than instruction," though various "reflections upon life" can be extracted from their writings and "treasured up" by the reader (III, 158, 159).

When writers are casual to instruct, it is up to the reader to deduce his own "precepts" from their works; but in many cases this is hardly possible. Milton's epic is morally superior to its predecessors precisely because it is literally true: "The ancient epick poets, wanting the light of Revelation, were very unskilful teachers of virtue: their principal characters may be great, but they are not amiable. The reader may rise from their works with a greater degree of active or passive fortitude, and sometimes of prudence; but he will be able to carry away few precepts of justice, and none of mercy" (*Life of Milton*, I, 179). As moral teachers Homer and Virgil are incomplete and imprecise. They fail to teach the whole of natural morality (fortitude, prudence, justice, temperance); they omit Christian morals altogether (faith, hope, charity); and the reader, though he may be influenced by their works, is frustrated in the desire to "carry away" specific instructions for virtue. *Paradise Lost* is altogether different in its close dependence on revealed truth, like the lessons in the Book of Common Prayer, Hooker's comment on which is quoted under "precept" in the *Dictionary*: "The custom of lessons furnishes the very simplest and rudest sort with infallible axioms

[20]Disapproving of Fielding's ethic, Johnson cannot very well approve of the narrator who teaches it. But Fielding's mode of narrative ought surely to appeal to him more than the ambiguous first-person mode of *Moll Flanders* or *Roderick Random* (novels which he may well have in mind in *Rambler* 4). If Johnson had ever written a critique of *Clarissa*, he would have had to go beyond general praise of knowledge of the heart and explain his claim, contradicting the experience of many eighteenth-century readers, that Lovelace does not represent a dangerously seductive example (see the *Life of Rowe*, II, 67).

and *precepts* of sacred truth, delivered even in the very letter of
the law of God." Perhaps Johnson remembered this sentence
when he wrote later of Shakespeare's casual "precepts and
axioms."

It stands to reason that only an explicitly moral writer like
Milton would be a rich source of memorable precepts. A biographer, however, is in an excellent position to offer them as often
as he likes. We have noticed that Savage possessed some of the
very faults that Johnson detested in Tom Jones; but Tom is an
attractively idealized young hero and lover, while Savage was a
real man whose faults can be analyzed and warned against even
as they are forgiven. Johnson says of a poet he greatly admired:
"Butler had not suffered life to glide beside him unseen or
unobserved. He had watched with great diligence the operations
of human nature and traced the effects of opinion, humour,
interest, and passion. From such remarks proceeded that great
number of sententious distichs which have passed into conversation, and are added as proverbial axioms to the general stock of
practical knowledge" (*Life of Butler*, I, 213). The same words
could easily be applied to Johnson himself. In the *Lives of the
Poets*, as we shall now go on to see, he at last enjoys perfect
freedom to pursue the moral issues that lie at the boundary
between art and life and to add his own wise axioms to the
general stock of knowledge. Criticism in the *Lives* is grounded on
the biographical reality, the "truth" so important to Johnson,
that Shakespeare maddeningly lacked. It is this new context, I
think, and not any major shift in his moral preoccupations, that
causes Johnson to speak so much more favorably of the imagination throughout the *Lives*. "Poetry pleases," he now tells us, "by
exhibiting an idea more grateful to the mind than things themselves afford" (*Life of Waller*, I, 292). This notion, which had been
the *radix malorum* in *Rambler* 4, *Rasselas*, and the *Preface to Shakespeare*, is presented here almost indulgently. Specific works will
still arouse Johnson's wrath, but in the biographical context he
can afford to relax his comprehensive suspicion of art.

6   *The Greatness of the* Lives

Much of the best literary work in the later eighteenth century was done in what we have come to call intellectual prose, a kind of writing in which factual truth is as important as the traditional pleasures of literary art. If the proper study of mankind was man, readers wanted to know about real men. A long series of great works sought to define the nature and limits of human achievement, and it is with these rather than with treatises on aesthetics that the *Lives of the Poets* belong.

The Nature of Johnson's Achievement

Johnson seeks to do for the British poets what Gibbon did for the Romans in the *Decline and Fall*, a work that has been variously called satiric, epic, elegiac, and tragic. But Johnson had to face other difficulties than the historian, who could still entertain a conception of literal truth, however it might be organized and mediated through the writer's imagination. The biographer of the poets was obliged to combine, if he could, critical evaluation with objective narrative. To rise above mere antiquarianism, he must constantly pass judgment. The *Lives of the Poets* have analogues in the work of a number of Johnson's contemporaries, and surpass them all. They draw upon antiquarian or annalistic biography, but transcend it; they combine literary history and the analysis of specific authors in a way not hitherto accomplished.

Some measure of Johnson's achievement is afforded by comparison with the complementary labors of the brothers Warton, both of whom were (at least at times) his friends. Joseph Warton's ambitious *Essay on the Genius and Writings of Pope* is intended to communicate a wealth of criticism and learning by way of commentary on a single poet. But it is a jumble, or, as Johnson more tactfully said in his review of the first volume in 1756, "a very curious and entertaining miscellany of critical remarks and

literary history" (1825 *Works*, VI, 37). Warton's discussion,
though ostensibly organized about specific poems of Pope, is
filled with quotations from classical and modern authors and
makes no sustained attempt to explore the "genius" of its title.
Rather, it is intended, by sheer weight of knowledge and taste, to
establish Pope's classification below the level of "our only three
sublime and pathetic poets; Spenser, Shakespeare, Milton."[1]
Pope becomes the occasion for a polemical argument about
literary kinds.

Warton does not undertake biography or try to estimate
Pope's character, but neither does he offer criticism of a very
searching kind. He admires *The Rape of the Lock*, for instance, but
devotes all of his forty-five pages to a discussion of mock-heroic
precedents, to accounts of supernatural beings in other poets
(such as Shakespeare's fairies) and to vague praise of the success
with which Pope has managed his: "The transformation of
women of different tempers into different kinds of spirits, cannot be too much applauded" (p. 231). With justice Johnson
comments in his review, "There is, in his remarks on this work,
no discovery of any latent beauty, nor any thing subtle or striking; he is, indeed, commonly right, but has discussed no difficult
question" (p. 44). Johnson has been charged with merely following Warton in his remarks on *The Rape of the Lock*, especially in
reacting to Warton's denial of its originality. It would be more
just to say that Johnson rightly reacts against a special kind of
pedantry, in which an unexamined and rhapsodic idea of "true"
taste is combined with niggling arguments about historical influence. Warton and others had treated Pope's sylphs and gnomes
as phenomena in literary history; Johnson treats them as evidence by which to determine "from what sources the power of
pleasing is derived" (*Life of Pope*, III, 232). His own account of
Pope's mock-epic machinery, depending as it does on this fidelity to the reader's response, offers impressive reasons for the
excellence of the poem.

Yet Joseph Warton was an intelligent man, and capable of
first-rate appreciative commentary in smaller compass (as his

[1]*Essay*, 4th ed. (1782), I, xii. The dedication to Young concludes, "In which of
these classes Pope deserves to be placed, the following work is intended to
determine" (p. xiii).

papers on Shakespeare in the *Adventurer* show). He stumbled
only when he tried to enlarge his mode of miscellaneous running
commentary into a full-scale evaluation of a poet's work. His
brother Thomas was no more successful in the attempt to organize a narrative around the chronology of literary history. The
ambitious *History of English Poetry*, which never got beyond the
sixteenth century, is more chaotic by far than the *Essay on Pope*
and submerges every writer in a welter of information about his
contemporaries.

Against the uncertain achievement of the Wartons, Johnson's
use of the biographical mode looks extremely impressive. The
fact that the booksellers suggested the *Lives* is irrelevant; it was
Johnson who chose to swell the projected prefaces into elaborate
surveys of the poets' lives and works. For this he had few precedents: there was plenty of biography, but not much biography
that seriously attempted criticism. William Mason's feeble *Gray*
was no help.[2] Johnson's most important predecessor was probably Izaak Walton, whose *Lives* he often praised and with whom
he shared a preference for biography that illuminates character
by means of striking details and rises to a morally exemplary
level. But Johnson's method is far subtler than that of Walton,
who tended to read backward from the mature man to reconstruct an ideal picture of his youth, and—in accordance with the
character-tradition in which he worked—to simplify discor-
dant elements in the life in order to emphasize a central conception of personality.[3] It would be absurd to say that Johnson never
shows bias, never distorts. But the uniformity he postulates in a
poet tends to be uniformity of mental powers, not of behavior.
He is much more open than Walton to contradictory or even

[2]Boswell has perhaps given this work an undeserved reputation by proposing it as a model for the *Life of Johnson*. It is a model only in that it reprints Gray's
letters (though altering them shamefully, as we now know). It is not a critical
biography. When it was published Johnson described it to Mrs. Thrale as
"Gray's letters prefixed by Mason to his poems," and called it dull (*Letters*, II,
28).

[3]See John Butt, *Biography in the Hands of Walton, Johnson, and Boswell* (Los
Angeles, 1966), and David Novarr, *The Making of Walton's Lives* (Ithaca, N.Y.,
1958). Walton not only glosses over the excesses of the youthful Donne, but also
makes a highly selective use of specific information, as in treating Hooker's
temporary expulsion from Oxford in such a way as to emphasize his integrity
but conceal his early leanings toward Calvinism (Novarr, p. 286).

irrational behavior; to motives that can only be guessed at; to friendships and enmities that are important in a man's life but look inexplicable to the detached observer.

Walton is therefore what Johnson rightly calls him, a "great panegyrist" (*Life*, II, 364) who tells us that Hooker at eighteen "seemed to be filled with the Holy Ghost, and even like St. *John Baptist*, to be sanctified from his Mothers womb, who did often bless the day in which she bare him," and who reports the vision of Christ that Donne saw at the moment of dying. Of Donne he says, "Thus *variable*, thus *vertuous* was the Life; thus *excellent*, thus *exemplary* was the Death of this memorable man."[4] Johnson's most Waltonian performance is the *Life of Savage*: "Such were the Life and Death of *Richard Savage*, a Man equally distinguished by his Virtues and Vices, and at once remarkable for his Weaknesses and Abilities" (*Savage*, p. 135). In many ways this *Life* is a secularized and disillusioned adaptation of Walton. Instead of Donne's beatific vision we find a deathbed of terrible emptiness: "The last Time that the Keeper saw him was on *July* the 31st, 1743; when *Savage* seeing him at his Bed-side said, with an uncommon Earnestness, *I have something to say to you, Sir*, but after a Pause, moved his Hand in a melancholy Manner, and finding himself unable to recollect what he was going to communicate, said *'Tis gone*" (p. 135).

One of the great strengths of Johnson's *Lives* is that this moral breadth is preserved even when the emphasis becomes primarily literary. Walton saw Donne and Herbert as saints who happened to have written poetry. In the *Lives* Johnson must concentrate on the poems, and on biography chiefly as it accounts for the poems, but he is able to do so without compromising his fundamental belief that human life must be seen and judged as a whole. To be sure, a man's writings are not synonymous with his character, and good poems are not always written by good men. "That Poetry and Virtue go always together is an opinion so pleasing that I can forgive him who resolves to think it true" (*Life of Gray*, III, 437). Johnson is commendably cautious in establishing relations between poetry and biography; he makes fun of attempts to deduce Thomson's character from his poems, in

---

[4]Izaak Walton, *Lives*, ed. George Saintsbury (Oxford, 1927), pp. 166, 82.

contrast to later critics who read *The Seasons* as evidence of Thomson's benevolence, tenderness, honesty, and piety.[5] Nevertheless, both poems and lives must be judged in the light of truth. In the *Rambler* moral judgments had to be conveyed through fictitious narratives and labored allegories; in the *Lives* they can be visibly grounded on specific moments of human reality. However great was his commitment to general truths, Johnson expressed them best when he could give them specific embodiment. "He has a penetrating insight into character," Cowper wrote after reading the *Lives*, "and a happy talent of correcting the popular opinion, upon all occasions where it is erroneous; and this he does with the boldness of a man who will think for himself, but, at the same time, with a justness of sentiment that convinces us he does not differ from others through affectation, but because he has a sounder judgement."[6]

But if he sought to embrace lives and works in a single conception, Johnson was nonetheless cautious about forcing the connections between them. When the *Lives* were to be printed separately from the poems to which they had been conceived as prefaces, he proposed two possible titles: *An Account of the Lives and Works of some of the most eminent English Poets* and *The English Poets biographically and critically considered* (*Letters*, II, 426). In their modesty these titles suggest that biography and criticism, though they should cast light on each other, cannot actually merge. A defense of the apparent casualness of this position must be deferred to the detailed argument of the next chapters, but it may be useful to generalize about the shrewdness of Johnson's biographical insight and the appropriateness of the moral criticism that follows from it.

The *Lives* are, first of all, lives. As was observed in the last chapter, biography held a special fascination for Johnson, partly

---

[5]See Ralph Cohen, *The Art of Discrimination: Thomson's* The Seasons *and the Language of Criticism* (Berkeley and Los Angeles, 1964), pp. 105-19. Similarly, Pope had deduced from the *Iliad* that Homer must have been "of a warm Temper," pious, patriotic, "addicted to a chearful, sociable Life," and partial to the female sex (*Essay on the Life, Writings, and Learning of Homer*, in Twickenham Ed., *Poems*, VII, 50-51).

[6]William Cowper to William Unwin, 21 March 1784, *Correspondence*, ed. Thomas Wright (New York, 1904), II, 179. Cowper adds, "This remark, however, has his narrative for its object, rather than his critical performance."

because he loved to learn about human beings, but more especially because of its dependence on presumably verifiable truth.
However urgently he might prefer that poetry suppress minute
details, in biography he demanded them. Reynolds could denounce "the minute discriminations, which distinguish one object of the same species from another" and command the painter
to "consider nature in the abstract, and represent in every one
of his figures the character of its species" (*Discourses*, No. 3, p.
35). But Johnson wrote to Mrs. Thrale that an intelligent traveler
should detect "minute discriminations" (*Letters*, I, 340) and in
Rambler 60 deplored the vagueness of most biographers. In his
early *Life of Browne* he speaks explicitly of "those minute
peculiarities which discriminate every man from all others,"
which are "irrecoverably lost" unless the subject's friends take
care to preserve them (1825 *Works*, VI, 494). And again in the
Life of Addison he laments that "the delicate features of the mind,
the nice discriminations of character, and the minute
peculiarities of conduct are soon obliterated" (*Lives*, II, 116).

So far as painting was concerned, Johnson seems actually to
have repudiated Reynold's ideal: "I had rather see the portrait of
a dog that I know, than all the allegorical paintings they can shew
me in the world" (*Miscellanies*, II, 15). One reason, no doubt, was
his opinion that painting could only be static and illustrative:
"When I observed to him that Painting was so far inferiour to
Poetry, that the story or even emblem which it communicates
must be previously known, and mentioned as a natural and
laughable instance of this, that a little Miss on seeing a picture of
Justice with the scales, had exclaimed to me, 'See, there's a
woman selling sweetmeats;' he said, 'Painting, Sir, can illustrate,
but cannot inform'"(*Life*, IV, 321). But the literalism of the
portrait, in which "truth is of the greatest value" (*Life*, V, 219),
implies a happy freedom from the anxieties of art. "The value of
every story," Johnson told Boswell, "depends on its being true. A
story is a picture either of an individual or of human nature in
general: if it be false, it is a picture of nothing" (*Life*, II, 433). An
imaginative picture of "human nature in general" involves, as we
have seen, moral ambiguities that caused Johnson great distress.
Biography, like the portrait, is firmly rooted in the specificity of a
single human life. In fact, it escapes all the complications of

Aristotle's probable impossibilities, with attendant contempt for unlikely events that may really have happened. "Such a purpose, formed at such an age and successfully prosecuted, delights as it is strange, and instructs as it is real" (*Life of Sheffield*, II, 167).

In estimating Johnson's excellence as a biographer we will find it helpful to start with the (perhaps heretical) notion that he is not at his best in the *Life of Savage*, published in 1744 and reprinted with few changes in the *Lives of the Poets* nearly forty years later. The *Savage* is a brilliant work, full of shrewd insights into human behavior, expressed in a style in which irony is perfectly balanced with sympathy.

With these Expectations he was so enchanted, that when he was once gently reproach'd by a Friend [very likely Johnson] for submitting to live upon a Subscription, and advised rather by a resolute Exertion of his Abilities to support himself, he could not bear to debar himself from the Happiness which was to be found in the Calm of a Cottage, or lose the Opportunity of listening without Intermission, to the Melody of the Nightingale, which he believ'd was to be heard from every Bramble, and which he did not fail to mention as a very important Part of the Happiness of a Country Life.

　　While this Scheme was ripening, his Friends directed him to take a Lodging in the Liberties of the Fleet, that he might be secure from his Creditors, and sent him every Monday a Guinea, which he commonly spent before the next Morning, and trusted, after his usual Manner, the remaining Part of the Week to the Bounty of Fortune. [P. 111]

But in addressing the less amusing aspects of Savage's character, Johnson is not so convincing. Savage's habitual tendency to betray and defame his benefactors is repeatedly glossed over, sometimes by turning the accusation back upon his friends. Steele may have been disillusioned by discovering that Savage, whom he had repeatedly helped, was ridiculing him, but on the other hand Savage "was not likely to learn Prudence or Frugality" from Steele, and "perhaps many of the Misfortunes which the Want of those Virtues brought upon him in the following Parts of his Life, might be justly imputed to so unimproving an Example" (p. 15).

The central problem is that in the *Savage*, as nowhere else in his writings, Johnson allows personal sympathy to paralyze his native skepticism. For whatever psychological reasons—he

probably saw many of his own faults in Savage, and in forgiving
him could forgive himself—Johnson consistently accepts Savage's version of every story. Thus he reports that Savage divided
his last guinea with the prostitute who had given perjured evidence against him at his murder trial, and goes on to comment,
"This is an Action which in some Ages would have made a Saint,
and perhaps in others a Hero, and which, without any hyperbolical Encomiums, must be allowed to be an Instance of uncommon Generosity, an Act of complicated Virtue; by which he at
once relieved the Poor, corrected the Vicious, and forgave an
Enemy; by which he at once remitted the strongest Provocations,
and exercised the most ardent Charity" (p. 40). Had the anecdote been reported of Dryden or Pope, Johnson would surely
have considered the possibility that the action was ostentatious,
performed in order to be boasted of; and the possibility approaches certainty in light of Savage's obsessively role-playing
personality. The man who bit the hands that fed him might easily
choose, as a dramatic gesture, to feed the mouth that bit him.

On a more fundamental level, Johnson does not submit to
scrutiny the story of maternal persecution from which the whole
of his narrative flows.

It is not indeed easy to discover what Motives could be found to
overbalance that natural Affection of a Parent, or what Interest could
be promoted by Neglect or Cruelty. . . . It was therefore not likely that
she would be wicked without Temptation, that she would look upon
her Son from his Birth with a kind of Resentment and Abhorrence;
and instead of supporting, assisting, and defending him, delight to see
him struggling with Misery; that she would take every Opportunity of
aggravating his Misfortunes, and obstructing his Resources, and with
an implacable and restless Cruelty continue her Persecution from the
first Hour of his Life to the last. [P. 6]

It is *not* likely that the woman would have behaved thus. The
conduct that excites Johnson's violent reproof—resentment,
abhorrence, delight in seeing misery, restless cruelty—can surely
be explained on the hypothesis that she sincerely believed Savage to be an impostor. She would then be, in her own eyes, the

victim, and Savage the persecutor. Savage almost certainly believed his story, but Johnson's intimate knowledge of his instability might have led him to wonder whether the story was based in fact. And at the very least he might have considered that Mrs. Brett, the putative mother, could be understood as a normal human being rather than a frightening monster by the simple assumption that she, like Savage, really believed in the truth of her own assertions.

These issues matter because the *Life of Savage* is an example of inverted hagiography. We have noticed Izaak Walton's tendency to emphasize spiritual states in the service of a didactic lesson. Young Jack Donne the rakehell is lost in Dr. Donne the dying saint. The reader readily accepts the conventions of Walton's genre and is not offended by obvious failures to explore motivation. The problem in the *Savage* is that Johnson tries to do both, moving uncertainly between the impulses to explain and to forgive. The final paragraph of the work proposes a moral for conduct, much as Walton might:

This Relation will not be wholly without its Use, if those, who languish under any Part of his Sufferings, shall be enabled to fortify their Patience by reflecting that they feel only those Afflictions from which the Abilities of *Savage* did not exempt him; or if those, who in Confidence of superior Capacities or Attainments disregard the common Maxims of Life, shall be reminded that nothing will supply the Want of Prudence, and that Negligence and Irregularity, long continued, will make Knowledge useless, Wit ridiculous, and Genius contemptible. [P. 140]

Yet the preceding paragraph had struck a very different note: "Those are no proper Judges of his Conduct who have slumber'd away their Time on the Down of Plenty, nor will a wise Man easily presume to say, 'Had I been in *Savage's* Condition, I should have lived, or written, better than *Savage*.' " Johnson concludes the *Life* by declaring that Savage's story may console those who suffer and provide a negative example for those whose imprudence might destroy their hopeful prospects. But that lesson is available only to a reader, on the down of plenty or elsewhere, who is willing to be a judge of Savage's conduct. The negative example is useless if even a wise man should say that in Savage's condition he would have lived and written like Savage.[7]

Thus the *Life of Savage* should be seen as the early work that it is, experimental rather than perfected. It is filled with splendid things. The note of compassion is noble. But in the *Lives of the Poets* Johnson will explore motivation more strenuously and will draw moral lessons from specific modes of behavior rather than from an all-embracing conclusion in the manner of Walton. And in another respect the *Savage* cannot serve as model for the *Lives of the Poets*: it is the biography of a man who happens to be a writer, much as the subject of the *Life of Boerhaave* is a man who happens to be a physician and theologian.[8] It is enough to assert that Boerhaave accomplished great things, just as it is enough to assert that Savage might have done so; the interest is in the exemplary story, not in the achievements themselves. It appears that Johnson may have intended to write a new *Savage* for inclusion in the *Lives* before eventually letting the old one stand.[9] Many of the first readers of the *Lives* objected that disproportionate weight was given to a very minor poet, and it is quite true that Johnson makes no attempt to justify Savage's importance as a poet or, if he thinks him unimportant, to analyze the limitations of his verse. "My Province is rather to give the History of Mr. *Savage*'s Performances, than to display their Beauties, or to obviate the Criticisms, which they have occasioned" (p. 54). As Johnson partly sees, this is evasive, for the dead Savage "now ceases to influence Mankind in any other Character" than that of

[7]On the complexity of Johnson's sympathies and judgments, see William Vesterman, "Johnson and *The Life of Savage*," *ELH*, 36 (1969), 659-78. John A. Dussinger's imaginative reading represents Savage as imprisoned in a determinist system, where he is what he has to be ("Style and Intention in Johnson's *Life of Savage*," *ELH*, 37 [1970], 564-80). It should be added that Johnson's lifelong horror of determinism complicates his attitude, compelling him to believe that Savage could surely change his life if he would only try (even while perceiving all too clearly that he *cannot* try). Conceivably Mrs. Brett serves Johnson as an agent of evil, playing her role in a universe in which "nothing in reality is governed by chance" (*Rambler* 184), as a way of escaping the suspicion that Savage ricochets helplessly among the jostling atoms of a Lucretian universe.

[8]I discuss Boerhaave as an exemplary figure in *Samuel Johnson and the Tragic Sense*, pp. 74-75.

[9]See Clarence Tracy's Introduction to the *Savage*, pp. xxxv-xxxvi.

an author (p. 139). Still, the actual badness of his poetry is treated as irrelevant, and most of the quotations from it are omitted from the version in the *Lives*. We must simply take Johnson's word for it that Savage had a talent that society wrecked and encouraged Savage himself to wreck. In many ways Johnson's Savage anticipates the damaged poets lamented by Wordsworth and his contemporaries, especially Chatterton, "the marvelous Boy"; but while they formulated a theory of poetry to which the age was supposed to be inimical, Johnson grounds his exemplum on a moral basis. If Savage had been luckier, if his character had been less pliant, he *might* have done great things; but we shall never know.

A more satisfactory model for the treatment of character in the *Lives* is suggested by Johnson's sketch of his old employer Edward Cave:

He was a friend rather easy and constant, than zealous and active; yet many instances might be given, where both his money and his diligence were employed liberally for others. His enmity was, in like manner, cool and deliberate; but though cool, it was not insidious, and though deliberate, not pertinacious.

His mental faculties were slow. He saw little at a time, but that little he saw with great exactness. He was long in finding the right, but seldom failed to find it at last. His affections were not easily gained, and his opinions not quickly discovered. His reserve, as it might hide his faults, concealed his virtues; but such he was, as they who best knew him have most lamented.[10]

In this remarkably frank sketch, printed in Cave's own magazine, Johnson has effectively summarized his character in two ideas—coolness and slowness—which are developed with a precision that allows us to form a firm impression of the man.

A great source of interest in the *Lives of the Poets* is in seeing Johnson strive for the same kind of masterful comprehension of men whom he can know only from published accounts or the recollection of survivors. At times he is confident that a poet and his works can be summed up in a single vision, as when Addison's posture of moderation in society is implicitly linked with the

[10]1825 *Works*, VI, 435. This text is Johnson's 1781 revision, with only trivial changes in the paragraphs quoted, of the version printed in the *Gentleman's Magazine* in 1754.

tepidity of his poetry.[11] Many of the minor *Lives*—for instance, of the amiable Fenton and the inoffensive Gay—reflect this confidence. But the major *Lives* show Johnson struggling energetically to deduce the outline of complex personalities without distorting the available evidence.

The first paragraphs of the first *Life* set the tone for everything that follows. Johnson projects immense control and absolute confidence as he relates the events of Cowley's life, introducing both personal and general reflections without ever seeming to digress. At the outset he tells us that Cowley's biography has been written by the great Dr. Sprat "with so little detail that scarcely any thing is distinctly known, but all is shewn confused and enlarged through the mist of panegyrick" (*Lives*, p. 1). Writing a century later, Johnson must disentangle the truth as best he can from the relations of "the morose Wood" and "the courtly Sprat" (p. 15). The personal note is effortlessly brought in when he tells us that Cowley's mother "had her solicitude rewarded by seeing her son eminent and, I hope, by seeing him fortunate." Stories of Cowley's early ability to excel in languages without learning grammar give rise to a Ramblerian digression—"This is an instance of the natural desire of man to propagate a wonder"—which is resolved by producing further evidence: "But in the author's own honest relation, the marvel vanishes." Even a general disquisition on the nature of genius, with an allusion to Sir Joshua Reynolds, is offered with complete naturalness as a comment on Cowley's early acquaintance with *The Faerie Queene*, by which "he became, as he relates, irrecoverably a poet" (pp. 1-3).

As the *Life of Cowley* moves forward, Johnson establishes still more decisively his role as wise commentator and moralist as well as investigator of fact. Fact must come first, as it did not for the courtly Sprat: "So differently are things seen and so differently are they shown; but actions are visible, though motives are secret" (p. 15). But the facts, once established, cry out for comment. "From the obloquy, which the appearance of submission to the usurpers brought upon him, his biographer has been very

---

[11]See James L. Battersby, "Patterns of Significant Action in the 'Life of Addison,'" *Genre*, 2 (1969), 28-42.

diligent to clear him. . . . Yet let neither our reverence for a
genius, nor our pity for a sufferer, dispose us to forget that, if his
activity was virtue, his retreat was cowardice. . . . He that is at the
disposal of another may not promise to aid him in any injurious
act, because no power can compel active obedience. He may
engage to do nothing, but not to do ill" (pp. 10-11). If passages
like this cannot be safely recommended as models for other
biographers, the reason points to one measure of Johnson's
excellence. Few biographers are great moralists, able to handle
such topics with Johnsonian authority.

   Johnson does not judge Cowley here by impossible standards
of saintly perfection, but by the same system of practical ethics
that he develops in the *Rambler*: a system which, like his aesthetics, is never promulgated in detail but is called forth and mod-
ified by the complications of actual life. The *Lives* are filled with
fine aphoristic observations on human behavior, for instance on
Harley's equivocation before his loss of power: "Not knowing
what to do he did nothing; and with the fate of a double-dealer at
last he lost his power, but kept his enemies" (*Life of Swift*, III, 17).
Always the pregnant generalization arises from reflection on
those "minute peculiarities" that Johnson prized in biography.

Gay was the general favourite of the whole association of wits; but they
regarded him as a play-fellow rather than a partner, and treated him
with more fondness than respect. . . . Gay is represented as a man easily
incited to hope, and deeply depressed when his hopes were disappointed. This is not the character of a hero; but it may naturally imply
something more generally welcome, a soft and civil companion. Whoever is apt to hope good from others is diligent to please them; but he
that believes his powers strong enough to force their own way, commonly tries only to please himself. [*Life of Gay*, II, 268, 272]

Johnson's success in reconstructing character is especially apparent in the *Dryden* and *Pope*, which will be discussed in separate
chapters, but may be observed even in the *Lives* that call forth
some measure of personal hostility. The *Life of Swift*, for instance, not only treats the works unfairly but follows the most
censorious of Swift's earlier biographers.[12] Yet it is full of telling

---

[12] As Wayne Warncke shows, Johnson follows Orrery rather than Delaney or
Deane Swift in emphasizing Swift's avarice, "singularity," and pride ("Samuel
Johnson on Swift: The *Life of Swift* and Johnson's Predecessors in Swiftian
Biography," *Journal of British Studies* 7 [1968], 56-64).

insights. Johnson acutely defines Swift's inverted hypocrisy: "The suspicions of his irreligion proceeded in a great measure from his dread of hypocrisy: instead of wishing to seem better, he delighted in seeming worse than he was" (*Lives*, III, 54). A general remark on political servility—"No man . . .can pay a more servile tribute to the Great, than by suffering his liberty in their presence to aggrandize him in his own esteem" (p. 21)— stands as a brilliantly accurate analysis of Swift's relation to Harley and Bolingbroke. Its justness derives from its congruence with Swift's own disillusioned scrutiny of behavior. Johnson would not apply so stern a test to the humble Gay. In discussing Swift's personality, he is concerned to explain a special kind of limitation, so that the phrase "he washed himself with oriental scrupulosity" (p. 55) becomes a central clue. And he sees the importance of Swift's "delight in revolving ideas from which almost every other mind shrinks with disgust. The ideas of pleasure, even when criminal, may solicit the imagination; but what has disease, deformity, and filth upon which the thoughts can be allured to dwell?" (p. 62). However one may choose to answer the question, Johnson puts it cogently and it can hardly be ignored.

As these examples suggest, Johnson moves freely from biographical narrative to moral reflection. Since his subjects are poets as well as men, moral reflection, in turn, continually extends into passages of literary criticism. Modern critics have often denounced this tendency, and Johnson's defenders have been anxious to quote the occasional passage in which he seems to protect criticism from didacticism: "With the philosophical or religious tenets of the author I have nothing to do; my business is with his poetry" (*Life of Akenside*, III, 417). But Akenside after all is pretty small fry. Johnson can afford to make this concession to a minor and not very alarming poet; moreover, the *Life of Akenside* as a whole undermines the concession, since Johnson makes plain his distaste for the poet's Nonconformist background and Whiggish politics. And on a more fundamental level the distinction survives: Johnson would certainly extend moral disapproval to Akenside's poems if they reflected the "tenets" he disapproves of. More likely he agrees with his biographical source in thinking that Akenside outgrew his "republican" follies.[13]

A full and complex treatment of these matters occurs in the *Life of Milton*, which implies, as Lawrence Lipking has said, "that the very independence, impatience, and ardor for fame which make a man impossible to live with or like may help make a poet great."[14] There is ample support in the eighteenth century for such a view of Milton. In examining the epic, we noticed Dennis's praise of Milton's contempt for literary authority; Bishop Hurd believed that when Milton rejected rhyme "his love of liberty, the ruling passion of his heart, perhaps transported him too far."[15] But although Johnson saw Milton's relation to Homer very much in this way, he found it necessary to keep his view of Milton's personality from contaminating his view of *Paradise Lost*. It is one thing to argue that the poem reflects a daring spirit, and quite another to admit, as Johnson will not, that Milton's political interests were inseparable from his religious ones and are present in the poem.

There is no need to rehearse the details of Johnson's antipathy to Milton's politics, an attitude which was hardly new with him and which, like many of his other attitudes, derives partly from his reaction to what he regarded as whitewashing biographers.[16]

[13] "He was warmly attached to the cause of civil and religious Liberty," says the biographer whom Johnson followed, and "he and his friend Mr. Dyson were understood, in early life, to be such strenuous advocates for liberty in its most extensive sense, as to have some tincture of republicanism in their notions. But no sufficient proof of this is deducible from Dr. Akenside's poems . . . . If there be any truth in the supposition, that Dr. Akenside and his friend entertained republican ideas in their youth, it is probable that they might afterwards soften the rigour of their sentiments" (*Biographia Britannica* [2d ed., 1778], I, 105).

[14] *Ordering of the Arts in Eighteenth-Century England*, p. 439.

[15] For Dennis, see p. 93 above; Richard Hurd, "A Dissertation on the Idea of Universal Poetry" (1764), *Works* (London, 1811) II, 24.

[16] Johnson chose (very much as in the *Life of Swift*) to follow hostile biographers who opposed Milton for moral and political reasons and to ignore the more favorable accounts of those who knew him best. The paradox of the poet and poem had been treated by earlier writers, for instance Thomas Yalden (one of the little poets in Johnson's *Lives*), who wrote in 1698 (I quote the text in *The Works of the British Poets*, ed. Robert Anderson [1795], VII, 762):

His feelings must have been exacerbated by the fact that many radicals in his time saw Milton as a symbol of the republican ideal and resistance to tyranny.[17] For them *Paradise Lost* was the greatest expression of this ideal; for Johnson it must not be. A central theme of his biographical survey is Milton's hatred of obedience: "Milton's republicanism was, I am afraid, founded in an envious hatred of greatness, and a sullen desire of independence; in petulance impatient of controul, and pride disdainful of superiority. He hated monarchs in the state and prelates in the church; for he hated all whom he was required to obey. It is to be suspected that his predominant desire was to destroy rather than establish, and that he felt not so much the love of liberty as repugnance to authority" (*Lives*, I, 157). This reads like a description of Milton's Satan, an analogy that would have been acceptable enough to Blake, but not to Johnson. The enraged anarchist can have no place in an epic poem whose purpose is "to shew the reasonableness of religion, and the necessity of obedience to the Divine Law" (p. 171).

What Johnson does, therefore, is to assume a complete separation between Milton's religion and his politics. In the biographical section he rejects out of hand a familiar charge by declaring Milton "untainted by any heretical peculiarity of opinion" (p. 155). It may indeed be, as modern scholars argue, that all trace of heresy is carefully excluded from *Paradise Lost*. But Johnson will admit it on no occasion whatever, for to do so would endanger his conviction of the pious rectitude of the poem. In his earnestness to make Milton orthodox he even proposes the touching but preposterous idea that if he neglected family prayer, it "was

---

These sacred lines with wonder we peruse,
And praise the flights of a seraphic muse,
Till thy seditious prose provokes our rage,
And soils the beauties of thy brightest page.

Johnson's irritation seems to have been stirred up in particular by Jonathan Richardson's biographical sketch, which sought to refute all objections to Milton's political and domestic character. Johnson calls Richardson "the fondest of his admirers" (*Lives*, I, 134) and says that while he was diligent in his inquiries he "discovers always a wish to find Milton discriminated from other men" (p. 138).

[17]See David V. Erdman, *Blake: Prophet against Empire* (New York, 1969), pp. 34-35.

probably a fault for which he condemned himself, and which he intended to correct, but that death, as too often happens, intercepted his reformation" (p. 156).

The liabilities in Johnson's solution are obvious; it makes impossible any recognition of the prophetic Milton whom Blake so deeply admired and quoted in his annotations to Reynolds: "A Work of Genius is a Work 'Not to be obtaind by the Invocation of Memory & her Syren Daughters. but by Devout prayer to that Eternal Spirit. who can enrich with all utterance and knowledge & sends out his Seraphim with the hallowed fire of his Altar to touch & purify the lips of whom he pleases'". Northrop Frye contrasts with this the Hobbes-Locke theory of art as memory decorated by fancy.[18] Johnson regards *Paradise Lost* in precisely the Lockean way that Blake repudiated: it represents the combination and recombination of literally true "images" from the Bible, together with embellishments of various kinds. Johnson's sense of Milton the man cannot enhance his sense of the poem, for he has no sympathy with the vision of a New Jerusalem in England's green and pleasant land. For him the "saints" are merely canting opportunists, and the satire of *Hudibras* is essentially correct. Least of all is Johnson prepared to consider the ways in which Milton's political experience contributes to the greatness of *Paradise Lost*.[19]

These are undeniable limitations, but not disastrous ones. For in refusing to do what he could not have done sympathetically, Johnson is able to preserve a sympathetic reading of *Paradise Lost* and one which (within its limits) does make full allowance for the poet's aspiring mind. Against the Romantic view that Milton was secretly of Satan's party, C. S. Lewis retorted that he was "enchanted" with the principle of hierarchical discipline and that in

---

[18]Blake, note to Reynolds's third *Discourse*, quoting Milton's *Reason of Church Government, Poetry and Prose*, p. 635; Frye, *Fearful Symmetry* (Princeton, 1947), p. 163.

[19]"His experience of great political events," Helen Gardner writes, "gives the poem much of its dramatic reality, and the disappointment of his hopes, personal and political, gives it depth. A weight of human experience and knowledge of men and a weight of human suffering is in the poem which the Milton of the 1640's could not have brought to it" (*A Reading of Paradise Lost* [Oxford, 1965], p. 97). This seems a highly Johnsonian theme, and one must regret Johnson's unwillingness to imagine it.

imagining Satan he was releasing precisely those aspects of himself that all men possess but attempt to control.[20] Johnson's treatment allows for the *possibility* of both interpretations, though it does not face them directly. Biographically, we are shown a Milton quick to resent oppression by any authority, hence able to imagine how Satan might feel even though Satan is wrong. Artistically, Milton has written a wholly orthodox poem in which all of Satan's psychologically convincing responses are shown to be grossly misconceived. "To make Satan speak as a rebel, without any such expressions as might taint the reader's imagination, was indeed one of the great difficulties in Milton's undertaking, and I cannot but think that he has extricated himself with great happiness" (p. 173). In the first part of the *Life* Johnson is concerned with Milton's deepest psychological impulses; in the second part with *Paradise Lost* as a work of art, not as autobiography. For this reason, not just for structural ones, the invocations are treated as "digressions" and "extrinsick paragraphs" (p. 175). Johnson sees their excellence but does not wish to interpret the poem as an expression of Milton's preoccupations. In his tactful refusal to force biographical interpretation on the poem, he encourages us to appreciate it as two things at once: an ambitious effort of the human mind, and a coherent artifact that deserves to be understood on its own terms.

In this sense the Milton of the biographical section is fully present in *Paradise Lost*. As early as 1642, when his controversial writing was infected with "the puritanical savageness of manners," Milton was able to foresee the great work to which his life should be dedicated. In *The Reason of Church Government* "he discovers, not with ostentatious exultation, but with calm confidence, his high opinion of his own powers; and promises to undertake something, he yet knows not what, that may be of use and honour to his country" (p. 102). And the final paragraph of the *Life of Milton* celebrates the fulfillment of that great promise:

He was naturally a thinker for himself, confident of his own abilities and disdainful of help or hindrance; he did not refuse admission to the thoughts or images of his predecessors, but he did not seek them. From his contemporaries he neither courted nor received support; there is in

[20]*A Preface to Paradise Lost* (Oxford, 1942), pp. 78, 98-99.

his writings nothing by which the pride of other authors might be gratified or favour gained, no exchange of praise nor solicitation of support. His great works were performed under discountenance and in blindness, but difficulties vanished at his touch; he was born for whatever is arduous; and his work is not the greatest of heroick poems, only because it is not the first. [P. 194]

Given Johnson's opinion of Milton's life, this generous conclusion is the right one: the poem is greater than the man. *Paradise Lost* is a permanent work of genius that draws on the best side of the poet's impatience of authority and shows his willingness to attempt the hardest genre, to vie with the greatest masters. Milton accepts the only true authority that is relevant here, the authority of God, and keeps close to sacred truth. *Paradise Lost* might have been dragged down by the surly republican, but instead it is the truest expression, as the controversial tracts are not, of a profoundly independent mind.

Finally, we must look at Johnson's practice when moral issues are directly raised by the poems themselves. An excellent example is his criticism of the panegyrics of Waller. Johnson is admirably fair in assessing the best of Waller's celebratory poems, *A Panegyric to My Lord Protector*, although Cromwell is hardly one of Johnson's favorite historical figures. An earlier biographer had complained, "One can hardly suppress indignation to see the tribute which is only due to virtue and piety, prostituted to usurpation, and cruelty."[21] Johnson knows better than to confuse his opinions of Cromwell and of Waller's poem: "His choice of encomiastick topicks is very judicious, for he considers Cromwell in his exaltation, without enquiring how he attained it; there is consequently no mention of the rebel or the regicide. All the former part of his hero's life is veiled with shades, and nothing is brought to view but the chief, the governor, the defender of England's honour, and the enlarger of her dominion. The act of violence by which he obtained the supreme power is lightly treated, and decently justified" (*Life of Waller*, I, 269). Johnson goes on to say that Cromwell's power, though necessary, was nonetheless illegal; but this is a reflection on Cromwell rather

---

[21]Percival Stockdale, *The Works of Edmund Waller* (1772), p. l (i.e., roman numeral 50).

than the poem. What matters is that Waller has praised Cromwell without grossly distorting the truth. In the same way
Johnson could accept Prior's praise of William of Orange,
though he himself regarded William as "one of the most worthless scoundrels that ever existed" (*Life*, II, 342). "King William
supplied copious materials for either verse or prose. His whole
life had been action, and none ever denied him the resplendent
qualities of steady resolution and personal courage" (*Life of Prior*,
II, 185).

Johnson reacts very differently, however, to Waller's *To the
King, upon His Majesty's Happy Return*. The indictment deserves to
be read at length:

> Soon afterwards the Restauration supplied him with another sub-
> ject; and he exerted his imagination, his elegance, and his melody with
> equal alacrity for Charles the Second. It is not possible to read, without
> some contempt and indignation, poems of the same author, ascribing
> the highest degree of "power and piety" to Charles the First, then
> transferring the same "power and piety" to Oliver Cromwell; now
> inviting Oliver to take the Crown, and then congratulating Charles the
> Second on his recovered right. Neither Cromwell nor Charles could
> value his testimony as the effect of conviction, or receive his praises as
> effusions of reverence; they could consider them but as the labour of
> invention and the tribute of dependence.
>
> Poets, indeed, profess fiction, but the legitimate end of fiction is the
> conveyance of truth; and he that has flattery ready for all whom the
> vicissitudes of the world happen to exalt must be scorned as a prosti-
> tuted mind that may retain the glitter of wit, but has lost the dignity of
> virtue. [*Life of Waller*, I, 270-71]

By the lights of much modern criticism, this is irrelevant: we
must read the poem to Charles II as if we knew nothing of
Waller's other poems or of Charles himself. Johnson's position is
uncompromisingly moral. But it is also aesthetic; the second
panegyric is not so good as the first, and Johnson detects a crucial
insincerity inside as well as outside it. Waller applied the attributes of Cromwell to Charles because Charles had few attributes
of his own. "The *Congratulation* is indeed not inferior to the
Panegyrick either by decay of genius or for want of diligence, but
because Cromwell had done much, and Charles had done little.
Cromwell wanted nothing to raise him to heroick excellence but

virtue; and virtue his poet thought himself at liberty to supply. Charles had yet only the merit of struggling without success, and suffering without despair. A life of escapes and indigence could supply poetry with no splendid images" (pp. 271-72). Waller could therefore say nothing splendid about Charles without hyperbolic invention. One indication of his difficulty is the wholesale transposition of Cromwell's attributes; another, which Johnson probably has in mind as well, is the general exaggeration of the imagery.[22]

In Johnson's view the aesthetic judgment is simply reinforced by the moral one. We are not surprised to find the second poem inferior, since Waller has prostituted his aesthetic integrity to write it. For Cromwell he had only to draw a veil over unpleasant features; for Charles he must say the thing that is not. Waller's poems, in Johnson's opinion, reflect a radical insincerity that is visible at all points in his life, whether in the "ignominy" he covered himself with in "Waller's Plot" (p. 264) or in a speech that exhibits "the language of a man who is glad of an opportunity to rail, and ready to sacrifice truth to interest at one time, and to anger at another" (p. 274). There is some evidence that the most perceptive of Waller's contemporaries saw him in just this way.[23]

Johnson's notorious criterion of sincerity, so misguided when

[22] As Stockdale noticed, "The similies, by which [Waller] would illustrate the clemency of the king, unhappily convey the ideas of ravage and desolation" (ibid., p. liii). He was probably thinking of such lines as 63-72, in which the people respond to the returning king "like powder set on fire," while the sea "No longer will from her old channel stay; / Raging, the late got land she overflows, / And all that's built upon 't, to ruin goes." Even more astonishingly, Waller compares Charles returning to England to Jupiter raping Semele (ll. 33-36).

[23] Lady Ranelagh wrote to her brother Robert Boyle in 1660, "I know his calling as a poet gives him license to say as great things as he can, without intending they should signify any more, than that he said them, or have any higher end, than to make him admired by those, whose admirations are so volatile, as to be raised by a sound of words; and the less the subject he speaks of, or the party he speaks to, deserves the great things he says, the greater those things are, and the greater advance they are to make towards his being admired, by his poetical laws" (Boyle's *Works* [1749], V, 556). Rochester wrote with evident irony of Waller's talent for panegyric: "He best can turn, enforce, and soften things, / To praise great *Conquerors*, or to flatter *Kings*" ("An Allusion to Horace," ll. 57-58).

he applies it to *Lycidas*, can often be justified on similar grounds. Consider the often-quoted comment on Cowley's *Mistress*: "The basis of all excellence is truth: he that professes love ought to feel its power. Petrarch was a real lover, and Laura doubtless deserved his tenderness. Of Cowley we are told by Barnes, who had means enough of information, that, whatever he may talk of his own inflammability and the variety of characters by which his heart was divided, he in reality was in love but once, and then never had resolution to tell his passion" (*Life of Cowley*, I, 6). As theory this cannot stand up—the love poet need not be a lover—but although Johnson is theoretically mistaken, he may still be right enough about Cowley's *Mistress*.

The passage just quoted occurs, after all, in the biographical part of the *Life of Cowley*. Rather than taking it to mean that "a man not in love can never write love poetry," one might read it instead as meaning "I am not surprised to find that the author of the *Mistress* was mechanically playing with Petrarchan conceits rather than writing out of genuine feeling." When Johnson comes to discuss the work critically rather than biographically, he talks about its effect on the reader rather than its origin in the mind of the poet.

Cowley's *Mistress* has no power of seduction; she "plays round the head, but comes not at the heart." Her beauty and absence, her kindness and cruelty, her disdain and inconstancy, produce no correspondence of emotion. His poetical account of the virtues of plants and colours of flowers is not perused with more sluggish frigidity. The compositions are such as might have been written for penance by a hermit, or for hire by a philosophical rhymer who had only heard of another sex; for they turn the mind only on the writer, whom, without thinking on a woman but as the subject for his talk, we sometimes esteem as learned and sometimes despise as trifling, always admire as ingenious, and always condemn as unnatural. [P. 42]

Johnson may be wrong to use the poems as biographical evidence, but he is not therefore wrong about the poems. Modern readers prefer Donne's love poetry to Cowley's, if they read Cowley's at all, and perceive in Donne (though it need not prove his "sincerity") precisely that pressure of feeling that is absent in the conceits of Cowley. We feel that Cowley, as Johnson puts it, "fatigues his fancy, and ransacks his memory" (p. 7) to write a

kind of poetry ill suited to his talents. Modern ideas about the
lyric as dramatic speech can in fact dwell on the same aspects of
poems that Johnson does, though they will not refer them to the
poet's biography in so direct a way. We may no longer demand
sincerity, but we certainly demand the illusion of sincerity.
"When he wishes to make us weep," Johnson says of an elegy by
Cowley, "he forgets to weep himself" (p. 37).

Practical Criticism in the *Lives*

When Johnson's moral or aesthetic assumptions seemed in-
convenient, it used to be the custom to recommend the *Lives*
instead for the cogency of their detailed criticism. While they do
contain a great deal of practical criticism, it needs defense, or at
least explanation, on two counts. First, it is filled with highly
particularized negative judgments that may seem to overbalance
the more generalized praise. And second, Johnson does not
attempt the comprehensive kind of practical criticism preferred
by many modern critics, so that if he is to be defended on that
basis he may seem arbitrary and impressionistic. "It should be
clear," George Watson observes, "that Johnson would not shine
in a modern practical-criticism class. His mind does not settle: it
darts." There is some truth to that, and perhaps many of his
specific judgments really are arbitrary and impressionistic. But
Johnson's mode of criticism also exhibits, as Watson goes on to
say, "a gift for perceiving relationships, certainty of judgment,
breadth."[24] I shall try to show that a genuine critical method does
underlie the practical criticism in the *Lives*, even if it is not in the
end the most valuable aspect of Johnson's critical performance.

Ever since the *Lives* were published, readers have been struck
by their combination of generalized praise and highly specific
blame. It is easy to conclude, with Edmund Cartwright, that the
best analogy for Johnson's "microscopical sagacity" is in *Candide*:
"What a wonderful genius is this Pococurante! Nothing can
please him!"[25] Johnson is sometimes unfair. The willful dis-

---

[24]*The Literary Critics* (Harmondsworth, Penguin Books, 1964), pp. 82, 83.
[25]*Monthly Review*, 66 (1782), 126, 127.

memberment of Gray's odes can only be explained by hostility to
a school of poetry in general and to Gray in particular. But his
procedure is not usually so arbitrary as it may appear, for it
derives from a considered view of the possibilities of criticism.

"Had Gray written often thus," Johnson declares at the end of
that *Life*, "it had been vain to blame, and useless to praise him"
(*Lives*, III, 442). He has just mentioned some lines from the *Elegy*
that we are sure to admire: "I have never seen the notions in any
other place; yet he that reads them here persuades himself that
he has always felt them." When the reader and the critic are
certain to agree that a poem is great, Johnson sees no point in
minute analysis. And as the tribute handsomely suggests, any
hostility he may feel toward Gray would be discharged in vain
against the *Elegy*, just as the lines are so self-evidently fine that it
would be "useless" to praise them.

Johnson's method of general praise and specific blame has led
some readers to suspect disingenuousness in the praise, but the
notion of the common reader affords a full explanation of his
procedure. No one can be persuaded to like a poem against his
will. It follows that if Johnson admires a poem, he is mainly
concerned to define—not prove—its excellence in terms that will
seem just to other admirers. If he likes a poem but suspects that
his readers do not, he has little hope of being able to dissuade
them—certainly not within the limited space available in the
critical sections of the *Lives*. On the other hand, when his opinion
is negative he apparently feels an obligation to defend it. If he
thinks that readers agree with him, of course, then no argument
is necessary: when Akenside's odes "are once found to be dull all
further labour may be spared, for to what use can the work be
criticised that will not be read?" (*Life of Akenside*, III, 420). But if
he dislikes a popular work he must give his reasons.

Johnson is thus the common reader when he celebrates and
the expert when he blames. When he praises, it does not occur to
him to intervene between the satisfied reader and the poem that
communicates satisfaction. Instead he tries to show, by means of
carefully chosen phrases, that he shares and can define the
general quality of that satisfaction. A perfect description of this
ideal is given by Gibbon after reading Longinus: "Till now, I was
acquainted only with two ways of criticizing a beautifull passage;

The one, to shew, by an exact anatomy of it, the distinct beauties of it, and from whence they sprung; the other, an idle exclamation, or a general encomium, which leaves nothing behind it. Longinus has shewn me that there is a third. He tells me his own feelings upon reading it; and tells them with such energy, that he communicates them."[26] Johnson attempts to do just this, describing the effect of a work upon the reader rather than its formal properties as objective phenomena.

In this Johnson falls between two great critical traditions, as is shown by the special nature of his perennial interest in the author. "When any work has been viewed and admired the first question of intelligent curiosity is, how was it performed?" (*Life of Butler*, I, 213). But Johnson has little of the neoclassical critic's interest in the technical problems of the writer. He sees rhyme, for example, from the reader's point of view (it keeps the structure of the verse in one's mind), whereas Dryden describes the ways in which the apparent constraint of rhyme can liberate, by directing and stimulating, the poet's imagination. On the other hand, Johnson does not share the enthusiasm of many of his contemporaries for the mysteries of bardic inspiration and does not write the natural history of souls in the manner of Sainte-Beuve. Rather his emphasis is on the qualities of mind which the reader perceives *inside* the poems: "Whatever Prior obtains above mediocrity seems the effort of struggle and of toil. He has many vigorous but few happy lines; he has everything by purchase, and nothing by gift; he had no 'nightly visitations' of the Muse, no infusions of sentiment or felicities of fancy.... His expression has every mark of laborious study; the line seldom seems to have been formed at once; the words did not come till they were called, and were then put by constraint into their places, where they do their duty, but do it sullenly" (*Life of Prior*, II, 209). The subject here is the Prior who is visible in his poetry. Johnson is concerned with achievement, not with the wish to achieve.

It is true that his biographical approach can lead to statements that look dubious today, as when he says of Dryden, "It was throughout his life very much his custom to recommend his works by representation of the difficulties that he had encountered, without appearing to have sufficiently considered that where there is no difficulty there is no praise" (*Life of Dryden*, I, 338-39). To be sure, a work must possess or lack value in itself, regardless of the ease or difficulty with which it was performed. But in thinking along these lines Johnson appreciates the peculiar excellence of a work—its originality, in the modern sense—by realizing what went into its creation. The modern scholar often sees the works he reads as part of a fixed canonical sequence; he has known most of them by name long before he read them, and they have the solidity of objects in a landscape. Johnson on the other hand sees them as feats of skill, achievements won from the void. One feels like giving small praise to an easy accomplishment—a work should require art and be seen to embody it—though one gives high praise to a man who accomplishes with ease what is difficult for all other men.

In seeking to echo the proper response of the reader, Johnson emulates Dryden's character of Shakespeare, "a perpetual model of encomiastick criticism; exact without minuteness, and lofty without exaggeration" (*Life of Dryden*, I, 412). To achieve such a standard is harder than it looks. Too often we are put off with something like Oldisworth's praise of Edmund Smith: "His contrivances were adroit and magnificent; his images lively and adequate; his sentiments charming and majestick. . . ." This is not criticism. As Johnson comments, "The praise is often indistinct, and the sentences are loaded with words of more pomp than use" (*Life of Smith*, II, 7, 11).

Johnson's success in this mode appears everywhere in the *Lives*, for instance in the character of Goldsmith whose accuracy was praised by Burrowes, or in the description of Thomson's poetry that influenced generations of later critics.[27] R. S. Crane has pointed out that Johnson was only one of many eighteenth-century critics who liked to argue by means of "manipulations of contraries or of positive and privative terms."[28] If the danger of

[27] For Burrowes, see p. 64 above. As Ralph Cohen shows, Johnson's response to Thomson is receptive and open, in spite of his supposed prejudices, and many later admirers of Thomson found it valuable (*Art of Discrimination*, pp. 452-53).

[28] "English Neoclassical Criticism: An Outline Sketch," in *Critics and Criticism*, p. 381.

this mode is that it may conjure up false antitheses, our study of Johnson's prose style suggests that it can also be a valuable critical tool. Certainly it can furnish a useful corrective to the modern tendency to force home a single, all-explaining idea without regard for possible qualifications. And in the *Lives* it allows Johnson to define the essential qualities of each poet's verse, small or great, in a concise statement that the reader should then expand by reflecting on his own experience of the poems.

His songs are upon common topicks; he hopes, and grieves, and repents, and despairs, and rejoices, like any other maker of little stanzas: to be great he hardly tries; to be gay is hardly in his power. [*Life of Sheffield*, II, 175]

His numbers are such as mere diligence may attain; they seldom offend the ear, and seldom sooth it; they commonly want airiness, lightness, and facility; what is smooth is not soft. His verses always roll, but they seldom flow. [*Life of Prior*, II, 210]

These passages can only have meaning for the reader who will test them against the poems, which of course were originally printed together with the *Lives* that introduced them.

Johnson's summary judgments should not be taken merely as evidence (as is sometimes charged) that he would not bother to reread the poems. Apart from the fact that his memory should never be underestimated,[29] he is often equally curt when he clearly expects the reader to have a specific text before him. Waller's "poem upon Sallee has forcible sentiments, but the conclusion is feeble" (*Life of Waller*, I, 288). More largely, Johnson's decisive judgments presuppose the active cooperation of the reader. "It is hard to conceive that a man of the first rank in learning and wit, when he was dealing out such minute moral-

---

[29]Long before the *Lives* Johnson wrote, "It will not easily be imagined of Langbaine, Borrichitus or Rapin, that they had very accurately perused all the books which they praise or censure; or that, even if nature and learning had qualified them for judges, they could read for ever with the attention necessary to just criticism" (*Rambler* 93). Doubtless this may apply to Johnson himself. But his writings (and conversation) are filled with quotations drawn from an extraordinary memory; see for instance his illustration of the "obscure corners" in which Broome found fragments to borrow: "His lines to Fenton . . .brought to my mind some lines on the death of Queen Mary, written by Barnes, of whom I should not have expected to find an imitator" (*Life of Broome*, III, 80-81).

ity in such feeble diction, could imagine, either waking or dreaming, that he imitated Pindar" (*Life of Cowley*, I, 44). Johnson presumes that the reader can see for himself what is so obviously weak in this "puny poetry" (p. 47) and moves at once to authoritative judgment.

If Johnson's tendency to general summary can be defended, what can be said for the apparently hostile particularity of his negative criticism? Anna Seward saw the author of the *Lives* as a brutal angel of death: "False criticism, on the pale horse of that despot, is the pest of the present times, trampling beneath its 'armed hoofs,' the richest and rarest flowers of genius."[30] Sometimes, as in the critique of *Lycidas*, Johnson perhaps means to overcompensate for the extravagant praise of other critics. One reviewer at least saw the *Life of Gray* in that light: "As the twig inclined too much one way, we are obliged to Dr. Johnson for bending strongly towards the other, which may make it strait at last."[31] Still, his negative criticisms are often outrageous, for example in the titanic denunciation of Gray's *Favorite Cat*; when he dislikes a poem Johnson has a disagreeable tendency to pretend he has never heard of a metaphor.

The sense of outrage in the *Life of Gray* can only be explained by a potent moral and aesthetic animosity. As a writer thirty years later explained it, "His insensibility to the higher poetry, his dislike of a Whig university, and his scorn of a fantastic character, combined to produce that monstrous example of critical injustice which he entitles the *Life of Gray*."[32] Mingled with dislike of Gray's character, politics, and friends is a general opposition to what Gray and his admirers considered the higher poetry, an opposition that supplies an important submerged theme in the *Life of Pope*. But this explanation of Johnson's animus is hardly a justification of his critical method. We have seen that in his positive commentary he avoided circumstantiality; the criticism of Pope's epitaphs is relegated to an appendix as "being too minute and particular to be inserted in the *Life*" (*Lives*, III, 254). But it is not simply that Johnson tends to be cir-

---

[30]*Letters* I, 191-92 (4 Oct. 1786).
[31]*Critical Review*, 52 (1781), p. 89.
[32]*Memoirs of Sir James Mackintosh* (London, 1835), II, 171 (entry for December 1811), in *Johnson: The Critical Heritage*, ed. J. T. Boulton, p. 354.

cumstantial only when he blames. It is virtually true as well that he cannot descend to circumstantiality *without* blaming. Gibbon sarcastically observed that the survey of Pope's epitaphs, judicious though it is, shows Johnson's habit of parsing syntax and meaning with unforgiving rigor.[33]

The point about metaphor is worth returning to. Consider Johnson's dismemberment of a "broken" (we would say mixed) metaphor in Addison's *Letter from Italy*:

> "Fir'd with that name—
> I bridle in my struggling Muse with pain,
> That longs to launch into a nobler strain."

To *bridle a goddess* is no very delicate idea; but why must she be *bridled*? because she *longs to launch*; an act which was never hindered by a *bridle*: and whither will she *launch*? into a *nobler strain*. She is in the first line a *horse*, in the second a *boat*; and the care of the poet is to keep his *horse* or his *boat* from *singing*. [*Life of Addison*, II, 128]

It may have been careless of Addison to involve the idea of the muse with that of Pegasus, but only Johnson would be so literal about "launch," and only he would insist on attributing the "strain" to the horse or boat rather than the poet whose inspiration is represented by the muse. Robert Potter very rightly commented, "Our author here strikes at the root of metaphor."[34] Perhaps no reader would have been seriously bothered by Addison's lines if Johnson had not placed them under his microscope. And one has to ask why he has done so. The *Letter from Italy*, he says, "has been always praised, but has never been praised beyond its merit. It is more correct, with less appearance of labour, and more elegant, with less ambition of ornament, than any other of his poems." Why then does he continue, "There is, however, one broken metaphor, of which notice may properly be taken"? No doubt he saw himself as a guardian of "correct-

---

[33]Gibbon quotes an inscription on a sultan's tomb—"O ye who have seen the glory of Alp Arslan exalted to the heavens, repair to Maru, and you will behold it buried in the dust"—and comments that Johnson, "who has severely scrutinised the epitaphs of Pope, might cavil in this sublime inscription at the words 'repair to Maru,' since the reader must already be at Maru before he could peruse the inscription" (*Decline and Fall of the Roman Empire*, Ch. 57, note 40).

[34]*Art of Criticism*, p. 90.

ness" in writing and accuracy in reading, but this tendency to expose a specific weakness in an otherwise admired poem does suggest a certain belligerence; and as Potter says, it depends on a literalism that no metaphor can sustain.

The *Life of Gray*, where Johnson's hostility is more than usually obvious, is particularly full of analyses of this kind. Johnson refuses to understand the pleasant ironies of the *Favorite Cat*: "If what glistered had been 'gold,' the cat would not have gone into the water; and, if she had, would not less have been drowned" (*Lives*, III, 434). A phrase in the *Eton College* ode draws a more extended objection: "Gray thought his language more poetical as it was more remote from common use: finding in Dryden 'honey redolent of Spring,' an expression that reaches the utmost limits of our language, Gray drove it a little more beyond common apprehension, by making 'gales' to be 'redolent of joy and youth' " (p. 435). "Redolent" must mean odor-giving; spring can suggest odors though it does not itself emit them; joy and youth cannot. So also in *The Progress of Poesy* Johnson objects to a "stream of music" that rolls through a landscape: "If this be said of Musick, it is nonsense; if it be said of Water, it is nothing to the purpose" (p. 436).

To be sure there are other eighteenth-century critics who support Johnson in this rigorous literalism.[35] But one should be wary of assuming, with or without such support, that such passages represent Johnson's unvarying conception of metaphor, so that, in Northrop Frye's words, "in Johnson's strictures on the music and water metaphor of Gray's *Bard* [*sic*] we can see what intellectual abysses, for him, would open up if metaphors ever passed beyond the stage of resemblance."[36] In the first place, Johnson is perfectly capable of admiring poetry in which metaphor is used in this way, as in the "though deep, yet clear" lines in *Cooper's Hill*, discussed in chapter 1. A theoretical objection that did not suffice to dampen his enthusiasm for Denham's lines is allowed to demolish Gray's. "Gray seems in his rapture to

[35]Lord Kames, surveying Thomson's *Seasons*, objects to "*Moving* softness, Freshness *breathes, Breathing* prospect, *Flowing* spring, *Dewy* light, *Lucid* coolness," on the grounds that "the figurative and proper meanings" have "no connexion whatever" (*Elements of Criticism*, II, 279).

[36]"Towards Defining an Age of Sensibility," in *Eighteenth-Century English Literature: Modern Essays in Criticism*, ed. James L. Clifford (New York, 1959), p. 317.

confound the images of 'spreading sound' and 'running water'"
(p. 436). Johnson hates Pindarism and will not permit Gray to
press language beyond its literal bounds in the service of "rapture," real or feigned. Second, Johnson is quite prepared to
accept similar effects when his hostility is not involved. On the
Eton College ode he comments: "His supplication to father
Thames, to tell him who drives the hoop or tosses the ball, is
useless and puerile. Father Thames has no better means of
knowing than himself" (pp. 434-35). One defender wrote bitterly, "Had Mr. Gray been the first person that had ever called
upon a river, or had he presumed to do so after the publication
of the Lives of the English Poets, nothing could have been said in
his defence"; and another cited Nekayah's apostrophe to the
"great Father of Waters" in *Rasselas*.[37] But one may simply quote
Johnson's own comment on *1 Henry IV*, I.iii.103:

> HOTSPUR. of swift Severn's flood;
> Who then affrighted with their bloody looks,
> Ran fearfully among the trembling reeds,
> And hid his crispe head in the hollow bank

This passage has been censured as sounding nonsense, which represents a stream of water as capable of fear. It is misunderstood. "Severn"
is here not the "flood" but the tutelary power of the flood, who was
frighted, and hid his head in "the hollow bank." [Yale *Works*, VII, 461]

If the Severn has a tutelary power so may the Thames.

A more general acceptance of metaphor can be illustrated
many times over in the Shakespeare notes, where Johnson is
commenting on lines that seem to require interpretation but is
not deliberately searching out objects of censure. Hazlitt, in a
telling phrase, objects to "the ordinary routine of his imagination" and proposes a passage from *The Winter's Tale* as the sort of
thing Johnson would be unable to appreciate:

> Daffodils
> That come before the swallow dares, and take
> The winds of March with beauty; violets dim,
> But sweeter than the lids of Juno's eyes,
> Or Cytherea's breath.

[37][William Tindal], *Remarks on Dr. Johnson' Life, and Critical Observations on the
Works of Mr. Gray* (1782), p. 37. Nekayah's speech (which of course may be
intended ironically by Johnson) is mentioned by a correspondent in the *Gentleman's Magazine*, 69 (1799), p. 29.

Hazlitt says that "violets dim" suggests "an image like 'the sleepy eye of love,' " and concludes that to anyone who cannot perceive this, "the allusion to 'the lids of Juno's eyes' must appear extravagant and unmeaning."[38] In fact Johnson does have a note on these lines, though Hazlitt probably never looked it up. While he suspects that "our authour mistakes Juno for Pallas, who was the 'goddess of blue eyes,' " he does not brand the lines with extravagant unmeaning: "Sweeter than an 'eye-lid' is an odd image: but perhaps he uses 'sweet' in the general sense, for 'delightful' " (Yale *Works*, VII, 303).

The problem, then, is not whether Johnson knows how to read a metaphor, but why his theory handles metaphor so roughly. The answer, I think, is that metaphor is closely allied with imagination, in its negative Johnsonian sense. So long as he is simply reading a passage in Shakespeare or Dryden, Johnson is likely to accept metaphor as a normal mode of poetic communication. In fact he says of Dryden, almost indulgently, "He delighted to tread upon the brink of meaning, where light and darkness begin to mingle; to approach the precipice of absurdity, and hover over the abyss of unideal vacancy. This inclination sometimes produced nonsense, which he knew . . .and sometimes it issued in absurdities, of which perhaps he was not conscious" (*Life of Dryden*, I, 460). Dryden's outrageousness is seen as a form of play, producing nonsense or absurdity—as the poet often realizes perfectly well—but producing nothing threatening in the larger context of Dryden's harmonious and reasonable verse. Always the imagination must be controlled by judgment, which Johnson sees as perfecting, not limiting it. Young's thoughts, for example, are weak because they "appear the effects of chance, sometimes adverse and sometimes lucky, with very little operation of judgement" (*Life of Young*, III, 393). When Johnson strikes at the root of metaphor it is because he senses a threat to the very concept of meaning, whether in a casual lapse that Addison's judgment should have corrected, or more dangerously in a theory of poetry by which Gray attempts to subvert the English language.

[38]William Hazlitt, Preface, *Characters of Shakespeare's Plays* (1818), Worlds Classics ed. (Oxford, 1955), pp. xxxiv-xxxv.

If my view is right, Johnson is not so much concerned with the nature of tropes as with the nature of the mind. Consider the puns that so excite his indignation in the *Preface to Shakespeare*. Addison had attacked puns, not as tiresome foolery, but as "false wit" that perverts a fundamental operation of the mind. In 1794, ten years after the *Lives*, Walter Whiter was commenting on passages in Shakespeare in a way that inverts the value system of Addison and Johnson:

> "Beshrew his soul for me,
> He *started* one poor *heart* of mine in thee."
> (*Twelfth Night* IV.i.62)

Dr. Johnson has remarked on this passage, that an equivoque was intended between *heart* and *hart*; and Mr. Malone observes, that *heart* in our Author's time was frequently written *hart*, and that "Shakspeare delights in playing on these words." This is certainly true; yet I am persuaded that no quibble was here intended; but that the equivocal word suggested to the unconscious Poet a term which was allied to one of its significations.—It is here extremely worthy of the reader's observation, that the Poet will be sometimes entangled in the dangers of a petty quibble, or betrayed into the quaint application of a familiar expression by the same association, which on another occasion will supply him with the most poetical ideas, and suggest the most delicate touches of metaphorical imagery.[39]

Whiter's account of metaphor springing from the poet's unconscious mind looks forward to Coleridge, who calls for readers "accustomed to watch the flux and reflux of their inmost nature, to venture at times into the twilight realms of consciousness, and to feel a deep interest in modes of inmost being, to which they know that the attributes of time and space are inapplicable and alien, but which yet can not be conveyed save in symbols of time and space" (*Biographia*, Ch. 22, II, 120). Johnson, on the contrary, sees art—especially in its power of generalizing—as taking us *outside* ourselves, not deeper within ourselves, and putting us in contact with the external world of physical and social reality.

In these terms it is not surprising that Johnson should prefer

[39]*A Specimen of a Commentary on Shakespeare*, ed. Alan Over and Mary Bell (London, 1967), p. 87.

simile to metaphor and should demand of both that they operate
in a series of one-to-one correspondences.[40] When Johnson
praises such an effect, it is usually a progression of analogies that
add up, in his own term, to a "parallel."[41] His mind unwraps a
metaphor like a parcel. Johnson's ideal is one of analogy or
illustration, while Coleridge calls for symbolism in language
drawn from religion, as Wordsworth makes explicit: "The concerns of religion refer to indefinite objects, and are too weighty
for the mind to support them without relieving itself by resting a
great part of the burthen upon words and symbols. . . . In all this
may be perceived the affinity between religion and
poetry; . . .poetry—etherial and transcendent, yet incapable to
sustain her existence without sensuous incarnation."[42] For a
Johnsonian similitude to work, the tenor must not seem too
remote from the vehicle, like Cowley's conceits which turn the
mind "more upon the original than the secondary sense, more
upon that from which the illustration is drawn than that to which
it is applied" (*Life of Cowley*, I, 45). But the similitude is equally
useless if tenor and vehicle belong to the same species. "As a king
would be lamented, Eleonora was lamented. . . . This is little
better than to say in praise of a shrub that it is as green as a tree,
or of a brook, that it waters a garden as a river waters a country"
(*Life of Dryden*, I, 441). Coleridge's conception, on the other
hand, implies that images in and of themselves can take on the
heightened meaning of symbol. "Like a green field reflected in a
calm and perfectly transparent lake, the image is distinguished
from the reality only by its greater softness and lustre" (*Biographia*, II, 121).

But if Johnson distrusts the imagination, he also reverences it.
Art is dangerous but invaluable. I have tried here to explain the
grounds on which Johnson dismembers metaphor, but as the
examples of Dryden and Shakespeare show, this tendency need
not get in the way of good criticism. In general terms, however, it
is well to recognize that detailed criticism tends to express the

[40]See Hagstrum's excellent discussion, *Samuel Johnson's Literary Criticism*, pp.
117-22.
  [41]See his discussions of poetry compared by Denham to the Thames (*Lives*, I,
78-79); pleasure compared by Young to quicksilver (III, 398); and a student
compared by Pope to an Alpine traveler (III, 229).
  [42]*Essay supplementary to the Preface* (1815), *Prose Works*, III, 65.

censor in Johnson, not the appreciative reader. He will expose
the occasional lapse from correctness in an admired poet like
Addison or Pope and will sternly denounce perfectly ordinary
metaphors in a poet like Gray whom he detests. In a way he is
doing on a small scale what the Augustan satirists did at large,
generalizing favorable descriptions and particularizing negative
ones.[43] Two conclusions should be drawn. One is that Johnson's
detailed hostile criticisms are not the best place to look for
evidence of his literary theory. Another is that they need not be
taken as proof of a debilitating critical dyspepsia, since parallel
examples can be found in many if not most other critics. Coleridge, disturbed by the literal implication of the myth in
Wordsworth's *Intimations* ode, attacks the eighth stanza in positively Johnsonian terms: "Now here, not to stop at the daring
spirit of metaphor which connects the epithets 'deaf and silent,'
with the apostrophized *eye*: or (if we are to refer it to the preceding word, philosopher) the faulty and equivocal syntax of the
passage; and without examining the propriety of making a 'master *brood* o'er a slave,' or the *day* brood *at all*; we will merely ask,
what does all this mean? In what sense is a child of that age a
philosopher? In what sense does he *read* 'the eternal deep'?" (*Biographia*, Ch. 22, II, 111). Even more clearly Johnsonian passages
can be found in Yvor Winters when his wrath is aroused.[44] But it
would not be easy to use these passages to prove Coleridge's or
Winters's incompetence as readers of verse. And one must remember that critics have not always been expected to praise
indiscriminately every part of a work they admire.

Still, it is well to accept the fact that Johnson is not really a great
practical critic. His negative judgments reflect serious limitations
in the breadth of his taste,[45] and his positive ones, though gener-

---

[43]See Irvin Ehrenpreis on "negative particularity," *Literary Meaning and
Augustan Values* (Charlottesville, Va., 1974), pp. 45-47.

[44]Thus on Wordsworth's "Westminster Bridge" sonnet: "The river does not
glide at its own sweet will, and this is very fortunate for London; the river glides
according to the law of gravitation, and a much better line could have been
made of this fact. Of the last two lines, the houses are good, the two exclama-
tions are mere noise" (*Forms of Discovery* [Chicago, 1967], p. 168).

[45]See M. H. Abrams, "Dr. Johnson's Spectacles," *New Light on Dr. Johnson*, ed.
F. W. Hilles (New Haven, 1959), 177-87. Johnson's friend Burney held that his
great defect as a critic was "the want of taste for almost all poetry except heroic
and didactic" (review of Robert Anderson's *Life of Samuel Johnson*, *Monthly
Review*, 2d ser., 20 [1796], 23).

ous, are of use mainly to readers who already agree with his admiration of the poems in question. We are never told why the lines in Gray's *Elegy* "to which every bosom returns an echo" are different from the thoughts which "have nothing new" in the *Ode on the Spring* or those in *Eton College* which every beholder equally thinks and feels (*Lives*, III, 434). The heart of Johnson's achievement is rather to be found in his continual appeal to the reader to make value judgments on poems and on life itself. Johnson's critical program is profoundly conservative, unlike that of Coleridge, who in Hazlitt's image "threw a great stone into the standing pool of criticism, which splashed some persons with the mud, but which gave a motion to the surface and a reverberation to the neighbouring echoes, which has not since subsided."[46] Johnson's criticism is intended to have the effect that he defines in wit and admires in Gray's *Elegy*: you may not have thought like this before, but you feel as if you had. The effect is not of sudden illumination but of strengthened conviction. Johnson is least successful, on the other hand, when he is throwing stones into the criticism of *Lycidas* or Gray's odes.

Above all, Johnson at his best speaks for the common reader: for his deepest instincts that no criticism can wish away. Consider once more the judgment of *Paradise Lost*: "None ever wished it longer than it is." Against the want of human interest by which Johnson accounts for this, one may place his mention of Otway's *Orphan*. Though he does not admire either play or playwright greatly, he is compelled to admit that in appealing to "the heart," Otway has secured the attention of succeeding generations. "If the heart is interested, many other beauties may be wanting, yet not be missed" (*Life of Otway*, I, 245). Similarly, Johnson ends his note on *The Merry Wives of Windsor*, "The conduct of this drama is deficient; the action begins and ends often before the conclusion, and the different parts might change places without inconvenience; but its general power, that power by which all works of genius shall finally be tried, is such, that perhaps it never yet had reader or spectator, who did not think it too soon at an end" (Yale *Works*, VII, 341). No one wishes *Paradise Lost* longer than it

---

[46]William Hazlitt, *The Spirit of the Age* (1825), *Complete Works*, ed. P. P. Howe (London, 1932), II, 28 (final par. of the chapter on Godwin).

is, but *Paradise Lost* is immeasurably greater than *The Merry Wives of Windsor*.

Here as so often Johnson directly attacks the assumption common to many critics, that we can teach ourselves to enjoy literature in proportion as we admire it. It would be more honest to admit that some of the greatest works are deficient in the power to command every kind of delight, though that deficiency certainly does not exalt Rowe above Milton. And it is far from being simply a matter of forbidding greatness, for wit itself can weary the reader, as it does in *Hudibras*, if other kinds of pleasure are neglected.

Uniformity must tire at last, though it be uniformity of excellence.... If inexhaustible wit could give perpetual pleasure no eye would ever leave half-read the work of Butler; for what poet has ever brought so many remote images so happily together? It is scarcely possible to peruse a page without finding some association of images that was never found before. By the first paragraph the reader is amused, by the next he is delighted, and by a few more strained to astonishment; but astonishment is a toilsome pleasure; he is soon weary of wondering, and longs to be diverted. [*Life of Butler*, I, 212]

As modern critics show when they begin by quoting Johnson, *Paradise Lost* violates the usual expectations of the common reader, and any valid interpretation of it must begin by accepting that fact. Our first response to a poem may not be our best, or the one most likely to produce lasting enjoyment. We may learn, for instance, to appreciate Milton on angelic corporeality by coming to understand the richness of his ideas about the relation between body and spirit. But we ought not to pretend that a dramatization of angelic corporeality was precisely what we expected in literary works. Johnson reminds us always to stay in touch with our fundamental instincts and the deepest sources of our literary pleasure. If we can accommodate ourselves to *Paradise Lost*, it can satisfy those instincts and give us that pleasure; but it may not do so at a first or a cursory reading. Often the common reader will find himself unable to enlarge his comprehension as the poem demands. He should then be honest with himself and admit that it wearies him, an admission that reflects on him as well as on the poem. Milton would have been still greater if he could have commanded the reader's unquenchable curiosity as Homer and Shakespeare do, but in failing to command it he is nevertheless a great genius and his poem a masterpiece.

Literary History and Biography

The true greatness of the *Lives* rests not upon criticism considered as a discipline in itself—Johnson called it, after all, one of the "subordinate and instrumental arts" (*Rambler* 208)—but upon a broad conception of literary history as a branch of human history. Like most neoclassical critics Johnson believed that art has developed rather than simply changed. But he is not vulnerable to Blake's complaint against Reynolds: "If Art was Progressive We should have had Mich Angelo's & Rafaels to Succeed & to Improve upon each other But it is not so. Genius dies with its Possessor & comes not again till Another is Born with It."[47] The right note is struck in a sentence (also denounced by Blake) that Johnson contributed to Reynolds's dedication to the king: "The regular progress of cultivated life is from necessaries to accommodations, from accommodations to ornaments" (*Discourses*, p. 3). Johnson sees a progressive improvement in English *versification*, placed on the proper basis by Denham and Waller, strengthened by Dryden, and perfected by Pope. Johnson's ear was formed by the couplet, and he does suggest that if Milton "had written after the improvements made by Dryden, it is reasonable to believe that he would have admitted a more pleasing modulation of numbers into his work" (*Life of John Philips*, I, 318). But it does not follow that Johnson is insensitive to the power of Milton's verse. "To degrade the sounding words and stately construction of Milton, by an application to the lowest and most trivial things, gratifies the mind with a momentary triumph over that grandeur which hitherto held its captives in admiration" (p. 317).

In finding English poetry brick and leaving it marble, Dryden acted in part as a brilliant technician. "Some improvements had been already made in English numbers, but the full force of our

---

[47]Annotation to Discourse 6, *Poetry and Prose*, p. 645.

language was not yet felt: the verse that was smooth was commonly feeble. If Cowley had sometimes a finished line he had it
by chance. Dryden knew how to chuse the flowing and the
sonorous words; to vary the pauses and adjust the accents; to
diversify the cadence, and yet preserve the smoothness of his
metre" (*Life of Dryden*, I, 466). These technical effects, clearly, are
the expression of a powerful mind. They are not merely
mechanical skills. But neither are they the whole of poetry. Pope
studied "correctness" not because it was easy but because it is so
hard to be correct without being tedious. Roscommon "is
perhaps the only correct writer in verse before Addison," but his
writing is distinguished at best for absence of faults, and Johnson
derides the excuse that he lacked imagination only because his
judgment was so severe (*Life of Roscommon*, I, 235). If in Pope's
versification "art and diligence have now done their best" (*Life of
Pope*, III, 251), that is because Pope had not only the "sedate and
quiescent quality" of good sense but also "genius; a mind active,
ambitious, and adventurous, always investigating, always aspiring; in its widest searches still longing to go forward, in its highest
flights still wishing to be higher; always imagining something
greater than it knows, always endeavouring more than it can do"
(p. 217).

As these passages suggest, Johnson's real interest in literary
history was not in the evolution of form and technique but in the
creative leaps of genius. His celebrated analysis of the metaphysical poets is not original in what it describes, having been anticipated in many details by the pedantic Theobald.

Wit lying mostly in the Assemblage of *Ideas*, and in the putting Those
together with Quickness and Variety, wherein can be found any Resemblance, or Congruity, to make up pleasant Pictures, and agreeable
Visions in the Fancy; the Writer, who aims at Wit, must of course range
far and wide for Materials. Now, the Age, in which *Shakespeare* liv'd,
having, above all others, a wonderful Affection to appear Learned,
They declined vulgar Images, such as are immediately fetch'd from
Nature, and rang'd thro' the Circle of the Sciences to fetch their Ideas
from thence. But as the Resemblances of such Ideas to the Subject must
necessarily lie very much out of the common Way, and every piece of
Wit appear a Riddle to the Vulgar; This, that should have taught them
the forced, quaint, unnatural Tract they were in, (and induce them to

follow a more natural One,) was the very Thing that kept them attach'd
to it. The ostentatious Affectation of abstruse Learning, peculiar to
that Time, the Love that Men naturally have to every Thing that looks
like Mystery, fixed them down to this Habit of Obscurity. Thus became
the Poetry of DONNE (tho' the wittiest Man of that Age,) nothing but a
continued Heap of Riddles.[48]

While Johnson's definition of metaphysical poetry resembles
Theobald's, the real originality lies in his willingness to take it
seriously and to respond to the strength of mind that it embodies.[49] If the metaphysicals finally fail it is in the extreme
specialization of their poetics: despite their great intelligence
they forgot to trace "intellectual pleasure to its natural sources in
the mind of man" and instead "paid their court to temporary
prejudices" (*Life of Cowley*, I, 18).

Johnson's emphasis on the individuality of imagination is thus
ideally suited to literary biography, rather than to conventional
literary history, which describes the evolution of style and genre
as if it took place in a region remote from human beings. Poems
are written by poets. *Paradise Lost* could have been written by no
one but Milton—it is certainly not the inevitable product of the
mutations of epic—whereas Macpherson's Ossianic poems could
have been written by "many men, many women, and many
children" (*Life*, I, 396). As our study of genre indicates, Johnson
understands that poets imitate each other; indeed, it is the feeble
poets like Blackmore who imagine themselves self-created, and
the masters like Milton who most ambitiously measure themselves against the exalted dead. But "no man ever yet became
great by imitation" (*Rambler* 154, V, 59). To the extent that a poet
can breathe new life into a familiar form, he is an inventor and
not an imitator. To the extent that the form controls his imagination, he is weakened by it. Johnson's contemporaries understood
these issues well.[50]

In the end, therefore, the subjects of Johnson's *Lives* appear as
contemporaries in the fullness of literary achievement. Every
great writer is unique, and the critic must find appropriate terms

[48]Preface, *The Works of Shakespeare*, ed. Lewis Theobald (1733), I, xlvi.
[49]David Perkins emphasizes Johnson's concern with mental energy in
"Johnson on Wit and Metaphysical Poetry," *ELH*, 20 (1953), 200-217.
[50]See Bate, *The Burden of the Past*.

to describe the special qualities of mind that inform his writings.

The Chronicle is a composition unrivalled and alone: such gaiety of fancy, such facility of expression, such varied similitude, such a succession of images, and such a dance of words, it is vain to expect except from Cowley. His strength always appears in his agility; his volatility is not the flutter of a light, but the bound of an elastick mind. His levity never leaves his learning behind it; the moralist, the politician, and the critick, mingle their influence even in this airy frolick of genius. To such a performance Suckling could have brought the gaiety, but not the knowledge; Dryden could have supplied the knowledge, but not the gaiety. [*Life of Cowley*, I, 37-38]

Poets and poems, life and works, throw light upon each other as Johnson ponders them. And the great Dryden is invoked here as a poet whom Cowley in certain ways excels, not as a standard toward which Cowley should have been working.

The *Lives of the Poets* form a flexible and capacious whole. At the level of entertainment they are filled with delightful anecdotes, such as the story of Oxford dismissing Rowe, who expected a diplomatic appointment if he learned Spanish, with the cold remark that he envied him the pleasure of reading *Don Quixote* in the original (*Lives*, II, 71), or the account of the specialized sensuality of John Philips, whose "sovereign pleasure" as a schoolboy "was to sit hour after hour while his hair was combed by somebody, whose service he found means to procure" (*Lives*, I, 312). At the level of moral reflection, they offer an extended meditation on the rarity of human achievement, and are filled with the fading light of once brilliant reputations.

It is reported that the juvenile compositions of Stepney made grey authors blush. I know not whether his poems will appear such wonders to the present age. One cannot always easily find the reason for which the world has sometimes conspired to squander praise. [*Life of Stepney*, I, 310-11]

It would now be esteemed no honour, by a contributor to the monthly bundles of verses, to be told that, in strains either familiar or solemn, he sings like Montague. [*Life of Halifax*, II, 47]

Even the most trivial details in the *Lives* gain value from Johnson's determination to rescue all that he can from the dark. He likes to quote Latin epitaphs, in which a man's life and character are given a kind of permanence in stone. And he feels genuine sorrow that so little is known about men of talent.

> In what character Butler was admitted into that Lady's service, how long he continued in it, and why he left it, is, like the other incidents of his life, utterly unknown.
>
>   . . . . .
>
> In this mist of obscurity passed the life of Butler, a man whose name can only perish with his language. The mode and place of his education are unknown; the events of his life are variously related; and all that can be told with certainty is, that he was poor. [*Lives*, I, 203, 209]

Finally, it is well to emphasize that the *Lives* succeed because they reflect Johnson's own powerful individuality, combining intellectual energy, moral authority, and rhetorical wit. The last of these is visible everywhere, quite apart from the occasional passage on which time has conferred an accidental charm: "Benjamin, the eldest son, was disinherited and sent to New Jersey, as wanting common understanding" (*Life of Waller*, I, 277). Johnson's account of the Puritans whom Butler satirized, for instance, is enhanced by the irony in his own style: "We have never been witnesses of animosities excited by the use of minced pies and plumb porridge, nor seen with what abhorrence those who could eat them at all other times of the year would shrink from them in December (*Life of Butler*, I, 215). And he is fond of sharpening his mode of balanced clauses to an epigrammatic point: "In his translations from Pindar he found the art of reaching all the obscurity of the Theban bard, however he may fall below his sublimity: he will be allowed, if he has less fire, to have more smoke" (*Life of A. Philips*, III, 324-25). The joke was traditional, but Johnson expresses it with characteristic wit.[51]

Behind all the miscellaneous matter in the *Lives*, behind every digression and associative transition, we feel the presence of Johnson himself. The *Lives* are held together partly by the theme of human achievement and failure, partly by our simple interest in biography and literary history, but above all by the pressure of

---

[51] It seems to go back to line 143 of the *Ars Poetica*. Addison says that Lee's thoughts "are wonderfully suited to Tragedy, but frequently lost in such a Cloud of Words, that it is hard to see the Beauty of them: There is an infinite Fire in his Works, but so involved in Smoak, that it does not appear in half its Lustre" (*Spectator* 39).

a lively and versatile mind. And just as Johnson reminds us not to forget the poet in the poems, so there is no need to suppress our own interest in Johnson when we read the *Lives*. We may not share his dislike of those who clamor for liberty, but if we know his biography we can appreciate that he has himself experienced "that indistinct and headstrong ardour for liberty which a man of genius always catches when he enters the world, and always suffers to cool as he passes forward" (*Life of Lyttelton*, III, 446). It is especially pleasant to come upon a description of Addison's relations with Steele that clearly reflects Johnson's with Boswell: "It is not hard to love those from whom nothing can be feared, and Addison never considered Steele as a rival; . . .Addison, who knew his own dignity, could not always forbear to shew it by playing a little upon his admirer; but he was in no danger of retort: his jests were endured without resistance or resentment" (*Life of Addison*, II, 81). Nor are we offended when Johnson shows himself directly. The eloquent memorial to Garrick and Gilbert Walmesley, in the *Life of Smith*, seems anything but extraneous. These men (one famous, one obscure) are part of the past in which Johnson and his subjects once lived; they are important to Johnson, and we feel their living presence, in his unexpected tribute, more keenly than we do that of Edmund Smith.

This book will close with a study of two of the finest *Lives*, the *Dryden* and *Pope*, where Johnson's special excellence can be discussed in a detailed context. Matthew Arnold, choosing these and four others for an edition that could serve as "a *point de repère*, or fixed centre, . . .for the student of English literature," observed that the *Lives of the Poets* give us "Johnson mellowed by years, Johnson in his ripeness and plenitude, treating the subject which he loved best and knew best." As Arnold saw clearly, they are valuable because the ripeness and plenitude are combined with a confident, even aggressive individuality. "The more we study him, the higher will be our esteem for the power of his mind, the width of his interests, the largeness of his knowledge, the freshness, fearlessness, and strength of his judgments."[52]

---

[52]*The Six Chief Lives from Johnson's* Lives of the Poets (London, 1886), pp. xii, xiii, xxvi. The first edition appeared in 1878. The other *Lives* are the *Milton*, *Swift*, *Addison*, and *Gray* (leaving out, most notably, the *Cowley*).

Many critics lecture the reader. Johnson, like Arnold himself, even when he is most idiosyncratic, impels the reader to emulate his breadth and energy of mind. The *Lives* are full of insights into specific writers and works, but above all they are exemplary: they are written from a great fullness of experience and communicate a memorable way of thinking about literature and life.

7   Dryden: The Power of Mind

THE FIRST READERS of the *Life of Dryden* agreed that it was excellent. Not only was it obviously written *"con amore,"* as the reviewer in the *Gentleman's Magazine* said, but Johnson's enthusiasm had been translated into an impressively coherent achievement. Even an unfriendly writer in the *London Review* testified, "The character of Mr. Dryden, our author hath traced out with a masterly hand." And Robert Potter, pausing in his attack on the *Lives* a decade later, conceded that "our author has written this great poet's life with candour, analized his character with much ingenuity, and dismissed him with a genteel and just eulogium."[1]

These testimonies deserve notice because modern authorities have felt that the *Lives of the Poets*, this one included, are seriously defective both biographically and critically.[2] The *Life of Dryden* is a good test case: it tends to ramble, it contains inaccuracies and odd disproportions of emphasis, and its critical remarks may seem sketchy and arbitrary. Yet it deserves to be recognized as a masterpiece of biographical criticism: not the misreading of poems through external information about the poet's life, but

---

[1]*Gentleman's Magazine*, 49 (1779), 364; *London Review*, 9 (1779), 262; Potter, *Art of Criticism*, p. 66. The *London Review* was edited by William Kenrick, who had been a splenetic enemy of Johnson since the Shakespeare edition of 1765; his reviewer (who might be himself) describes the *Lives* as "cobbled up, as a bookseller's job, with that slow haste peculiar to the author," and denounces them as *"Tory* prefaces" (p. 258). His praise and Potter's suggest that the excellence of the *Life of Dryden* was taken for granted; whatever were the weak points of the *Lives*, they did not lie there.

[2]George Watson says that "The *Lives* were written in haste, in the confidence of a great reputation, and there is a good deal in them that is formula-ridden and inconclusive. . . .[Johnson] is writing to a recipe, and he does not stir his ingredients. . . . He makes singularly little attempt to exploit biography for critical purposes. His notion of the creative act is not so much naive as non-existent" (*The Literary Critics*, pp. 93, 95, 96). Richard D. Altick, though more sympathetic to Johnson, concludes that "his narratives often lack balance. . . . Johnson usually was content to offer a loosely arranged miscellany of facts rather than a coherent portrait. . . . In general Johnson lacked the integrating, shaping talents that the very greatest artists in biography should possess" (*Lives and Letters* [New York, 1966], pp. 56-57).

the analysis of life and poems as aspects of a single whole. In showing how Dryden overcomes his defects as man and artist, Johnson leads us to appreciate the poetry for the mental powers that inform it. The *Life of Dryden* is intended to teach us how to value, and indeed how to read, a poet whose intellectual strength carries us irresistibly forward through poems that are disappointingly uneven. Dryden has no *Paradise Lost*. His life is not dedicated to preparing himself to write a single astonishing masterpiece. But his genius is evident everywhere in his highly miscellaneous works, and he surpasses Milton (in Johnson's view, at least) in the crucial ability to command the ungrudging attention of the reader.

I propose to discuss this *Life* in approximately its own sequence, erratic though that may sometimes appear, for Johnson's subject is Dryden's mind, and his leisurely, discursive narrative helps us to develop our own view of that subject rather than having it imposed on us from the outset. I do not mean that every omission and digression is carefully calculated to produce this effect. But the procedure does encourage us to come to terms with a complex and often perplexing poet in our own way, weighing the various kinds of evidence even as Johnson weighs them. The *Life* moves forward with a cumulative richness that would be falsified by a thematic summary of its "conclusions."

The first paragraph announces two themes: the greatness of the subject and the inherent limitations in the usual way of dealing with it. "Of the great poet whose life I am about to delineate, the curiosity which his reputation must excite will require a display more ample than can now be given. His contemporaries, however they reverenced his genius, left his life unwritten; and nothing therefore can be known beyond what casual mention and uncertain tradition have supplied" (*Lives*, I, 331). Johnson thus opens with a sense of raised expectation, of much that must be accomplished and of the difficulties that impend. He is not simply apologizing in advance for the scarcity of information about Dryden, for the scarcity is itself interesting. No one who knew him felt impelled (as Milton's admirers did) to record the details of his life.

In assessing the biographical part of the *Life*, we have first to consider its apparent disproportions. A surprising amount of space is given to pamphlet attacks on Dryden, particularly that of Elkanah Settle, together with what Johnson believed to be Dryden's reply. The quantity of this material cannot perhaps be defended, but its presence can. "Such was the criticism to which the genius of Dryden could be reduced, between rage and terrour. . . . But let it be remembered, that minds are not levelled in their powers but when they are first levelled in their desires" (p. 346). What is important is that on this level Dryden is indistinguishable from Settle: he can write greater poems than Settle but cannot excel him in scurrilous abuse. Here is one of many instances where we see Dryden stooping when he need not have stooped; it reveals a weakness in him. It is no help, incidentally, to point out that only three paragraphs of Dryden's reply seem to be his, since these are not obviously superior to the rest. If the other paragraphs quoted by Johnson are actually by Shadwell and Crowne, then we discover that Dryden was not only prepared to descend to Settle's level but could do it without visible embarrassment in the company of Shadwell and Crowne. The issue is altered only if one believes, as may indeed be the case, that none of the pamphlet is by Dryden.[3]

Johnson had reasons, then, for taking up the Settle controversy; but can he be justified for doing it at such length? If we want the *Life of Dryden* to exhibit the harmonious proportions of a work of art, he cannot. But rightly or wrongly he regards such proportions with some disdain. He wants to learn whatever he can about Dryden's character, for which there is little direct evidence except in his writings, and is too sensible to expect the poems to be trustworthy guides. Something may therefore be learned by following Dryden through the spontaneous explosions of a pamphlet battle. "As the pamphlet, though Dryden's, has never been thought worthy of republication and is not easily to be found, it may gratify curiosity to quote it more largely" (p. 343). It does gratify curiosity. Like Milton's prose tracts, though less brilliantly, it revives the spirit of a bygone age of uncivil argument. And it reduces the "great poet" of Johnson's opening

[3] For the three-paragraph theory, see James M. Osborn, *John Dryden: Some Biographical Facts and Problems* (Gainesville, Fla., 1965), p. 33. For the argument against Dryden's authorship, see Charles E. Ward, *The Life of John Dryden* (Chapel Hill, N.C., 1961), pp. 328-29.

paragraph to "poor Dryden," stung by Settle into "venting his malice" (p. 345).

Moreover the affair permits Johnson to introduce the sort of moral reflection whose absence would make the *Lives of the Poets* tidier but much less impressive. At the end of the passage in question he concludes, "Enough of Settle" (p. 354). But Settle refuses to go away:

Elkanah Settle, who had answered *Absalom*, appeared with equal cour-age in opposition to *The Medal*, and published an answer called *The Medal Reversed*, with so much success in both encounters that he left the palm doubtful, and divided the suffrages of the nation. Such are the revolutions of fame, or such is the prevalence of fashion, that the man whose works have not yet been thought to deserve the care of collecting them; who died forgotten in an hospital; and whose latter years were spent in contriving shows for fairs, and carrying an elegy or epithalamium, of which the beginning and end were occasionally var-ied, but the intermediate parts were always the same, to every house where there was a funeral or a wedding—might with truth have had inscribed upon his stone

"Here lies the Rival and Antagonist of Dryden." [P. 375]

Of course this is a digression, but it is an impressive one, and it has its place in the *Life*. Dryden descended unnecessarily from his proper greatness to quarrel with Settle, and the measure of his greatness is that the best thing Settle ever did was to quarrel with Dryden.

Another kind of objection deserves special notice, for it helps to define the nature of Johnson's biographical method. As James M. Osborn rightly observes, we get little sense of Dryden's per-sonality, more of which is evident in the letter to his sons printed by Johnson as an appendix (pp. 479-81) than in all the rest of the *Life*.[4] But it is not so much that Johnson ignores the subject—he is willing to speculate on the personalities of Swift and Milton and Pope—as that hardly anything of Dryden's personality was recorded by anyone. "Of his petty habits or slight amusements tradition has retained little. Of the only two men whom I have found to whom he was personally known, one told me that at the house which he frequented, called Will's Coffee-house, the ap-

[4]Osborn, pp. 37-38.

peal upon any literary dispute was made to him, and the other related that his armed chair, which in the winter had a settled and prescriptive place by the fire, was in the summer placed in the balcony; and that he called the two places his winter and his summer seat. This is all the intelligence which his two survivors afforded me" (pp. 408-9). Mark Van Doren's attempt to conjure up a real being from these scraps of information only shows how tenuous they are: "His coffee-house dictatorship has long been proverbial in English literary history; 'the great patriarch of Parnassus' who ruled by the fire in winter and out on the balcony in summer is the most striking figure between the blind Milton and the rolling Johnson."[5] Not very striking. Boswell, in fact, recording the story, did not notice the pun on "summer seat" (as in "country seat") and gave it as "chair" instead (*Life*, III, 71).

Johnson sees that there is little use in trying to reconstruct Dryden's personality from what remains. Yet we are not wholly without information. We know little about his mannerisms and peculiarities, but we do know that younger writers deferred to his authority. This suggests that his mind was more formidable than his personality and that the tradition about Will's is valuable in that light. "He has been described as magisterially presiding over the younger writers, and assuming the distribution of poetical fame; but he who excels has a right to teach, and he whose judgement is incontestable may, without usurpation, examine and decide" (p. 396).

In this as in other aspects of the *Life of Dryden*, Boswell and later readers have thought they saw a good deal of Johnsonian self-portrait. This is true in some respects, though of course not in others. But if the *Life* is not a conventional biography, neither is it the rambling testimonial to a private affection. In the *Life of Pope* Johnson makes the famous statement "If the reader should suspect me, as I suspect myself, of some partial fondness for the memory of Dryden, let him not too hastily condemn me; for meditation and enquiry may, perhaps, shew him the reasonableness of my determination" (*Lives*, III, 223). The esteem expressed here is for Dryden's mental powers as contrasted with Pope's, not for Dryden the man. To the latter Johnson is surpris-

[5]*John Dryden: A Study of His Poetry* (New York, 1946), p. 236.

ingly hostile, for a reason that is central to his interpretation of
Dryden's achievement: throughout his life he allowed himself to
be less than he might have been, to fall short of full expression of
his powerful genius.

Such was the lesson of the imbroglio with Settle, and such is the
lesson of Dryden's long series of obsequious dedications. The
violence of Johnson's outrage needs to be seen in the context of
his consistently strong feelings on the subject:

Nothing has so much degraded literature from its natural rank, as the
practice of indecent and promiscuous dedication; for what credit can
he expect who professes himself the hireling of vanity, however profli-
gate, and without shame or scruple celebrates the worthless, dignifies
the mean, and gives to the corrupt, licentious, and oppressive, the
ornaments which ought only to add grace to truth, and loveliness to
innocence? Every other kind of adulteration, however shameful, however mischievous, is less detestable than the crime of counterfeiting
characters, and fixing the stamp of literary sanction upon the dross and
refuse of the world. [*Rambler* 136, IV, 356]

In exalting worthless patrons—Johnson's tone does not suggest
that many can be worthy—the author cheapens himself, and
does so solely for the most immediate and temporary rewards.
Johnson therefore scorns to dedicate the *Rambler* or any other of
his works. "The supplications of an author never yet reprieved
him a moment from oblivion; and, though greatness has sometimes sheltered guilt, it can afford no protection to ignorance or
dulness. Having hitherto attempted only the propagation of
truth, I will not at last violate it by the confession of terrors which
I do not feel: Having laboured to maintain the dignity of virtue, I
will not now degrade it by the meanness of dedication" (*Rambler*
208, V, 317).

Johnson's language in these passages expresses intense moral
anger. In the *Life of Dryden* three decades later he is not inclined
to mitigate Dryden's offense by reference to the conventions of
his age, as Edmond Malone suggested he might have done.[6]

---

[6]"The encomiastick language which is sometimes found in his Dedications,
was the vice of the time, not of the man" (*Critical and Miscellaneous Prose Works of
John Dryden* [1800], I, 243).

This composition is addressed to the princess of Modena, then dutchess of York, in a strain of flattery which disgraces genius, and which it was wonderful that any man that knew the meaning of his own words could use without self-detestation. [P. 359][7]

In the meanness and servility of hyperbolical adulation I know not whether, since the days in which the Roman emperors were deified, he has been ever equalled, except by Afra Behn in an address to Eleanor Gwyn. When he has once undertaken the task of praise he no longer retains shame in himself, nor supposes it in his patron. As many odoriferous bodies are observed to diffuse perfumes from year to year without sensible diminution of bulk or weight, he appears never to have impoverished his mint of flattery by his expenses, however lavish. [P. 399]

The moral energy is reminiscent of the passages in the *Rambler*, but in deference to his subject Johnson is careful to convey it with ironic wit. It is not much of an extenuation to say that Dryden at his worst is not so bad as Afra Behn at hers. And the imagery of the final sentence nicely conveys the suggestion of Dryden as an odoriferous body and, in the metaphor of the mint, glances at the quid pro quo the dedications were intended to provoke: the patrons were to pay Dryden back in real money. If Dryden then complains of poverty, it is the complaint of the prostitute who has not received the customary fee.

It may be urged in Dryden's defense that any poet in his time was obliged to seek and please patrons and that much of his praise is intended as an elaborate social game. Also Johnson's own feelings about patrons were far from impartial. Still, Dryden's encomiums are extravagant even by Restoration standards, and Johnson is not convinced that he was "more delighted with the fertility of his invention than mortified by the prostitution of his judgement." As he remarks with some scorn, the worst shame of all would be that Dryden was a prostitute without

[7]What especially offends Johnson is the "attempt to mingle earth and heaven, by praising human excellence in the language of religion." Dryden's theme is the duchess's beauty, which (he says) distracts him from thoughts of anything else, and inspires such effusions as this: " 'Tis true, you are above all mortal Wishes: No Man desires Impossibilities, because they are beyond the reach of Nature: To hope to be a God, is Folly exalted into Madness: But by the Laws of our Creation we are oblig'd to adore him; and are permitted to love him too, at human Distance."

knowing it: "It is indeed not certain that on these occasions his judgement much rebelled against his interest. There are minds which easily sink into submission, that look on grandeur with undistinguishing reverence, and discover no defect where there is elevation of rank and affluence of riches" (p. 400).

The rigor of Johnson's moral analysis here can hardly be exceeded by anything in the *Life of Milton*, however much his strictures there have inflamed Milton's admirers to revenge. While one is reading this it is hard to believe that Dryden can be a poet for whom Johnson feels anything but bottomless contempt. Yet the effect of these judgments in the *Life* as a whole is not to undermine the appreciation, but rather to support it by contributing a valuable kind of perspective. As Lawrence Lipking observes, "Just as the *Life of Milton* may be considered a definitive study of the genius too independent and self-willed to be emulated, however admired, the *Life of Dryden* consistently pictures a genius vitiated by its willingness to please, to compromise with popular demand rather than insist on the best of which it is capable."[8]

This defines a paradox that calls for explanation: how does Johnson manage to combine both praise and blame without confusing or alienating the reader? The answer is surely that he achieves a union of criticism and moral judgment that few other critics can approach. When he relates literature to its author, Johnson is able to convince us of the essential justice of his moral insight. We are offended by the blanket indictment of fiction in *Rambler* 4, with the concealed implication that *Tom Jones* can only have been written by a very nasty man; we are even more irritated at the idea that Shakespeare's plays, in which the author is not visibly didactic, reveal a moral vacuum. But when Johnson has a firm grasp of his author's character he handles these matters far more persuasively. Any nonmoral response to his account of Waller's panegyrics—seeing them, for instance, simply as exercises in a genre to which truth is irrelevant—has the air of shamefaced special pleading; Johnson has defined an issue that we have to face, whether or not we accept his conclusions. Likewise, Dryden's dedications give an important insight into his

[8]*Ordering of the Arts*, p. 445.

character and his aesthetic conscience, and what we learn from them can be applied in other places as well. "He that could bear to write the dedication felt no pain in writing the preface" (p. 360).

We are further convinced of Johnson's moral authority because we see not merely that he has strong opinions but also that he is able to hold them while preserving a remarkable flexibility of response to specific situations. In the *Rambler*, where the focus is general, Johnson denounces servile dedication as if it ought to be punished by excruciating torture. In the *Life of Dryden* his opinions have not changed, but the note is rather one of sorrowful disappointment. Why should so fine a poet abase himself in this way, and what must that abasement tell us about the weaknesses at the heart of his poetry? Still, Dryden, like Savage, is a man, not a Rambler figure of the Obsequious Dedicator, and this evidence must be accommodated to the other kinds of evidence upon which we form our judgment of the man and the work.

Finally, it should be remembered that all of this is presented in the biographical section of the *Life*, interspersed with straightforward narrative and with literary criticism, rather than being reserved for the formal discussion of Dryden's character. The result (whether expressly intended by Johnson or not) is that our sense of his character is built up gradually, by reflection on a multitude of different circumstances. Throughout all the miscellaneous matter of this part of the *Life* two main threads are apparent: the first, Dryden's quest for poetic reputation (a noble ambition he shares with other great writers); and the second, an unhappy tendency to place obstacles in his own way. The former theme quickly reaches an apparent fruition. In 1667 Dryden "began . . .to exercise the domination of conscious genius, by recommending his own performance" (p. 338). Only a year later "he was now so much distinguished that in 1668 he succeeded Sir William Davenant as poet-laureat" (p. 340). But uneasy lies the head that wears the laurel; Settle enters the picture because he happened to write a successful play, "which was so much applauded as to make [Dryden] think his supremacy of reputation in some danger" (p. 342). Dryden's response is to write the pamphlet that Johnson quotes at such length, introducing it with a remark rather moral than critical: "Dryden could not now repress these emotions, which he called indignation, and others jealousy; but wrote upon the play and the dedication such criticism as malignant impatience could pour out in haste" (p. 342). Again and again Dryden is shown to be the worst enemy of his own much-desired greatness, stooping from his proper level to fling mud or diffuse perfume.

The most serious critical miscalculation in the *Life of Dryden* derives from this moral emphasis: the decision to treat the plays in the biographical rather than the critical section. This would not matter if Johnson took them seriously or if he gave all of them the kind of sympathetic reading that *The Conquest of Granada* receives (pp. 348-49). But he sufficiently confesses his distaste for "tracing the meanders of his mind through the whole series of his dramatick performances" (p. 336), choosing to see them essentially as potboilers and to make much of Dryden's own apologies for their deficiencies. In effect they serve as evidence for Dryden's fitful expressions of aesthetic conscience, to which the word *shame* is freely applied. "He therefore made rhyming tragedies till, by the prevalence of manifest propriety, he seems to have grown ashamed of making them any longer" (pp. 337-38). "The rants of Maximin have been always the sport of criticism, and were at length, if his own confession may be trusted, the shame of the writer" (p. 348).

The Dryden who emerges from the biographical section is thus not a very pleasing figure. In his main profession, the drama, he is seen as slipshod, indecent, and anxious to pander to popular taste. In his relations with others he is petulant, quarrelsome, and vain. The one great event in Dryden's private life, his conversion to Catholicism, is treated with scrupulous fairness and yet betrays an implication that Johnson wishes to believe the best while fearing the worst. "It is natural to hope that a comprehensive is likewise an elevated soul, and that whoever is wise is also honest. I am willing to believe that Dryden, having employed his mind, active as it was, upon different studies, and filled it, capacious as it was, with other materials, came unprovided to the controversy, and wanted rather skill to discover the right than virtue to maintain it. But enquiries into the heart are not for man; we must now leave him to his Judge" (p. 378). Although Johnson dismisses the charge that Dryden's conversion was simply a stratagem to ingratiate himself with James II, he leaves open—without giving any evidence—the suspicion that it was still less than wholly sincere. "It is natural to hope . . .I am willing to believe."

The function of the biographical section, then, is not to reconstruct Dryden's personality from a few wretched reports about his winter and summer seats. Its function, to which the whole body of the plays is sacrificed, is to establish the main lines of character that will be developed in the next section and then applied to the poems. By way of dismissing the possibility of anything else Johnson quotes what he himself calls the "wild story" of Dryden's funeral (pp. 389-92), in which a drunken young lord was supposed to have halted the mourners and delayed the burial for several weeks. No doubt he includes this partly, as Paul Fussell says, because he cannot resist its quality of "ghoulish farce."[9] But it may also reflect a serious frustration at Dryden's inexplicable colorlessness. Here is a poet much given to controversy, the victim of endless scurrilous attacks, about whom almost nothing of interest has been preserved. There is then an attractive irony in the story of his funeral, which makes him more productive of incident in death than in life. The man who filled his plays with "incredible love and impossible valour" (p. 349) never participated in anything remotely resembling the tragicomic excesses of Waller's Plot, and gives an opportunity for real narrative only when he has left his summer and winter seats for his coffin.

When at last Dryden is in his grave and we arrive at the survey of his character (pp. 394-410), we find that it holds no surprises. This section serves as a transition in two ways. It continues and summarizes the analysis, already begun, of Dryden's temperament and "character" in the ordinary sense; and it deliberately postpones a study of his *intellectual* character for the second half of the *Life*, where it can properly be deduced from his works. It is as though Dryden's mortal part were here disposed of, freeing Johnson and the reader to pursue his strengths and weaknesses where they really matter, in the world of the mind in which he is immortal.

[9]*Samuel Johnson and the Life of Writing* (New York, 1971), p. 267.

As in the *Life of Waller*, Johnson begins this section by quoting in full a formal character by someone who knew the poet. In the *Waller* the judgments of Clarendon are clearly too severe and need qualification, though Johnson's qualifications do not altogether dispel the severity. Here the character is a wholly favorable one by Congreve, Dryden's friend, protégé, and literary executor, obviously intended to dispel some of the hostility to Dryden's memory that was still current when it appeared seventeen years after his death. Rather oddly, Johnson has chosen to alter the original sequence of ideas in the sketch, perhaps in order to make us come at Dryden, once again, by way of his mind rather than his personality.[10] In any event, he goes on to devote thirty-two paragraphs to his own reflections on Dryden's character, showing little willingness to accept as authoritative Congreve's account of the poet's modesty and eagerness for friendship.

In the first place Congreve has shown Dryden's disposition "rather as it exhibited itself in cursory conversation, than as it operated on the more important parts of life. His placability and his friendship indeed were solid virtues; but courtesy and good-humour are often found with little real worth." As for the modesty, which is Congreve's interpretation of Dryden's notorious bashfulness in company, Johnson's opinion is severe: "The modesty which made him so slow to advance, and so easy to be repulsed, was certainly no suspicion of deficient merit, or unconsciousness of his own value: he appears to have known in its whole extent the dignity of his character, and to have set a very high value on his own powers and performances. He probably did not offer his conversation, because he expected it to be solicited; and he retired from a cold reception, not submissive but indignant, with such reverence of his own greatness as made him unwilling to expose it to neglect or violation" (p. 395).

One's first impulse may be to ask how Johnson can possibly know this, but in fact the passage is a good indication of his excellence as an intellectual biographer. As he sees very well, Dryden's prefaces and his self-defense against pamphlet enemies are anything but the work of a modest man. In just the

[10]The evidence for this suggestion, which can only be conjectural, is given in the Appendix, p. 229 below.

same way Johnson writes of Addison, "Of his habits, or external manners, nothing is so often mentioned as that timorous or sullen taciturnity, which his friends called modesty by too mild a name. . . . This modesty was by no means inconsistent with a very high opinion of his own merit. He demanded to be the first name in modern wit" (*Life of Addison*, II, 118-20). What is wrong is the affectation of modesty, not the consciousness of ability: "His own powers were such as might have satisfied him with conscious excellence" (p. 120). Milton was wiser than Addison in revealing "with calm confidence his high opinion of his own powers" (*Life of Milton*, I, 102), and similarly "it was the felicity of Pope to rate himself at his real value" (*Life of Pope*, III, 89). Like Milton and Pope, Dryden is great and need not be blamed for knowing it. "His modesty was by no means inconsistent with ostentatiousness: he is diligent enough to remind the world of his merit, and expresses with very little scruple his high opinion of his own powers; but his self-commendations are read without scorn or indignation: we allow his claims, and love his frankness" (p. 396).

In this discussion Johnson goes beyond the amiable platitudes of Congreve and exhibits insight of a high order. It is of course true that what he perceives in all of these poets is a confidence, not without arrogance, very similar to his own; but that is only to say that he is able, as in so many other instances, to generalize fruitfully from his private experience.[11] This insight leads to a double view of Dryden: on the one hand justly proud of his powerful abilities; on the other, pitiably mean in his stratagems of self-defense whenever he feels threatened. This view of Dry-

---

[11]"Though he was by nature diffident," Charles E. Ward says of Dryden, "he seems to have compensated somewhat by a self-confidence in his powers that was to strike some contemporaries as arrogance" (*Life of John Dryden*, p. 30). Exactly the same was true of Johnson, whose insecurity was probably none the weaker for being more successfully masked. As George Irwin writes, "Though Johnson was aware of his intellectual superiority, though, as Boswell says, he had a 'noble consciousness of his own abilities,' it was only an intellectual consciousness, a superficial awareness. He could not feel his superiority at the deeper emotional level, because he lacked that inner confidence which comes only with self-acceptance. He knew himself to be intellectually superior to most of his fellow students [at Oxford], but he did not *feel* that he was. Because of this painful breach between his thoughts and feelings, Sam Johnson strove incessantly for the balm of distinction" (*Samuel Johnson: A Personality in Conflict*, p. 44).

den had been fully formed many years before when Johnson discussed Dryden's specious defense of a much-derided line by producing a parallel in Virgil: "Every one sees the folly of such mean doublings to escape the persuit of criticism; nor is there a single reader of this poet, who would not have paid him greater veneration, had he shewn consciousness enough of his own superiority to set such cavils at defiance, and owned that he sometimes slipped into errors by the tumult of his imagination, and the multitude of his ideas" (*Rambler* 31).

What Johnson admires in Dryden, then, is the imagination and the ideas rather than the man. The rest of the character section continues to darken, conveying moral disapproval of an almost Olympian comprehensiveness. Dryden's indecency, for instance, is only made worse by the likelihood that it was cynically calculated.

His works afford too many examples of dissolute licentiousness and abject adulation; but they were probably, like his merriment, artificial and constrained—the effects of study and meditation, and his trade rather than his pleasure.

Of the mind that can trade in corruption, and can deliberately pollute itself with ideal wickedness for the sake of spreading the contagion in society, I wish not to conceal or excuse the depravity.—Such degradation of the dignity of genius, such abuse of superlative abilities, cannot be contemplated but with grief and indignation. What consolation can be had Dryden has afforded, by living to repent, and to testify his repentance. [Pp. 398-99]

So much for any defense of Dryden as no worse than his age.

After taking up several miscellaneous topics (Dryden's attitude toward priesthood, his passion for astrology, and so on), Johnson concludes, "So slight and scanty is the knowledge which I have been able to collect concerning the private life and domestick manners of a man, whom every English generation must mention with reverence as a critick and a poet" (p. 410). Not much is known about Dryden, and what little is known reveals him to be an unfortunate example of human weakness. But he does deserve "reverence," for in his works he largely overcomes his deficiencies and makes a virtue of the very narrowness that limits his attractiveness as a man. His genius, Johnson had written in another place, "was not very fertile of merriment, nor ductile to humour, but acute, argumentative, comprehensive, and sublime."[12]

After eighty pages on biography and character, Johnson turns to Dryden's intellectual achievement with obvious pleasure. "Dryden may be properly considered as the father of English criticism, as the writer who first taught us to determine upon principles the merit of composition" (p. 410). This is to assign him a very high place, one analogous to that of Aristotle, "the father of criticism" (*Life of Cowley*, I, 19), but remarkably enough there is no discussion of Dryden's actual opinions, which would be the main theme of any modern survey of his criticism. The famous "Heads of an Answer to Rymer," in fact, are printed at the end of the *Life* only so that "no particle of Dryden may be lost" (p. 471). Johnson does not ask himself why Dryden never published his answer to Rymer or whether it differs from the criticism he did publish.

The purpose of Johnson's discussion is to define the powers of mind that inform the criticism as a whole. The limitations are obvious: Dryden's formal learning (his "literature") was not extensive, and his involvement in controversy and self-justification vitiates much of what he says. "His occasional and particular positions were sometimes interested, sometimes negligent, and sometimes capricious. . . . When all arts are exhausted, like other hunted animals, he sometimes stands at bay. . . . What he wishes to say, he says at hazard. . . . His scholastick acquisitions seem not proportionate to his opportunities and abilities" (pp. 413-16). In these respects we see the same limitations that have occupied so much of the biographical section. But what really matters is that "the criticism of Dryden is the criticism of a poet . . . where delight is mingled with instruction, and where the author proves his right of judgement by his power of performance" (p. 412).

Dryden's greatness is seen as inseparable from his impatience with the laborious scholarship of a Rymer, who struggles toward truth "through thorns and brambles" (p. 413). His mind moves rapidly but is not therefore shallow. Johnson says in the *Preface*

---

[12]Final note on *Romeo and Juliet*, Yale *Works*, VIII, 957. Johnson's point is that Dryden, who made a joke about Mercutio, could never have created him; Dryden's abilities were of a different kind from Shakespeare's, narrower but nonetheless impressive.

that Shakespeare could draw wisdom from other sources than the classics. As for Dryden,

his works abound with knowledge, and sparkle with illustrations. There is scarcely any science or faculty that does not supply him with occasional images and lucky similitudes; every page discovers a mind very widely acquainted both with art and nature, and in full possession of great stores of intellectual wealth. . . . A mind like Dryden's, always curious, always active, to which every understanding was proud to be associated, and of which every one solicited the regard by an ambitious display of himself, had a more pleasant, perhaps a nearer, way to knowledge than by the silent progress of solitary reading. [P. 417]

Here at last Johnson can praise without reservation: to evaluate the power of the critical prose is to pay tribute to a master. It is not that Dryden—any more than Aristotle—can be accepted as an oracle. Johnson had written in an earlier *Life*, "To the critical sentence of Dryden the highest reverence would be due, were not his decisions often precipitate and his opinions immature" (*Life of Butler*, I, 217). What matters is that by participating in "the impetuosity of his genius" (p. 417) we are spurred into thought. What we value in Dryden is not specific opinions but something very like what Johnson called in Burke a perpetual "stream of mind" (*Life*, II, 450).

The brief description of Dryden's prose style supports this evaluation while paying homage to qualities at the opposite extreme from Johnson's own.

None of his prefaces were ever thought tedious. They have not the formality of a settled style, in which the first half of the sentence betrays the other. The clauses are never balanced, nor the periods modelled; every word seems to drop by chance, though it falls into its proper place. Nothing is cold or languid; the whole is airy, animated, and vigorous: what is little is gay; what is great is splendid. . . . Though all is easy, nothing is feeble; though all seems careless, there is nothing harsh; and though since his earlier works more than a century has passed they have nothing yet uncouth or obsolete. [P. 418]

Johnson is having a bit of fun with his own style, exemplifying precisely those features that are absent in Dryden's in a playful imitation of "Though deep, yet clear, though gentle, yet not dull." But there is also a handsome tribute here to a mind different from his own. "He who writes much," Johnson goes on, "will not easily escape a manner, such a recurrence of particular modes as may be easily noted." Johnson's style was forever being parodied; Dryden's "could not easily be imitated, either seriously or ludicrously," for it is altogether free of idiosyncrasy. And it seems evident that Johnson envies Dryden's fluency. "He that has once studiously formed a style," as he says in the *Life of Pope*, "rarely writes afterwards with complete ease" (III, 160).

The survey of Dryden's critical powers forms a suitable bridge between the two halves of the *Life*. Having described Dryden's mind in general terms, Johnson can now show it at work in the poems. In introducing this section, he touches on Dryden's role in literary history, a topic that will be dealt with again at the end of the *Life*. The reason it appears here is that in perfecting the couplet Dryden was not simply doing a favor to later poets, but was developing the truest expression of his own mind. We are not required to accept Johnson's assumptions about literary teleology, but we can respect the clarity with which he sees how much better Dryden is than Denham and Waller. "Their works were not many, nor were their minds of very ample comprehension" (pp. 419-20). Dryden is a giant standing on the shoulders of dwarfs.

But of course there are two aspects to Dryden's achievement. Though in one sense he was a perfectionist who "refined the language, improved the sentiments, and tuned the numbers of English Poetry" (p. 419), in another sense his poems, like his criticism, are the product of accidental occasions and careless haste. "His faults of negligence are beyond recital. Such is the unevenness of his compositions that ten lines are seldom found together without something of which the reader is ashamed" (p. 464). The mind that could urge its progress irresistibly through a "tumult of imagination" (*Rambler* 31) was well qualified to give force and sonority to the feeble numbers of Waller and Denham, but something more is still wanted: the teleological pattern awaits the advent of Pope.

Here it may be fairly charged that Johnson's acute understanding of Dryden's mind leads him to undervalue a certain aspect of the poetic achievement, which is that Dryden makes a virtue of the fact that most of his poems are occasional. When he takes up this subject Johnson handles it with great judiciousness and, once again, with insight that derives from his own experience.

The exigencies in which Dryden was condemned to pass his life are reasonably supposed to have blasted his genius, to have driven out his works in a state of immaturity, and to have intercepted the full-blown elegance which longer growth would have supplied. Poverty, like other rigid powers, is sometimes too hastily accused. If the excellence of Dryden's works was lessened by his indigence, their number was increased; and I know not how it will be proved that if he had written less he would have written better; or that indeed he would have undergone the toil of an author, if he had not been solicited by something more pressing than the love of praise. [Pp. 423-24]

But this is a negative verdict: Dryden's poems might not have been better if he had spent more time on them, but they are not so good as we could wish. "In an occasional performance," Johnson continues, "no height of excellence can be expected from any mind, however fertile in itself, and however stored with acquisitions."

On Johnson's behalf it may be urged that he may not be thinking of the longer poems, even though we have come to see that Dryden's most generalized works, such as *Religio Laici*, can accurately be called occasional in inspiration. Johnson recognizes that "as Dryden's genius was commonly excited by some personal regard he rarely writes upon a general topick" (p. 376), but he seems to assume that the smaller poems, though first-rate of their kind, deserve no searching critical examination. "In this volume are interspersed some short original poems [as opposed to translations], which, with his prologues, epilogues, and songs, may be comprised in Congreve's remark, that even those, if he had written nothing else, would have entitled him to the praise of excellence in his kind" (p. 456).

Johnson has placed himself in an awkward position here, for, as he seems partly to realize, the conditions that produce occasional poems are exactly the ones best suited to Dryden's genius. "Not only matter but time is wanting. The poem must not be delayed till the occasion is forgotten. The lucky moments of animated imagination cannot be attended; elegances and illustrations cannot be multiplied by gradual accumulation: the composition must be dispatched while conversation is yet busy and admiration fresh; and haste is to be made lest some other event should lay hold upon mankind" (p. 425). Dryden of all writers is the most fertile of spontaneous felicities, and compositions that "must be furnished immediately from the treasures of the mind" (p. 425) are ideally suited to his powers.

Nonetheless, Johnson has located something important in Dryden's poetry that holds it back from the highest excellence, even if he has not perfectly defined it. A hasty poem on a temporary subject may be a good one, but it is likely to be ephemeral. "Occasional poetry," he says in the *Life of Rowe*, "must often content itself with occasional praise" (II, 67). Modern Dryden criticism, allied with scholarship that seeks out the contemporary contexts of occasional verse, tends to admire too much what it has labored to explain: the more we have been able to find out about a poet's allusions, the more interesting his poem seems to us. Here again Johnson testifies to the response of the common reader, whose interest cannot be forced, though his esteem may be. We cannot always like those works which we know we should admire. Johnson's brilliant and affectionate critique of *Hudibras* is little known just because—as he foresaw—*Hudibras* itself has largely been forgotten.

Of *Hudibras* the manners, being founded on opinions, are temporary and local, and therefore become every day less intelligible and less striking. . . . Much therefore of that humour which transported the last century with merriment is lost to us, who do not know the sour solemnity, the sullen superstition, the gloomy moroseness, and the stubborn scruples of the ancient Puritans; or, if we know them, derive our information only from books or from tradition, have never had them before our eyes, and cannot but by recollection and study understand the lines in which they are satirised. Our grandfathers knew the picture from the life; we judge of the life by contemplating the picture. [*Life of Butler*, I, 213-14]

Whatever the specialist may persuade himself, Dryden often suffers from the same handicap. Rich with implication though *Religio Laici* and *The Hind and the Panther* are, they lack something that *Mac Flecknoe* has, for we need to know nothing more about Shadwell than Dryden tells us (and indeed tells us wrongly, since Shadwell was hardly the amiable cretin of Dryden's poem). Pope, in his unwearied care to improve his poems, seems to have

understood this matter well. *The Rape of the Lock* is inspired by
an obscure family quarrel, but its interest depends not at all on
our knowledge of it.

After the general introduction to Dryden's poems, Johnson
surveys them in chronological order. Again it looks as if he is
inept in matters of proportion, for by far the greatest space is
given to several early poems and to the late translation of Virgil.
But this is not a defect if we remember that his subject is Dryden's
poetic genius rather than a systematic critique of each of the
major poems. Seen in this light, there is much to be said for a
study of the poet's development at the start of his career and a
summary of his mature achievement as reflected in the one work
on which he bestowed long and diligent labor. No doubt Johnson
has taken pains to reread the early poems and is anxious to make
use of this reading, but it does not follow that the use he makes of
it is inappropriate.

The survey of Dryden's first published poems is intended to
show him learning to throw off "the ambition of forced conceits"
(p. 426) that at first captivated him, as in the schoolboy elegy on
Hastings, which is very properly dismissed in the biographical
section (pp. 332-33). Johnson makes no effort to assess these
poems as aesthetic wholes, but rather comments shrewdly on a
series of quotations from them. "In the verses to the lord chan-
cellor Clarendon . . .is a conceit so hopeless at the first view that
few would have attempted it, and so successfully laboured that
though at last it gives the reader more perplexity than pleasure,
and seems hardly worth the study that it costs, yet it must be
valued as a proof of a mind at once subtle and comprehensive"
(p. 428). The distinguishing features of Dryden's mind are thus
evident even while he struggles in the fetters of an obsolete
mode. Further on in the same poem occur "four lines, which
perhaps afford Dryden's first attempt at those penetrating remarks on human nature, for which he seems to have been
peculiarly formed." In the later poems, Johnson suggests, he was
wise enough to deal with subjects that were simpler and more
universal, and "did not often bring upon his anvil such stubborn
and unmalleable thoughts" (p. 429).

The extended study of *Annus Mirabilis* that follows supports
this view, though the poem is still seen as deficient in some

respects. It is written "with great diligence"(p. 430)—a perfect term for the impression it gives—and shows Dryden's characteristic powers still imperfectly adjusted to the subject he has chosen. "His description of the Fire is painted by resolute meditation, out of a mind better formed to reason than to feel" (p. 434). In his often denounced objection to "nautical language" (p. 433) Johnson detects a kind of pedantry: Dryden has learned these terms and is determined to show them off.

Likewise Johnson's discussion of *Absalom and Achitophel* is not really a critical analysis, but rather a series of reflections on the common reader's response to the poem. He is telling us not how to understand it but how to read it. Having praised the poem with great enthusiasm, he mentions three of its faults. The first, which no one has ever denied, is that the Biblical analogy must sometimes seemed forced: "Charles could not run continually parallel with David." The second and more important involves what the critic tends to forget, the fact that a work can be both excellent and tiresome. "A long poem of mere sentiments easily becomes tedious; though all the parts are forcible and every line kindles new rapture, the reader, if not relieved by the interposition of something that sooths the fancy, grows weary of admiration, and defers the rest" (p. 437). And finally Johnson points out the bathos of the ending in which a speech by Charles / David miraculously dispels the ominous revolt. It is no defense, though it is an explanation, to say that history had not yet worked itself out, or that Dryden wished to flatter Charles, or that he hoped Monmouth / Absalom would repent. "Who can forbear to think of an enchanted castle, with a wide moat and lofty battlements, walls of marble and gates of brass, which vanishes at once into air when the destined knight blows his horn before it?" (p. 437). The imagery is not merely playful. Dryden the hardheaded realist and political poet has abandoned reality for the wish-fulfilling fantasies of romance.

Johnson has now firmly established his interpretation of Dryden's poetry as expressive of his mind. The treatment of the later poems tends to be slight, and for some reason *Mac Flecknoe* is not mentioned at all, though in the biographical section it is called "a poem exquisitely satirical" (p. 383). The odes are praised rather extravagantly but too vaguely to convert readers, of whom there were many by the time of the *Lives*, for whom they represented obsolete bombast.[13] Of course we may wish that these poems had been treated more fully, but it is unlikely that the main lines of the analysis would have been much different.

Finally Johnson turns to Dryden's *Virgil*, which succeeded brilliantly in carrying out the principles of translation he had treated earlier (pp. 421-22). By way of introduction he mentions Dryden's version of Juvenal, which lacks "the dignity of the original," and his Persius, which "seems to have been written merely for wages, in an uniform mediocrity, without any eager endeavour after excellence or laborious effort of the mind" (p. 447). Had Dryden done no more than this for Virgil we could not have been surprised. Furthermore he was faced with greater obstacles than would later confront Pope, since "the discriminative excellence of Homer is elevation and comprehension of thought, and that of Virgil is grace and splendor of diction. The beauties of Homer are therefore difficult to be lost, and those of Virgil difficult to be retained" (pp. 447-48). But for once Dryden rose to the occasion, and amply fulfilled his role as a literary hero: "All these obstacles Dryden saw, and all these he determined to encounter. The expectation of his work was undoubtedly great; the nation considered its honour as interested in the event. . . . The hopes of the publick were not disappointed. He produced, says Pope, 'the most noble and spirited translation that I know in any language' " (pp. 448-49).

By way of illustrating Dryden's triumph Johnson quotes from an attack by Luke Milbourne. Dryden, to whom critics had given such pain throughout his life, is at last invulnerable to their impotent rage. "Such were the strictures of Milbourne, who found few abettors" (p. 453). Two competing translations are next described with measured irony: "Those who could find faults thought they could avoid them; and Dr. Brady attempted in blank verse a translation of the *Eneid*, which, when dragged into the world, did not live long enough to cry. I have never seen

[13]Gilbert Wakefield, in an edition of Gray, objected indignantly to Johnson's "extravagant encomiums" on Dryden's Killigrew ode,"a performance infinitely inferiour to any production of *Mr. Gray*; a model indeed of almost every vice of composition; full fraught with sentiments at once puerile, low, and turgid; and debased by meanness of expression" (*The Poems of Mr. Gray with Notes by Gilbert Wakefield, B.A.* [1786], p. 121).

it; but that such a version there is, or has been, perhaps some old catalogue informed me. With not much better success Trapp . . .attempted another blank version of the *Eneid*. . . .His book may continue its existence as long as it is the clandestine refuge of schoolboys" (p. 453). Dryden now reigns serene, though Shadwell had usurped the laurel. His critic and his competitors have gone with Elkanah Settle into the shades. Of Milbourne Johnson says that "the world has forgotten his book" (p. 449), and it is exhumed for a moment here only to exalt Dryden. Trapp's bitter fate is to survive as a crib, and Brady would not exist at all if he were not rescued from the flotsam of literary history by Johnson's capacious memory.

The discussion of Dryden's *Virgil* leads at once, by way of a refusal to compare it with later versions, to Johnson's central affirmation of Dryden's greatness as a poet, which in turn rises to an eloquent statement of literary value.

It is not by comparing line with line that the merit of great works is to be estimated, but by their general effects and ultimate result. It is easy to note a weak line, and write one more vigorous in its place; . . .but what is given to the parts may be subducted from the whole, and the reader may be weary though the critick may commend. Works of imagination excel by their allurement and delight; by their power of attracting and detaining the attention. That book is good in vain which the reader throws away. He only is the master who keeps the mind in pleasing captivity; whose pages are perused with eagerness, and in hope of new pleasure are perused again; and whose conclusion is perceived with an eye of sorrow, such as the traveller casts upon departing day. [P. 454]

This passage, which I have already quoted as describing the ideal receptiveness of the common reader, is the climax of the *Life of Dryden* and a testimony to Johnson's specific excellence as a critic. After everything that can be said against Dryden both as man and as poet, after all his failures to write poems wholly worthy of himself, still he is a master who holds the mind in pleasing captivity and communicates the pleasure without which literature is composed in vain. This view is eloquently confirmed when Johnson comes to comment on the *Aeneid* of Christopher Pitt: "If the two versions are compared, perhaps the result would be, that Dryden leads the reader forward by his general vigour and sprightliness, and Pitt often stops him to contemplate the excellence of a single couplet; that Dryden's faults are forgotten in the hurry of delight, and that Pitt's beauties are neglected in the languor of a cold and listless perusal; that Pitt pleases the criticks, and Dryden the people; that Pitt is quoted, and Dryden read" (*Life of Pitt*, III, 279).

The *Fables* are briefly dismissed—it is hard to know why Johnson is so severe—and the *Life* concludes with "a general survey of Dryden's labours," the theme of which is "a vigorous genius operating upon large materials" (p. 457). I shall not analyze this fine discussion in detail, since most of it has been anticipated elsewhere in the *Life*; it is filled with memorable statements whose aphoristic conciseness has been earned by the cumulative force of the *Life* as a whole.

With the simple and elemental passions, as they spring separate in the mind, he seems not much acquainted. . . . Sentences were readier at his call than images; he could more easily fill the ear with some splendid novelty than awaken those ideas that slumber in the heart. . . . He delighted to tread upon the brink of meaning. . . . There is surely reason to suspect that he pleased himself as well as his audience; and that these [rants], like the harlots of other men, had his love, though not his approbation. . . . Dryden was no rigid judge of his own pages. . . . What was said of Rome, adorned by Augustus, may be applied by an easy metaphor to English poetry embellished by Dryden, "lateritiam invenit, marmoream reliquit," he found it brick, and he left it marble. [Pp. 457-69]

This is not literary criticism as we are accustomed to practice it today; we must look elsewhere than in Johnson for scrupulous explications of Dryden's poems. More than that, Johnson does not seriously try to prove the very existence of this mental energy, this power of captivating the reader. His discussion might be more persuasive if it included illustrative quotations from Dryden's works. He may have neglected to provide these for any number of reasons (it did not occur to him; it occurred to him but he was lazy). More probably, however, he simply saw no use in doing so, for the same reason that explains his dogged defense of the *de gustibus* principle. By analysis of quotations one may easily show that Dryden has a fertile imagination and a mastery of the couplet form; one may possibly show (what is not so easy) that his poems are coherent wholes. This, however, is essentially description, such as Johnson does offer in his one extensive use of quotation, the account of the metaphysical poets in the *Life of Cowley*. What no amount of quotation and analysis can do is to persuade a hostile reader to *like* Dryden.

Essentially Johnson is offering an appreciation of Dryden's mind. He can hope to forestall our objections to Dryden's character and to the unevenness of the poems that such a character produces, by showing that these need not be inconsistent with a high regard for the poetry itself—the poetry rather than the poems. More than this Johnson will not do. Readers who feel they cannot like Dryden will not be compelled to do so by Johnson, though they may learn not to give irrelevant or inadequate reasons for their dislike. Readers who do like Dryden, on the other hand, will find their appreciation deepened and clarified by Johnson's example. If the *Life of Dryden* is not criticism in the usual sense, neither is it biography, if by that we mean an image of a man's everyday personality and a careful record of his affairs. It is, instead, an achievement of a very remarkable kind, a wholly convincing demonstration of Dryden's essential greatness. If it is neither biography nor criticism in the usual sense, it is something no less valuable, for it performs what Eliot called "the great, the perennial, task of criticism," which is "to bring the poet back to life."[14]

[14]T.S. Eliot, "Andrew Marvell," *Selected Essays* (London, 1951), p. 292.

8   Pope: The Fulfillment of Genius

THE LAST MAJOR PERFORMANCE in the *Lives of the Poets* is the *Life of Pope*. It attracted attention at once by its range and depth. "*Pope, agminis instar* [equal to an army] occupies the whole of the VIIth volume," wrote one of the first reviewers.[1] This *Life* is full of biographical detail and reflects an obvious affection on the part of the author; Boswell (repeating the phrase that was applied to the *Life of Dryden*) said that it was written "*con amore*" (*Life*, IV, 46). Not surprisingly it has generally been regarded as the finest of the *Lives*. Lately, however, it has come under attack in various ways and has been shown to be neither so unified nor so effortlessly persuasive as was formerly supposed.[2]

Much of the difficulty can be explained by the fact that once again Johnson is not writing literary criticism in the modern academic sense. In attempting to define the excellence of this *Life*, I shall concentrate not on its critical survey but on two main themes that dominate it and carry the reader through its most uneven stretches. The first is the analysis of Pope's powers of mind in relation to his character, to his works, and to Dryden in the famous comparison of the two poets. The second is the moral assessment of Pope as man and poet, exploring the ambiguities of his own preferred stance of moral censor and conscience of his age. Johnson deals very skillfully with the relations between art and life: he knows that the two are different, but also that they are interdependent, particularly in an avowed moralist like Pope.

A serious problem in the *Life of Dryden*, as we have seen, is the scarcity of biographical information. In writing about Pope,

---

[1] *Gentleman's Magazine*, 51 (1781), 226.
[2] Benjamin Boyce, "Samuel Johnson's Criticism of Pope in the *Life of Pope*," *Review of English Studies*, NS 5 (1954), 37-46, shows how desultory Johnson's research was and how often he depended on previous writers to stimulate his critical judgments. F. W. Hilles further documents this view in his interesting study "The Making of *The Life of Pope*," in *New Light on Dr. Johnson*, pp. 257-84. The various issues involved are well analyzed by Lawrence Lipking in *The Ordering of the Arts*, pp. 448-54.

Johnson could at last draw upon a marvelous wealth of information, ranging from the reminiscences of his friend Savage, through Spence's not yet published manuscript of anecdotes, to interviews with people like Lord Marchmont. In the index to the Hill-Powell edition of the *Life of Johnson* Pope occupies five columns, Shakespeare less than four, Milton and Dryden two each; the disproportion is due mainly to the frequency with which remarks about Pope's life and poems enter the ordinary conversation of people living only a generation later. For Johnson, Pope is the great modern poet.

Because so much biographical material is available, Johnson is able to deduce character from conduct with unusual confidence and to describe the poet's career with more coherence than was possible for Dryden. I shall not discuss every aspect of this impressive section, which occupies over a hundred pages (*Lives*, III, 82-196), but only those that contribute directly to establishing Pope's moral and intellectual character. As in the *Dryden*, the middle section of the *Life*, though presented as a formal character sketch, is developed from the evidence of the first section.

Having surveyed Pope's birth and early education, Johnson pauses for reflection at the point where Pope himself first paused. "Of a youth so successfully employed, and so conspicuously improved, a minute account must be naturally desired; but curiosity must be contented with confused, imperfect, and sometimes improbable intelligence. Pope, finding little advantage from external help, resolved thenceforward to direct himself, and at twelve formed a plan of study which he completed with little other incitement than the desire of excellence" (III, 86). For Pope's later life there will be more information, but the point has been made that he was an autodidact who formed his own mind almost without help. And we are made to see that the governing influence in Pope's life is "the desire of excellence," which was to become "voracity of fame" (p. 136) by the time he first collected his works at the age of twenty-nine. In a way the comparison with Dryden is foreshadowed here; Dryden, who was educated at a great school and university, "does not appear to have been eager of poetical distinction, or to have lavished his early wit either on fictitious subjects or publick occasions" (*Life of Dryden*, I, 333).

As Johnson moves forward through the biographical section,

he conveys a sense of unhurried ease, giving every incident or anecdote the amplitude it deserves, while establishing a number of points that will be developed later as manifestations of character. The boyhood friendship with Sir William Trumbull elicits the remark "Pope was through his whole life ambitious of splendid acquaintance, and he seems to have wanted neither diligence nor success in attracting the notice of the great" (p. 90). Just as "the desire of excellence" will become "voracity of fame," so this relatively mild judgment will later turn severe:

> Next to the pleasure of contemplating his possessions seems to be that of enumerating the men of high rank with whom he was acquainted, and whose notice he loudly proclaims not to have been obtained by any practices of meanness or servility; a boast which was never denied to be true, and to which very few poets have ever aspired. [P. 204]

> His scorn of the Great is repeated too often to be real: no man thinks much of that which he despises; and as falsehood is always in danger of inconsistency he makes it his boast at another time that he lives among them. [P. 211]

At the beginning, however, Johnson is gentler and more amused at the spectacle of the adolescent author initiating himself in the preoccupations of his career. "It is pleasant to remark how soon Pope learned the cant of an author, and began to treat criticks with contempt, though he had yet suffered nothing from them" (p. 91). This author's cant soon precipitates the unedifying dispute with John Dennis, from which neither party emerges with much credit. Pope is clearly subtler and wittier than his unwieldy opponent, but the controversy exhibits him in an unattractive role that he will often play again; he pretends to vindicate Addison rather than himself with "disingenuous hostility" and claims that he feels outrage only for his friend, though "Addison was not a man on whom such cant of sensibility could make much impression" (p. 106).

Pope, then, is above all an author: he lives to write, and shows equal parts of vanity and genuine love of excellence. Accordingly Johnson gives a long account of the translation of the *Iliad* (pp. 108-36), which represents the crucial turning point in Pope's career, making him supreme among English poets and wealthy as well. The complications of the venture are handled in an interesting narrative that combines striking quotations from Spence—Pope "wished, as he said, 'that somebody would hang him' " (p. 112)—and judicious pronouncements on disputed points—"it is not very likely that he overflowed with Greek" (p. 113). The protraction of the work is sympathetically viewed: "He that runs against Time, has an antagonist not subject to casualties" (p. 117). A long series of variant readings illustrates Pope's poetic care. And finally the publication of the work leads to the ruptures with Halifax and Addison, each of which is discussed with great penetration: "Their commerce had its beginning in hope of praise on one side, and of money on the other, and ended because Pope was less eager of money than Halifax of praise. . . . The reputation of this great work failed of gaining him a patron; but it deprived him of a friend. Addison and he were now at the head of poetry and criticism; and both in such a state of elevation, that, like the two rivals in the Roman state, one could no longer bear an equal, nor the other a superior" (pp. 127-28).

For the first time since the *Life of Savage* three decades earlier, Johnson is able to write with the confidence that he really *knows* his subject; instead of piecing together the evidence about Waller or Milton or Swift to guess at an ambiguous personality, he can move through the minutiae of biography with complete assurance that he knows what to look for and how to interpret it. He is not always fair to Pope, but he is very seldom irrelevant; even his ungenerous account of the famous grotto implies, as Maynard Mack has said, a shrewd sense of what it reveals about Pope's character.[3] Johnson apparently has no inkling of the symbolic meanings of the grotto that Mack has explored, but he is sensitive to its ethical implications.

The biography marches forward until it ends with Pope's death, the sorrow and love of his friends, and a tragicomedy surrounding the discovery of an unauthorized edition of Bolingbroke's *Patriot King* that leads to Pope's admirers squab-

---

[3]"Much in Pope's career, I think we must agree, *was* determined by an effort to extract ornament from inconvenience of a rather painful kind—to find, or make, some ground for pride in all too visible defects" (*The Garden and the City: Retirement and Politics in the Later Poetry of Pope* [Toronto, 1969], p. 61).

bling over his grave in a most unseemly manner. "Bolingbroke, however, was not yet satisfied; his thirst of vengeance excited him to blast the memory of the man over whom he had wept in his last struggles, and he employed Mallet, another friend of Pope, to tell the tale to the publick with all its aggravations. Warburton, whose heart was warm with his legacy and tender by the recent separation, thought it proper for him to interpose" (pp. 193-94). The effect is rather like that of the wild story about Dryden's funeral; the living have their own affairs to look to and carry on the spirit of controversy in which Pope had so eagerly taken part. Although Johnson here accepts Warburton's extenuation of Pope's conduct, he cannot let the subject alone and comes back to it with reflections that put the dead man on a level with the undignified survivors: "His unjustifiable impression of *The Patriot King*, as it can be imputed to no particular motive, must have proceeded from his general habit of secrecy and cunning: he caught an opportunity of a sly trick, and pleased himself with the thought of outwitting Bolingbroke" (pp. 200-201).

The special excellence of the *Life of Pope*, whatever its faults may be, lies in the way this kind of analysis is related to the works. In the *Dryden* a rather unpleasant personality was shown to be more or less irrelevant to the greatness of the poetry, though it helped to explain the unevenness of the poems. Here both poetry and poems are intimately related to character. Pope would not have chosen his subjects or developed his mode of versification if he had not been vain, cunning, and ambitious of lasting fame.

As the biographical section continues, Johnson's moral judgments are pronounced with increasingly magisterial weight: "The man who threatens the world is always ridiculous; for the world can easily go on without him, and in a short time will cease to miss him. I have heard of an idiot who used to revenge his vexations by lying all night upon the bridge. 'There is nothing,' says Juvenal, 'that a man will not believe in his own favour.' Pope had been flattered till he thought himself one of the moving powers in the system of life. When he talked of laying down his pen, those who sat round him intreated and implored, and self-love did not suffer him to suspect that they went away and laughed" (pp. 153-54). It seems outrageous to compare Pope with the idiot on the bridge, but Johnson makes the comparison work: the great poet is descending to absurdly childish behavior. Johnson took some pains with the sentence, which in the proof sheet (as Hill's note mentions) had read "an idiot who used to enforce his demands by threatening to beat his head against the wall." That would be too obvious, too childish; so Johnson substitutes the more passive "revenge" of the bridge. Immediately afterwards the tone of moral superiority, which might arouse resentment in the reader, is supported by an allusion to Juvenal (a severer satirist than Pope's Horace, and identified with Johnson through his two imitations).

The final effect of the passage is not of hostility, but rather of disappointment that Pope should diminish his own greatness and give the flatterers "who sat round him" an occasion to laugh at him. And as he so often does Johnson takes care to follow a negative passage with a favorable one, describing Pope's "filial piety" as warmly as Warburton's creature Ruffhead could do,[4] and concluding with the solemn statement "Whatever was his pride, to them he was obedient; and whatever was his irritability, to them he was gentle. Life has, among its soothing and quiet comforts, few things better to give than such a son" (p. 154).

Having developed Pope's character throughout the long biographical section, Johnson describes it more formally in the longest and most finished character section of any of the *Lives*, and effects a more convincing transition to the critical section than in any other *Life*. Beginning with an analysis of Pope's personality and moral character (pp. 196-223), he goes on to define his intellectual character both in itself and by contrast with Dryden's (pp. 216-223). In the opinion of George Sherburn, "He understood Pope's personality better than any one else has seemed to do. . . . One feels that on the whole Johnson understood Pope both man and artist better than any one can

---

[4] The story has often been told how Pope's arrogant commentator Warburton frightened off the inoffensive Spence from writing a biography, but could never get round to writing one himself. In the end he caused Owen Ruffhead to bring out *The Life of Alexander Pope* (1769) of which Johnson said, "He knew nothing of Pope and nothing of poetry' (*Life*, II, 166-67). Ruffhead has a long hymn to Pope's filial piety and loyalty to friends (pp. 484-98).

ever understand him now that he has been dead nearly two centuries."[5]

The nature of Johnson's understanding may be illustrated by the following passage:

> He was fretful and easily displeased, and allowed himself to be capriciously resentful. He would sometimes leave Lord Oxford silently, no one could tell why, and was to be courted back by more letters and messages than the footmen were willing to carry. The table was indeed infested by Lady Mary Wortley, who was the friend of Lady Oxford, and who, knowing his peevishness, could by no intreaties be restrained from contradicting him, till their disputes were sharpened to such asperity that one or the other quitted the house.
>
> He sometimes condescended to be jocular with servants or inferiors; but by no merriment, either of others or his own, was he ever seen excited to laughter. [P. 202]

This behavior is interesting in itself, as expressive of personality, but it has a larger interest too. Johnson remarks later on, "A man of such exalted superiority and so little moderation would naturally have all his delinquencies observed and aggravated: those who could not deny that he was excellent would rejoice to find that he was not perfect" (p. 215). It is after all because Pope was a great poet that we want to know about him, and the account Johnson has been giving is highly relevant to an understanding of a satirist. Pope, who so often expressed superiority to most of mankind, need not be surprised if mankind are eager to know his faults. And the faults Johnson describes are certainly reflected in the satires: Pope holds his laughter under strict constraints; he is condescending to inferiors; he is given to peevishness and capricious resentment; he is quick to quarrel and will not appear at a friend's table when it is "infested" (a nice term) by someone against whom he harbors a grudge.

Following the discursive and anecdotal treatment of Pope's general character comes the condensed and highly polished analysis of "his intellectual character" (p. 216), leading to the famous comparison with Dryden (which represents Johnson's fundamental effort to place Pope in literary history and will be discussed later). The third section of the *Life*, in which Pope's

[5]*The Early Career of Alexander Pope* (Oxford, 1934), pp. 13, 15.

works are taken up one by one, has always been regarded as relatively weak; it seems probable that Johnson wrote it without rereading the poems, recurring to some of his old *idées fixes* (sound-and-sense from the *Rambler*, the theodicy of the *Essay on Man* from the Jenyns review). While the critical section is far from valueless, it does not offer the most fruitful grounds for discussion.[6] What is most valuable in this section is the treatment of Pope's role as satirist. Johnson manages to do justice both to the integrity of the poems and to our interest, which refuses to be argued away, in the animus and motives that lie behind them. He does not give us an extended reading of the *Dunciad*, but he forces us to think about important questions that the *Dunciad* suggests in the admittedly blurry region between criticism and moral judgment.

Victorian critics took it for granted that Pope's satire was the malicious waspishness of a deformed personality, and even when they enjoyed it found ways to express moral disapproval. Macaulay, deploring a prose work in which Pope departs from his mastery of verse satire, likens him to "a wolf, which, instead of biting, should take to kicking, or a monkey which should try to sting." The issue for such critics is that Pope attacks not only mankind in general but specific people who can be shown to have been the object of personal resentment. The classic defense of Pope used to take two forms. First, it was argued that his enemies were bad writers and deserved contempt for failing to understand, in Geoge Sherburn's words, "that inferior writing

---

[6]F. W. Hilles discusses Johnson's carelessness in the critical section and shows that his comments are almost all inspired by two sources only, Warton and Ruffhead ("Making of *The Life of Pope*," pp 268-72). I would not defend everything in this section, but some parts of it have been condemned too strongly. Johnson's inclusion of his twenty-five-year-old essay on Pope's Epitaphs has been thought gratuitous, but it is intended to encourage "the cultivation of propriety" (p. 254) and thus is directed to the precise quality in which Pope desired to excel. Again, Johnson is wrong to dismiss Pope's Horatian imitations, but it is unjust to make the ad hominem retort that his own most ambitious poems are imitations. I imagine he included his own efforts in the judgment that "what is easy is seldom excellent: such imitations cannot give pleasure to common readers. . . . Between Roman images and English manners there will be an irreconcileable dissimilitude" (p. 247). This is not a fair appraisal of Pope's imitations, but it probably reflects a considered view that the kind of poetry in which Johnson had made his major attempts, many years before, was far from the noblest kind.

or pretentious claims to fame are crimes for a litterateur." The
second defense was that Pope's enemies were as bad as he.
According to Geoffrey Tillotson, "In judging the nature of
Pope's personal satire one has to remember that it does not stand
alone, that it exists in a thick context of abuse. Pope is not sharp,
cruel, nasty and his fellow satirists gentle and clean. They are all
as sharp, cruel, and nasty as they can be. And all of them,
including Pope, write as well as they can, that is, make as much of
their material as possible. Pope and the others always use against
a man as much as they can find—truth or rumour about his
person, character, history, habits." It follows that nothing is too
much for these desperate fellows, even the unedifying moment
when Pope administered an emetic to the bookseller Curll, a
stratagem that has been admired on the grounds that Pope was
too small to have physically beaten Curll. "Even in 1735," Sherburn remarks with mild surprise, "Curll could still remember the
emetic."[7] I should think he might.

The trouble with this defense is that its two parts, on close
examination, turn out to be contradictory. If bad writing is really
the object of Pope's wrath, why attack bad writers for personal
failings rather than for writing badly? And if the whole mass of
writers at that time were reckless in abuse and innuendo, why
regard Pope as rising above them in moral superiority? More
recently, therefore, a subtler defense has been put forward, in
which it is shown that Pope uses the accidental peculiarities of
individual victims to elaborate a vision of absolute evil; the victims are important only as emblematic figures in this moral
design. Leonard Welsted complained that Pope attacked him
and other writers not for their writing but for their lives, "calling
Gentlemen Scoundrels, Blockheads, Garreteers, and Beggars."
But this only shows, as Welsted's editor explains, "that most of
the Dunces were no more able to read satire properly than were
Pope's nineteenth-century critics. They were, as Pope quite
properly kept pointing out, very bad writers and very dull men.

---

[7]T. B. Macaulay, "The Life and Writings of Addison" (1843), in *Critical,
Historical, and Miscellaneous Essays* (New York, 1876), V, 395. Sherburn, pp. 150,
171 (though he does call the emetic episode "pitiful conduct," p. 172); Tillotson, *On the Poetry of Pope*, p. 33.

The *ethos* of the satiric *persona* was something they could not understand."[8]

The difficulty is that Pope presented himself, and his modern admirers wish to present him, as a moralist. If he is a moralist, then he must have some demonstrable right to moral authority. After the failure of the older defense, according to which one moralist is as good as another when the administration of emetics is the order of the day, it seemed best to locate moral authority within the poems, in the *personae* that Welsted failed to appreciate, rather than in the life of the poet. The obvious circularity of such a procedure has been ably demonstrated by Irvin Ehrenpreis, and need not be enlarged upon here.[9] To say that the device of the *persona* is not morally self-justifying is not to deny its importance in Pope's work, or the fact that he uses it rhetorically to persuade us of his moral rectitude. "For effective attack," Northrop Frye observes, "we must reach some kind of impersonal level, and that commits the attacker, if only by implication, to a moral standard. The satirist commonly takes a high moral line. Pope asserts that he is 'To Virtue only and her friends a friend,' suggesting that that is what he is really being when he is reflecting on the cleanliness of the underwear worn by the lady who had jilted him."[10]

I have dwelt on this issue because it is a central one in modern criticism of Pope and because Johnson is remarkably good at helping us to thread our way through this maze. It is sometimes asserted that Johnson disliked or feared satire, but I see little evidence of this. He told Boswell that "the sense of ridicule is given us, and may be lawfully used," in contradiction of a pious writer who "would have us treat all men alike" (*Life*, III, 379-80).

[8]Leonard Welsted, *One Epistle to Mr. A. Pope* (1730), in *Two Poems Against Pope*, ed. Joseph V. Guerinot, Augustan Reprint Society No. 114 (Los Angeles, 1965), pp. vi (Welsted's Preface), i (Guerinot's Introduction).

[9]"If we deduce the intention of a poem from the attitudes implicit in the sentiments of the poet, we shall inevitably discover that the speaker of the poem has sentiments appropriate to its purpose. ...If such an approach is valid, Pope was inept, because the speaker of the *Epistle* [*to Arbuthnot*] appeals continuously to history, resting his defense upon the verifiable truth of his data" ("Personae," *Literary Meaning and Augustan Values*, p. 55).

[10]*Anatomy of Criticism*, p. 225.

One way in which Johnson preferred Pope to Swift was almost
certainly Pope's reliance on "personal satire," attacks on identifi-
able individuals, as opposed to Swift's "general satire" on mankind.[11] In attacking individuals, what matters is that the satirist
choose a target who really deserves contempt. Johnson would
entirely agree with the principle in Swift's *Verses on the Death of Dr.
Swift:*

> He spar'd a Hump or crooked Nose,
> Whose Owners set not up for Beaux.
> True genuine Dulness mov'd his Pity,
> Unless it offer'd to be witty.

[467-70]

Shakespeare's Aguecheek, Johnson says, "is drawn with great
propriety, but his character is, in a great measure, that of natural
fatuity, and is therefore not the proper prey of a satirist" (Yale
Works, VII, 326).

Both Dryden and Pope, in Johnson's view, selected their principal targets justly. *Mac Flecknoe* is "a poem exquisitely satirical"
(*Life of Dryden*, I, 383), and the *Dunciad* is "perhaps the best
specimen that has yet appeared of personal satire ludicrously
pompous" (*Life of Pope*, III, 241). In the first version of the
Dunciad Theobald was the hero. Johnson tells us that Pope chose
Theobald in revenge for "having revised Shakespeare more
happily than himself" (p. 146), but Theobald deserved the
treatment he got and (as Johnson wryly noted earlier) had Pope
to thank for an undeserved measure of fame. "Theobald, thus
weak and ignorant, thus mean and faithless, thus petulant and
ostentatious, by the good luck of having Pope for his enemy, has
escaped, and escaped alone, with reputation, from this undertaking [of editing Shakespeare]. So willingly does the world
support those who solicite favour, against those who command
reverence; and so easily is he praised, whom no man can envy"

[11]Johnson condemns "the general lampooner of mankind" in *Idler* 45. Mrs.
Thrale reported on two occasions his "aversion to general satire"(*Miscellanies*, I,
223, 327). Of the second instance she added that "for the most part [he]
professed himself to feel directly contrary to Dr. Swift; 'who (says he) hates the
world, though he loves John and Robert, and certain individuals.' Johnson said
always, 'that the world was well constructed, but that the particular people
disgraced the elegance and beauty of the general fabric.'"

(*Preface*, p. 96). When Colley Cibber replaced Theobald it was unfortunate that Pope retained "the old books, the cold pedantry and sluggish pertinacity of Theobald" (*Life of Pope*, III, 186), but this is an aesthetic, not a moral judgment. Cibber too deserved what he got. Indeed Johnson had been accustomed to attack Cibber himself with an asperity that excited comment.[12]

Pope's victims, then, really are bad writers, and deserve to be censured as such. "He that writes," Johnson had said in *Rambler* 93, "may be considered as a kind of general challenger, whom every one has a right to attack; since he quits the common rank of life, steps forward beyond the lists, and offers his merit to the publick judgment. To commence author is to claim praise, and no man can justly aspire to honour, but at the hazard of disgrace." The same principle is stated in the *Life of Pope*: "An author places himself uncalled before the tribunal of criticism, and solicits fame at the hazard of disgrace. Dulness or deformity are not culpable in themselves, but may be very justly reproached when they pretend to the honour of wit or the influence of beauty. If bad writers were to pass without reprehension what should restrain them? . . . The satire which brought Theobald and Moore into contempt, dropped impotent from Bentley, like the javelin of Priam" (pp. 241-42). There are perhaps two allusions to Swift here: first to the lines about dullness offering to be witty, and second to the javelin (though it is not Priam's) with which Boyle pierces Bentley in *The Battle of the Books*.

So long as bad writing is at issue, the satirist's motives are not especially important. Undoubtedly Theobald and Cibber aroused Pope's special ire, but as bad writers they deserve re-

---

[12]Johnson had written, probably in 1741, "Great George's acts let tuneful Cibber sing; / For nature form'd the poet for the king" (Yale *Works*, VI, 70). In the *Compleat Vindication of the Licensers of the Stage* (1739) he had suggested that Cibber might be helpful in repairing heavily censored plays: "In many parts, indeed, the speeches will be imperfect, and the action appear not regularly conducted, but the poet laureate may easily supply these vacuities, by inserting some of his own verses in praise of wealth, luxury, and venality" (1825 *Works*, V, 342). Commenting on the phrase "the mists which poverty and Cibber had spread" in the *Life of Savage*, Edmund Cartwright wrote, "Whenever Dr. Johnson has occasion to speak of Cibber, it is with an acrimony that, in any other man, we should suspect must have proceeded from personal resentment" (*Monthly Review*, 65 [1781], 408).

buke; "he that refines the publick taste is a publick benefactor" (p. 242). Contrariwise, mistaken criticism of good writers (or scholars, like Bentley) will fail of its effect and can be dismissed as harmless. What is wrong—as Welsted maintained—is to attack bad writers for being bad men, as in the ambiguous suggestion that Burnet and Duckett were homosexuals (mentioned on p. 151), or the endless taunts of which Johnson says, "The great topick of his ridicule is poverty: the crimes with which he reproaches his antagonists are their debts, their habitation in the Mint, and their want of a dinner" (p. 204). Pope's defense would be that these men should have chosen some career that could provide financial support and that they lack even an economic reason for persisting in writing badly. But Johnson may yet be right about the rhetorical effect of Pope's attack: instead of despising the dunces' writings because of their innate worthlessness, he seems at times to despise them only because their authors are not rich. How strongly Johnson disliked this note of superiority we know from the Jenyns review: "This author and Pope, perhaps, never saw the miseries which they imagine thus easy to be borne. The poor . . .are not pained by casual incivility, or mortified by the mutilation of a compliment; but this happiness is like that of a malefactor, who ceases to feel the cords that bind him, when the pincers are tearing his flesh" (1825 *Works*, VI, 54-55).

Hervey as Sporus may indeed reflect evil incarnate, but Johnson, though he admires the *Epistle to Arbuthnot* precisely because Pope's self-vindication has called forth great poetry, will not allow the exaggerations of the Sporus passage to be excused on rhetorical or symbolic grounds. "As there is no stronger motive to exertion than self-defence, no part has more elegance, spirit, or dignity than the poet's vindication of his own character. The meanest passage is the satire upon Sporus" (p. 246). Of another instance Johnson says, "Aaron Hill, who was represented as diving for the prize, expostulated with Pope in a manner so much superior to all mean solicitation, that Pope was reduced to sneak and shuffle, sometimes to deny and sometimes to apologize: he first endeavours to wound, and is then afraid to own that he meant a blow" (p. 151). Nothing could be more telling than the allusion to Pope's own portrait of

Atticus / Addison, "Willing to wound, and yet afraid to strike."

The dunces, then, deserve to be ridiculed, but Pope is not always careful to limit his ridicule to dunces or to attack them on the proper grounds. And Pope's satires, furthermore, tell us a good deal about him; it is not by accident that he has chosen this mode or that he enjoys it so much. Johnson knows the difference between biography and criticism; the *Dunciad* is a better poem, not a worse one, because Pope felt his enmities so keenly. For that very reason it is relevant to discuss the animus that feeds the poems, as it feeds the work of other satirists. Dryden's contribution to Tate's continuation of *Absalom and Achitophel*, Johnson says, "for poignancy of satire exceeds any part of the former. Personal resentment, though no laudable motive to satire, can add great force to general principles. Self-love is a busy prompter" (*Life of Dryden*, I, 437). A great satire, moreover, is not a sermon; it may have moral implications but it has other implications too. "That the design was moral," Johnson says of the *Dunciad*, "whatever the author might tell either his readers or himself, I am not convinced" (p. 241).

Johnson's assessment is marvelously balanced in its willingness to see moral weakness without delivering moral denunciations like those of the Victorian critics of Pope the monkey. "In this design [of avenging himself on Theobald] there was petulance and malignity enough; but I cannot think it very criminal" (p. 241). The term *malignity* recurs throughout the *Life of Pope*: "to a cool reader of the present time" Pope's prose reply to Hervey "exhibits nothing but tedious malignity" (p. 179); "the incessant and unappeasable malignity of Pope" (p. 185); "his malignity to Philips" (p. 213). This sounds unpleasant enough, but Johnson is well aware that a person may reveal different qualities at the same time. "He was sometimes wanton in his attacks, and before Chandos, Lady Wortley, and Hill, was mean in his retreat. The virtues which seem to have had most of his affection were liberality and fidelity of friendship, in which it does not appear that he was other than he describes himself" (p. 213).

Pope is neither monkey nor saint. His motives and the works inspired by them must be judged alike as each occasion requires. The poems may have moral implications, but not simply because

Pope tells us so. A work like the *Dunciad* is inspired, as Jóhnson says of one of Dryden's critics, "by stronger resentment than bad poetry can excite" (*Life of Dryden*, I, 449) and does not represent a morally uniform whole. Likewise Pope really was a good friend and son, but it does not follow that we must accept everything he says of himself, particularly in his letters. "Of his social qualities, if an estimate be made from his Letters, an opinion too favourable cannot easily be formed; they exhibit a perpetual and unclouded effulgence of general benevolence and particular fondness" (p. 206). Benevolence and malignity are both characteristic of Pope.

Finally, returning to biography, we should remember that Pope lived to write and that his satires were part of his life; he agonized over their fate. The real problem in attacking Cibber is that Cibber and many of the other dunces, bad writers though they are, deserve but cannot be hurt by such heavy artillery.

Pope was ignorant enough of his own interest to make another change, and introduced Osborne contending for the prize among the booksellers. Osborne was a man entirely destitute of shame, without sense of any disgrace but that of poverty. He told me, when he was doing that which raised Pope's resentment, that he should be put into *The Dunciad*; but he had the fate of Cassandra. I gave no credit to his prediction till in time I saw it accomplished. The shafts of satire were directed equally in vain against Cibber and Osborne; being repelled by the impenetrable impudence of one, and deadened by the impassive dulness of the other. [P. 187]

As Cibber himself cheerfully remarked in his *Apology*, "My Superiors, perhaps, may be mended by him; but, for my part, I own myself incorrigible."[13] It is the story of Dryden and Settle all over again, and Pope suffers from a more delicate sensibility than Dryden's. One of the finest passages in the *Lives* relates the story of Jonathan Richardson the younger, who "attended his father the painter on a visit, when one of Cibber's pamphlets came into the hands of Pope, who said, 'These things are my diversion.' They sat by him while he perused it, and saw his features writhen with anguish; and young Richardson said to his

[13]*An Apology for the Life of Colley Cibber*, ed. B. R. S. Fone (Ann Arbor, Mich., 1968), p. 16.

father, when they returned, that he hoped to be preserved from such diversion as had been that day the lot of Pope" (p. 188).

I do not claim that Johnson gives us a complete criticism of the *Dunciad*; in interpreting the poem, we look to modern commentators rather than to him. His gaze is too exclusively moral, showing no interest in the element of fantasy, the magnificent antiworld that acquires a life of its own. He said absurdly of *Gulliver*, "When once you have thought of big men and little men, it is very easy to do all the rest" *Life*, II, 319). His own youthful attempts at Swiftian satire are ineffective partly because there is no trace of the manic energy of Swift's ironic speakers, or the fecundity of insane logic which they display. But there is undoubtedly a moral dimension in the *Dunciad*, and Johnson's orientation makes him exceptionally acute in analyzing it.

I should like to return now to the comparison between Dryden and Pope that concludes the elaborate "intellectual character" at the middle of the *Life*. This comparison has often been regarded, I suspect, as nothing more than a pleasant tour de force, a chance for Johnson to show off his abilities in a familiar and rather obvious genre (Homer / Virgil, Shakespeare / Jonson, Michelangelo / Raphael). In my view, however, it is an essential part of the *Life of Pope*, and represents almost the only way Johnson can come to terms with the central paradox of Pope's artistic achievement. This paradox is that everything Joseph Warton and others had said was perfectly true: Pope is, above all, cautious, correct, and uniform; yet these qualities are somehow combined with an aspiring genius of a kind Warton would not recognize in him.

Consider the terms Johnson chooses to describe Pope's mind: "Good Sense, a prompt and intuitive perception of consonance and propriety" (p. 216); "incessant and unwearied diligence" (p. 217); "he excelled every other writer in *poetical prudence*; he wrote in such a manner as might expose him to few hazards" (p. 219); "the style of Pope . . .is cautious and uniform" (p. 222); "the dilatory caution of Pope" (p. 223). All of this sounds like Matthew Arnold's characterization of Pope. But Johnson wants to assert that antitheses are often misleading. In Addison's case it may be true that caution and prudence impose serious limitations on his artistic achievement; in Pope's it is not.[14] "But good sense alone is a sedate and quiescent quality, which manages its possessions well, but does not increase them; it collects few materials for its own operations, and preserves safety, but never gains supremacy. Pope had likewise genius; a mind active, ambitious, and adventurous, always investigating, always aspiring; in its widest searches still longing to go forward, in its highest flights still wishing to be higher; always imagining something greater than it knows, always endeavouring more than it can do" (p. 217.) The question then is whether these two qualities— prudence and aspiring genius— can be united in the same poet. Warton was sure they could not.

We do not, it should seem, sufficiently attend to the difference there is, betwixt a MAN OF WIT, a MAN OF SENSE, and a TRUE POET. . . . Which of these characters is the most valuable and useful, is entirely out of the question: all I plead for, is, to have their several provinces kept distinct from each other; and to impress on the reader, that a clear head, and acute understanding are not sufficient, alone, to make a POET; . . . and that it is a creative and glowing IMAGINATION, "acer spiritus ac vis," and that alone, that can stamp a writer with this exalted and very uncommon character, which so few possess, and of which so few can properly judge.[15]

Against Warton's assertions Johnson can of course offer counterassertions—"in its highest flights still wishing to be higher"—but evidence of a more substantial kind is required if his opinion is to carry any more weight than Warton's.

Today we would have other ways of making such a case, for instance by close analysis of Pope's imagery and rhetorical wit. But as we have seen, this is seldom Johnson's mode: he uses it to attack but not to defend. What he does instead is to elaborate a brilliant comparison with Dryden that forces us to go beyond easy antitheses and to recognize that every great poet has his own

[14] See the discussion above of Johnson on Addison's style, p. 73.

[15] Joseph Warton, Dedication to Edward Young of *An Essay on the Genius and Writings of Pope*, 4th ed. (1782), I, iv-vi. Milton is the only poet whom Warton sees as uniting both "a sublime and splendid imagination" and "a solid and profound understanding"; the other writers he lists are Herodotus, Plato, Cicero, Livy, Tacitus, Galileo, Bacon, Descartes, Malebranche, Burnet, Berkeley, and Montesquieu (p. 120).

peculiar excellence, so that each must be read on his own terms. As David Daiches has well said of Johnson's analysis, "These images are not mere decoration; they are diagnostic and clarifying; they direct our attention to essential qualities of each poet. And though the conclusion is that Dryden comes just a fraction higher in the scale of poetic genius than Pope, the comparisons and contrasts between them are not made at the expense of either but rather to help the reader appreciate both." [16]

So it needs to be emphasized that the importance of Johnson's analysis does not lie simply in the assertion that Pope has imagination as well as judgment. Merely as assertion, this defense had already been attempted by the humble Ruffhead: "In short, he held all the faculties of his mind in such due subordination, that many, perhaps, have been hastily led to suppose his *creative* powers (since such they are to be called) deficient, because they are so castigated by his judgment, that they were not so obviously predominant in him, as in some other great writers, who have occasionally given way to the *irregular sallies* of imagination, and the *wild flights* of fancy (*Life of Pope*, p. 459). Johnson's formulation is more eloquent than this, but is not, in itself, any more a demonstration than Ruffhead's.

Johnson therefore turns to the Dryden / Pope comparison to make his point. It is worth noticing, since this was so traditional a form, that he is unusual in weighting the balance so evenly between the two poets. The Demosthenes / Cicero comparison was often made in antiquity, for instance by Longinus and Plutarch, with the preference clearly given to Demosthenes. Johnson's set piece most resembles that of Quintilian, for whom Cicero is the greater: "Demosthenes is more compact, Cicero more verbose; Demosthenes argues more closely, Cicero with a wider sweep; Demosthenes always attacks with a sharp-pointed weapon, Cicero often with a weapon both sharp and weighty; from Demosthenes nothing can be taken away, to Cicero nothing can be added; in the one there is more study, in the other more nature." Johnson sees Pope's virtues, as Quintilian does those of Cicero, as being a case of both / and rather than either / or. He possess exactness *and* energy; as Quintilian goes on to say, in

[16]*Critical Approaches to Literature* (London, 1956), p. 253.

imagery that Blake also uses, "He does not, as Pindar says, collect rain water, but overflows from a living fountain."[17] But for Quintilian this means that Cicero is clearly greater than Demosthenes: he can do everything Demosthenes can and more besides. A similar conclusion is reached in Dryden's famous comparison of Juvenal and Horace, in which he has to be cautious—Dorset, to whom the *Discourse on Satire* is dedicated, is supposed to be the new Horace—but admits his feeling that Horace's "wit is faint; and his salt, if I may dare to say so, almost insipid."[18]

The closest model for Johnson's comparison is undoubtedly Pope's own treatment of Homer and Virgil; yet even here the differences are important enough to deserve attention.

No Author or Man ever excell'd all the World in more than one Faculty, and as *Homer* has done this in Invention, *Virgil* has in Judgment. Not that we are to think *Homer* wanted Judgment, because *Virgil* had it in a more eminent degree; or that *Virgil* wanted Invention, because *Homer* possest a larger share of it: Each of these great Authors had more of both than perhaps any Man besides, and are only said to have less in Comparison with one another. *Homer* was the greater Genius, *Virgil* the better Artist. In one we most admire the *Man*, in the other the *Work*. *Homer* hurries and transports us with a commanding Impetuosity, *Virgil* leads us with an attractive Majesty: *Homer* scatters with a generous Profusion, *Virgil* bestows with a çareful Magnificence: *Homer* like the *Nile*, pours out his Riches with a boundless Overflow; *Virgil* like a River in its Banks, with a gentle and constant Stream.[19]

Clearly Johnson remembers this when he writes, "It is not to be inferred that of this poetical vigour Pope had only a little, because Dryden had more, for every other writer since Milton must give place to Pope" (p. 223). But Johnson's comparison differs from Pope's in a fundamental sense, in that it tries to define, as

[17]*Institutes of Oratory*, X.i, trans. J. S. Watson (London, 1856), II, 271-72. Plutarch's comparison of Demosthenes and Cicero follows his *Lives* of the two orators and is mainly concerned with personality rather than style. Longinus gives a brief comparison in Ch. 12 of *On the Sublime*. "The cistern contains: the fountain overflows" appears in the Proverbs of Hell in Blake's *Marriage of Heaven and Hell*.
[18]*A Discourse Concerning the Original and Progress of Satire* (1693), in *Of Dramatic Poesy and Other Critical Essays*, II, 130.
[19]Preface to the *Iliad* (1715), in Twickenham Ed., *Poems*, VII, 12.

well as to embellish, the distinctions it makes. Pope, that is, relies entirely on metaphors, not unlike the labored similes that are familiar to readers of Boswell's *Life*. Homer and Virgil are like two kinds of rivers, of heroes, of gods, and so forth. Johnson attempts to go beyond this sort of impressionistic tribute to specify just how the two poets differ *in their poetry*.

I do not mean, of course, that Johnson is indifferent to the power of metaphor. No sentence in the Life of Pope is better known than the statement "Dryden's page is a natural field, rising into inequalities, and diversified by the varied exuberance of abundant vegetation; Pope's is a velvet lawn, shaven by the scythe, and levelled by the roller" (p. 222). But we tend to forget that this is a description solely of prose style, which Johnson regards as ornamental and therefore as properly described by images of art versus nature. When he comes to define the kind of genius that informs the whole of a poet's work, he is at pains to support metaphor with accurate description. The set-piece comparison comes as the last of seven paragraphs, summarizing and extending the distinctions that have already been established: Dryden had as much judgment as Pope, but used it carelessly, while Pope always strove to do his best; Dryden was capable of more "comprehensive speculation" and Pope of "minute attention" (p. 222). Their prose styles are compared, in the passage already quoted, as suggestive of different tendencies of mind. Then follows the elaborate set piece, which needs to be read as a whole:

Of genius, that power which constitutes a poet; that quality without which judgement is cold and knowledge is inert; that energy which collects, combines, amplifies, and animates—the superiority must, with some hesitation, be allowed to Dryden. It is not to be inferred that of this poetical vigour Pope had only a little, because Dryden had more, for every other writer since Milton must give place to Pope; and even of Dryden it must be said that if he has brighter paragraphs, he has not better poems. Dryden's performances were always hasty, either excited by some external occasion, or extorted by domestick necessity; he composed without consideration, and published without correction. What his mind could supply at call, or gather in one excursion, was all that he sought, and all that he gave. The dilatory caution of Pope enabled him to condense his sentiments, to multiply his images, and to accumulate all that study might produce, or chance might supply. If the flights of Dryden therefore are higher, Pope continues longer on the wing. If of Dryden's fire the blaze is brighter, of Pope's the heat is more regular and constant. Dryden often surpasses expectation, and Pope never falls below it. Dryden is read with frequent astonishment, and Pope with perpetual delight. [Pp. 222-23]

This is, to be sure, more like Quintilian's or Pope's comparisons than a modern critical essay. But the exfoliation of metaphors at the end, which most resembles Pope's method, is the conclusion to a discussion that accounts at once for the objective features of the poetry and the circumstances of composition that lie behind it. Dryden's carelessness and Pope's diligent accumulation of materials are visible in their works, which inevitably reflect their mental habits. Above all, the effect of the poems on readers is the crucial factor: "Dryden is read with frequent astonishment, and Pope with perpetual delight."

Johnson concludes, "This parallel will, I hope, when it is well considered, be found just; and if the reader should suspect me, as I suspect myself, of some partial fondness for the memory of Dryden, let him not too hastily condemn me; for meditation and enquiry may, perhaps, shew him the reasonableness of my determination" (p. 223). This is precisely the insight, as I have argued, that Johnson means to express in the notion of the common reader: if we feel deep affection, then careful "meditation and enquiry" may well locate good reasons for it. And of course this is affection for the writer in his works, not for his personality as distinct from them.

Considerations like these explain Johnson's preference for Dryden, a preference he manages to express without diminishing his admiration for Pope's achievement. Johnson is capable, as M. H. Abrams has said of Coleridge, "alternately of dwelling on a poem as a poem, and on a poem as a process of mind."[20] What he admires in Dryden is the power of mind that creates better passages than any in Pope—higher flights, brighter fire—but he is ready to acknowledge in Pope the patient care that produces better poems. The distinction is not absolute: Pope has not produced perfect poems, but poems better than Dryden's. The point of the comparison is that the two poets are

[20]*The Mirror and the Lamp* (New York, 1958), p. 124.

quite obviously commensurable. Pope "professed to have learned his poetry from Dryden, whom, whenever an opportunity was presented, he praised through his whole life with unvaried liberality; and perhaps his character may receive some illustration if he be compared with his master" (p. 220). There would be little value in a comparison of either Dryden or Pope with Milton, whose greatness and limitations are of a radically different order.

There is yet more to be said about Johnson's distinctions between Dryden and Pope, if we consider that his general statement seems to have been perfectly acceptable to Joseph Warton, who said in his second volume, published after Johnson's *Life*, "Though *Dryden* be the greater genius, yet *Pope* is the better artist."[21] If we generalize beyond the conclusions of the Dryden / Pope comparison, we can see that Johnson arrives at his assessment by assuming a very different version of literary history from Warton's. Without mistaking Warton for a radical "pre-Romantic," it is fair to say that he and his allies gave their highest approval to a sort of essence of poetry that did not necessarily develop through history and could easily manifest itself in rude and unsophisticated eras. As Johnson's would-be disciple Stockdale retorted to Warton:

There perhaps never was a poet who softened, and mellowed such delicacy, and refinement, such dignity, and strength, with so liberal, and polite an ease as Pope. But such Poetry will not be admired by criticks of a vitiated, and insatiable taste. In a most happy selection of those ideas, and images which give a lively, and forcible pleasure to human nature; in their new, and beautiful connexion; in the spontaneous, but strong language of the heart, and passions, in which those ideas, and images are conveyed, *They* see nothing great; nothing above mediocrity. Their Gothick souls are only stimulated with the *transcendently* sublime; or, in other words, with the unnatural, the gigantick, and the incoherent.[22]

[21]*Essay*, II, 411. Probably both Warton and Johnson recalled Pope's opinion that "*Homer* was the greater Genius, *Virgil* the better Artist."

[22]Percival Stockdale, *Inquiry into the Nature and Genuine Laws of Poetry; including a Particular Defence of the Writings and Genius of Mr. Pope* (1778), pp. 128-29. Stockdale was irritated when Johnson made no reference to this work in the *Lives* and only a passing and dismissive reference to Stockdale's *Waller*. See John Hardy, "Stockdale's Defence of Pope," *Review of English Studies*, NS 18 (1967), 49-54. In later life Stockdale reversed his ground and celebrated the genius of Chatterton (see Lipking, pp. 466-70).

Stockdale has Gray in mind here, and Johnson's wrath against Gray is explained not so much by moral considerations as by the conviction that English poetry had taken a disastrous wrong turning. The sublime was for Johnson only one of several modes of poetic excellence, but the latest generation of critics had identified it as the essential mode and had looked for it in remote places. Not surprisingly he suspected that Macpherson had fabricated the Ossianic poems to satisfy a growing taste for the primitive and sublime. In the same way Johnson regarded Gray's Celtic explorations with disgust, as perverting the literary teleology whose telos had been Pope.

> The natural progress of the works of men is from rudeness to convenience, from convenience to elegance, and from elegance to nicety. . . .
> From the time of Gower and Chaucer, the English writers have studied elegance, and advanced their language, by successive improvements, to as much harmony as it can easily receive, and as much copiousness as human knowledge has hitherto required . . .Every man now endeavours to excel others in accuracy, or outshine them in splendour of style, and the danger is, lest care should too soon pass to affectation. [*Idler* 63, II, 198]

This was Johnson's hopeful ideal: Pope had brought English versification to its natural perfection. "Sir, a thousand years may elapse before there shall appear another man with a power of versification equal to that of Pope" (*Life*, IV, 46). But a race of barbarians was inexplicably rebelling against this benignant millennium.

Behind Johnson's assessment of Pope, therefore, lies the full weight of his sense of English literature. The thrust of Warton's criticism is to show that Pope's mind and versification are inadequate to the highest poetic achievement: "The Sublime and the Pathetic are the two chief nerves of all genuine poesy. What is there transcendently Sublime or Pathetic in POPE?" (*Essay*, I, x). Johnson is quite prepared to grant that other poets are greater than Pope in these respects—Milton in the sublime, Shakespeare in the pathetic—but Pope exhibits a third quality, the beautiful, which is not necessarily inferior to the others.[23] And by compar-

[23]See Hagstrum, Ch. 7.

ing Pope with Dryden, Johnson hopes to show that Pope's limitations are the function of his individual qualities of mind (caution, prudence, dislike of risk-taking) rather than of his art in its widest application.

Thus Gray's odes are placed in implied contrast, as the first critics of the *Lives* perceived, to the superior model of Dryden. "His poem *On the death of Mrs. Killigrew* is undoubtedly the noblest ode that our language ever has produced. The first part flows with a torrent of enthusiasm. 'Fervet immensusque ruit'" (*Life of Dryden*, I, 439). In answering Johnson's strictures on *The Progress of Poesy*, Robert Potter throws Johnson's torrent of enthusiasm back at him and quotes the Horatian source of his Latin tag to imply that it belongs to Gray rather than Dryden:

The first Stanza rolls along in the fervor of enthusiasm, various, sweet, and magnificent as its subject. Dr. Johnson says "he is one of those that are willing to be pleased, and therefore would gladly find the meaning of this first Stanza." Had the Critic been pleased to find the meaning of Horace, he could not have failed of finding the same pleasure from this passage, the high metaphorical expressions of which are drawn from thence;

> Monte decurrens velut amnis, imbres
> Quem super notas aluere ripas,
> Fervet, immensusque ruit profundo
> Pindarus ore.[24]

Similar terms had been applied to Gray's odes since their first publication, as in this review of *The Bard*: "What follows is all enthusiasm, exstasy, and prophetic fury, that alarms, amazes, and transports the reader."[25] It seems likely that Johnson is deliberately adapting the commonplaces of Gray criticism in the *Life of Dryden* and showing where he thinks they ought really to be applied. Potter in turn reappropriates them for Gray, a number of whose admirers expressed surprise and bewilderment at Johnson's high praise of the odes of Dryden.

In locating the torrent of enthusiasm in Dryden rather than

---

[24]*An Inquiry into Some Passages in Dr. Johnson's Lives of the Poets, particularly his observations on Lyric Poetry, and the Odes of Gray* (1783), p. 22. Johnson had parodied Potter's translation of Aeschylus (though Potter did not know this): see Yale *Works*, VI, 303-4. The quotation is from Horace, *Odes*, IV.ii.

[25]*Critical Review*, 4 (1757), 169.

Gray, Johnson was protesting against what he believed to be a false conception of the sublime in which the reader is a passive recipient of emotion. Gilbert Wakefield, another of Gray's champions, declared of the odes, "That spirit of lyrical inspiration, which they breathe—that divine glow of pathos, which at the same time melts and inflames the reader—cannot operate with their full effect, but on a congenial soul, attuned to the bold vibrations of enthusiastic poetry." Wakefield goes on to speak of "the torrent of sublimity, that pours along."[26] What Johnson dislikes is not sublimity in itself, but the paradoxical theory in which the poet works it up with great effort (imitating Pindar, Norse or Celtic poetry, or whatever) while the reader relaxes his mind and receives the torrent in a state of passivity.

The readers of Gray are thus halted at a stage from which, as Coleridge remarked, the intelligent reader must eventually pass, even if he loses as well as gains. "When no criticism is pretended to, and the Mind in its simplicity gives itself up to a Poem as to a work of nature, Poetry gives most pleasure when only generally and not perfectly understood. It was so by me with Gray's Bard, and Collins' odes. The Bard once intoxicated me, and now I read it without pleasure. From this cause it is that what *I* call metaphysical Poetry gives me so much delight."[27] In Johnson's view, sublimity relates to a great subject treated in the high style, not to a mode of writing or reading in isolation. He will sometimes use Burkean language to describe natural scenes in Wales or the Hebrides, [28] and in literature will praise the sublime when he believes that poetic elevation has been called forth by an elevated theme. Milton "had considered creation in its whole extent, and his descriptions are therefore learned. He had accustomed his imagination to unrestrained indulgence, and his conceptions therefore were extensive. The characteristick quality of his poem is sublimity" (*Life of Milton*, I, 177). Gray, on the other

---

[26]*Poems of Mr. Gray*, p. 75. Wakefield delivers a stern criticism of Johnson (pp. 17-18), but surprisingly concurs with Johnson's strictures on the "Favorite Cat" (pp. 27-28).

[27]*Inquiring Spirit*, ed. Kathleen Coburn (London, 1951), p. 156.

[28]See the account of Hawkeston Park in Wales in 1774: "The Ideas which it forces upon the mind, are the sublime, the dreadful, and the vast. Above, is inaccessible altitude, below, is horrible profundity" (Yale *Works*, I, 175). In the *Journey to the Western Islands*, published the next year, the Buller of Buchan is described in similar terms (Yale *Works*, IX, 19-20).

hand, seeks to be sublime by an artificial inflation of subject and language. "He has a kind of strutting dignity, and is tall by walking on tiptoe" (*Life of Gray*,III, 440). Johnson would have been appalled to know that his own death would be mourned in this very mode.[29]

Johnson's claim, then, is that Pope did have genius and knew how to use it, taking advantage even of those elements in his character that might seem unattractive. Dryden's genius is greater than Pope's: his mind is stronger and deeper. "He observed, that in Dryden's poetry there were passages drawn from a profundity which Pope could never reach" (*Life*, II, 85). While this statement is unfortunately not illustrated at length, Johnson is probably thinking of the same quality Coleridge noticed, the driving force with which Dryden develops an idea through a paragraph rather than closing it in a couplet.[30] But Pope is not

[29] Apollo's lyre
The band will fire:——
Loud!—louder yet!—proclaim wise JOHNSON's name. . . .

The Furies fly:
They mount on high,
And hover o'er the hallow'd bed.—
"No hope! no hope!" enrag'd they scream;
Their tangled hair,
The wanton air
Waves high.—
Sad, sullen, mute, aghast they seem;
They sigh!—
A horrid yell,
Their bosoms swell. . . .

An Ode on the Much lamented Death of Dr. Samuel Johnson. Written the 18th December, 1784. This unusual work, which is handsomely printed and cost a shilling, prophesies the victory of the Lamb of God and the extinction of Faction.

[30] One of Johnson's examples is apparently the passage from *Tyrannic Love* which he quotes from memory in the *Life of Dryden*, I, 458; I am at a loss to define the excellence of these lines, unless he means that Pope would consider a "passion" like love to be more simple and uniform than Dryden does (though this does not seem true of Pope). The other passage Johnson mentions is the character of Zimri, of which Coleridge speaks as follows: "You will find this a good gauge or criterion of genius—whether it progresses and evolves, or only spins upon itself. Take Dryden's Achitophel and Zimri—Shaftesbury and Buckingham; every line adds to or modifies the character, which is, as it were, a-building up to the very last verse; whereas, in Pope's Timon, &c., the first two or three couplets contain all the pith of the character, and the twenty or thirty lines that follow are so much evidence or proof of overt acts of jealousy, or pride, or whatever it may be that is satirized (*Table Talk*, p. 194, 6 Aug. 1832).

simply more diligent than Dryden; he uses his talent better, and produces a long series of great poems. The final pages of the *Life of Pope* (pp. 247-52) reiterate its two themes, that Pope's genius was entirely real and that he forms a fitting destination for the teleology whose uncertain heralds were Denham and Waller. "Pope had, in proportions very nicely adjusted to each other, all the qualities that constitute genius. He had Invention...Imagination...Judgement...colours of language" (p. 247).

From the last term Johnson proceeds to define some of Pope's excellences of versification. Dryden left English poetry marble, and Pope knew how to build with marble. Dick Minim's Warton-like decision in *Idler* 60— "Pope he was inclined to degrade from a poet to a versifier"—is a parody of the truth that his versification is a great achievement in English literary history. Sonorous though the couplet became in Dryden's hands, Pope made it more so, and even Dryden's *Virgil* could come to seem a little awkward. "Since the English ear has been accustomed to the mellifluence of Pope's numbers, and the diction of poetry has become more splendid, new attempts have been made to translate Virgil" (*Life of Dryden*, I, 453). Fine as Dryden's Virgil is, Pope's Homer "is certainly the noblest version of poetry which the world has ever seen" (*Life of Pope*, III, 119). The objection that it is unlike Homer is answered in three ways: it adds to Homer rather than altering him; it uses the form of verse most acceptable to Pope's contemporaries; and it would not be read by them if it did not. As always the common reader is the final judge. A more accurate version of Homer would still be only a version and would have no use. "To a thousand cavils one answer is sufficient; the purpose of a writer is to be read, and the criticism which would destroy the power of pleasing must be blown aside" (p. 240).

I have tried to show that Johnson has set up his defense of Pope in a very interesting way, but it must be admitted that his polemical intention was doomed to failure. The comparison of Dryden to Pope was a brilliant stroke for readers who agreed with Johnson that Dryden had genius and who could value Pope more if they thought carefully about his relation to Dryden. But it could have no effect for the many readers who preferred Gray to both Dryden and Pope. Such readers were inclined to seize upon Johnson's images of soaring and blazing and to apply them to the poet he despised: "Gray, as a poet of the lyre, appears to me to be more uniformly grand and majestic [than Dryden]. The mind is elevated by him to ethereal regions, and soars with eagle flight, without being forced to fall from its eminence, like the son of Daedalus. Gray wings his way on high like a glorious luminary, all stately, all regularly magnificent; Dryden rises like an air balloon, which now and then breaks, and tumbles precipitately down, contrary to the intention of the conductor of it, and to the great mortification of the gaping spectators." Thus Vicesimus Knox, who adds that "the above strictures may expose me to the anger of the irritable sons of Aristarchus." So much for Dryden; an American writer early in the next century performs the same operation upon Pope, announcing that "if I reverence Johnson, I love truth more": "His [Pope's] page is irradiated by little of that mysterious light, which is generated by this unknown power [of genius]. . . . In vain do we seek for the creative energies of invention, the sublime soarings of thought, and the audacious struggles of imagination, bursting forth from the confinement of reason."[31]

It is all too evident that Johnson is an imperfect critic of the poetry of the later eighteenth century: he saw some of its faults very clearly, but had no sympathy for what it was trying to do. But Eliot has not won universal acceptance for his notion that the only good critic is the one who can identify the best of his contemporaries. And Johnson's weakness in this respect seems less terrible now that the minor poets he disliked no longer look like the vanguard of a new dawn. "He spied the great Romantic beard," Saintsbury declared, "under the Pindaric and Horatian muffler—and he did not like it."[32] Even if this be true, there was much more muffler than beard.

Its polemical intention aside, the character of Dryden and

---

[31] Knox, *Winter Evenings, or Lucubrations on Life and Letters* (1787), No. 100; A. M. Walter, "On Pope," *Monthly Anthology and Boston Review*, 2 (1805), 233–38, alluding to the proverbial "Amicus Plato, sed magis amica veritas," which Walter Shandy construes, "Dinah was my aunt, but Truth is my sister" (*Tristram Shandy*, I. xxi).

[32] George Saintsbury, *A History of English Criticism* (Edinburgh, 1911), p. 226.

Pope is a splendid piece of work, recognizing the place of both poets in literary history while identifying what is distinctive and valuable in each. Qualities of mind are acutely discriminated as they appear in the poems, and Pope is shown to illustrate a major theme of the *Lives* by fulfilling—as Dryden could not—the potential of his genius. The brief *Lives* that follow have their interest, but the *Pope* is a fitting culmination for the *Lives of the Poets*, and a noble testimony to the amplitude of Johnson's powers.

9   *Conclusion*

THROUGHOUT THIS BOOK I have sought to show that Johnson's criticism is most valuable when it goes beyond the usual boundaries of formal literary analysis. That is not in the least to question the value of formal analysis; it is only to recognize that many critics perform it at least as well as Johnson, and that his special excellence lies elsewhere.

Much as he loved poetry, Johnson saw it as a branch of the larger category "writing" rather than as the exalted summit of belles lettres. His well-known statement "The only end of writing is to enable the readers better to enjoy life, or better to endure it" (1825 *Works*, VI, 66) appears in a review of a minor work of metaphysics and implies no crucial distinction between beautiful letters and other kinds. Still less did Johnson recognize any obligation to a generalized concept of "art," the synoptic vision of the *beaux arts* that was gaining importance in his time. Like Swift, he felt no visible embarrassment at being indifferent to music and the other arts, and showed a polite interest in painting only out of courtesy to his friend Reynolds.

Literature (as we use the term today) was of great interest to Johnson, but on the same plane as many other interests, including theology, moral philosophy, political and legal theory, biography, philology, and medicine. Nowadays the man who can reason expertly in all of these areas seems an extraordinary polymath, and of course Johnson was that. But it is polymathy of a distinct kind, preferring traditional wisdom to the radical program of the French philosophes and their British allies. In speculative philosophy Johnson did not care to go much beyond Locke, choosing to ignore the searching epistemological inquiry that now seems a central achievement of eighteenth-century thought. His range of interests closely resembles that of the great Renaissance humanists, the "heroes in literature"—of learned writing in its widest sense—whom he praises in *Rambler* 137.

Johnson understands that poetry and narrative fiction have their own special rules and differ from other forms of writing.

But these rules are not, to him, the most interesting things about them. And since art and its subspecies poetry are not endowed with unique value, the criticism that would explain them can enjoy no status of unique authority: it is nothing more than a "subordinate and instrumental art" (*Rambler* 208).

Johnson therefore strives to break down the barriers that isolate criticism—as in his contemporaries Lord Kames and even the Wartons—from the wide purview of humanist thought. Considered in themselves, works of literature are of course susceptible to all sorts of specialized analyses: the subjects and diction proper to pastoral, the nature of poetic meter, and so forth. Such analyses have their place, in Johnson's view, but they are narrow. A keen awareness of the limitations of existing criticism helps to condition his understanding of specific works: the hostility to pastoral theory out of which he condemns *Lycidas*; the thoughtful response to Addison on epic that partly determines his reading of *Paradise Lost*; the irritation with Joseph Warton's canons of poetry that elicits the fine appreciation of *The Rape of the Lock*. But always he subordinates these topics to the larger concerns subsumed under the name of "truth."

In judging poetry as a moralist, Johnson applies to it the same standards that he applies to writing in general and to life itself. What makes him remarkable is his simultaneous commitment to the principle that poetry must give pleasure. As he likes to express it, writing instructs, poetry instructs by pleasing. In other words, while poetry can claim no privileged exemption from the moral status of all other human activities, it has satisfactions to give that belong to it alone. We are to *judge* it by the same rigorous standards that Johnson as moralist urges us to bring to every aspect of life. But we *respond* to it on its own terms, and he warns us to be deeply suspicious of any criticism that ignores our response.

In demanding *dulce* as well as *utile*, Johnson demands a good deal, for more than most critics he recognizes that the reader must be his own judge of what gives delight. This emphasis is by no means identical with the "affective stylistics" so much discussed lately, a mode of inquiry that has had to accommodate itself to the general presuppositions of twentieth-century aesthetics. Johnson is not elaborating a theoretical mode for anatomizing literary works; he is paying homage to a fundamental sense of pleasure that defies analysis but in whose absence analysis must be sterile.

The ultimate value of Johnson's criticism lies in its quality of truth-telling. No critic can tell us *the* truth about literature, for notions of truth vary widely from person to person and generation to generation. Nor is it adequate to say that we may disagree with his answers but that he asks the right questions. Nobody asks *the* right questions. What Johnson preeminently does—at his most crabby as well as his most generous—is to offer us a model for our own critical reading. Reynolds said that Johnson taught his friends to think justly. His example encourages the reader of literature to start from his true response, to use his intelligence as well as his taste, and to tell the truth (to himself as well as others) about the judgments and preferences that result. Often a reader will be convinced by Johnson's conclusions; he would hardly be an exemplary critic if he always seemed mistaken. Still it is the example that matters most, just as in the *Journey to the Western Islands* Johnson teaches the reader how to be an intelligent traveler even if he himself is sometimes an imperfect one.

In striving to be true at once to moral and aesthetic standards, Johnson encourages his reader to recognize the difficulty and importance of doing justice to both. His best criticism seems almost always to derive from a tension between *dulce* and *utile*, in which he stubbornly refuses to falsify either demand at the expense of the other, even if being honest to his sense of both produces strain and sometimes paradox. He is seldom at his most stimulating when he deals with works which he regards as aesthetically defective, either because they set a dangerous precedent (Gray's odes) or because they are simply feeble (Blackmore's hopeless, though morally unexceptionable, epics). And he tells us little about works that he regards as aesthetically good but morally bad, such as *Gulliver's Travels* and *Tom Jones*—for it seems likely that he does appreciate their aesthetic power, though it suits him to deny it—and Pope's *Unfortunate Lady*. These offend him so much that even in conversation he will not discuss them at any length.

Johnson's best criticism is called forth, not by works that he knows how to "place," but by those that defy categorizing. Many great works, for instance, strike him as being aesthetically excellent but morally neutral—not vicious, so that condemnation is not clearly in order, but in some way unsettling and potentially dangerous. The most eminent examples are the poems of Homer and the plays of Shakespeare, irresistibly fascinating, mirrors of life rather than of books, but careless to instruct. One wishes that Johnson had written at length on Homer. At any rate, we have his anguished and moving response to *Othello* and *King Lear.*

Above all there are the works in which *utile* and *dulce* are so problematic and so intimately related that Johnson is aroused to an extended analysis that gives the fullest expression of his powers. He believes that *Paradise Lost* exhibits a dangerously idiosyncratic form of verse and that its nonhuman characters and fable violate the obligation to interest the common reader; yet how can it possibly be called aesthetically defective? The *Dunciad* claims to be moral, but is only equivocally so; and how can the obscenity, which is so central to its conception, be justified either morally or aesthetically? As for Dryden, can any of his poems stand up to rigorous scrutiny? Or may his aesthetic carelessness and slipshod morality be overlooked on the grounds that his poetry is greater than his poems? We may not agree with Johnson's answers to these questions, but he explores them in such depth as to awaken our own moral and critical faculties, so that we may try to reach answers of our own.

It needs to be emphasized that few critics have been really distinguished moralists. The *Lives of the Poets* exhibit three qualities seldom found in combination: Johnson excels as biographer in exploring the poets' minds, as moralist in relating biography to the tradition of humanist wisdom, and as critic in evaluating literary works in themselves rather than as mere expressions of personality. The *Lives* establish connections among these three modes so effortlessly that we do not always appreciate how remarkable the achievement is. By way of contrast it is instructive to think of Boswell, celebrated as author of the world's greatest biography. Boswell is supreme in the recreation of personality, but as moralist and critic he is, to put it kindly, far from prepossessing.

Johnson stands, moreover, at just the right historical distance to be peculiarly valuable for us. The eighteenth century no longer looks like a furious battleground between Classic and Romantic: the Classic ideal had lost its unity and conviction by Johnson's time, and the Romantic, though perhaps struggling to be born, found no spokesman in Britain before Blake who understood its nature and had the courage to break with the past. Johnson occupies a sort of calm eddy between these two great currents, untroubled by his clearsighted perception of the limitations of Classicism, unmoved by the fumbling experiments of a rather pallid avant garde. This relative independence of literary movements has its advantages. Dryden's and Coleridge's criticism is inseparable from their practice of poetry and their hopes for it. Johnson's derives from the great humanist tradition of moral inquiry and lacks any programmatic or prophetic emphasis. He is sometimes compared with Matthew Arnold, and certainly he would have agreed with Arnold's pronouncement "It is important to hold fast to this: that poetry is at bottom a criticism of life; that the greatness of a poet lies in his powerful and beautiful application of ideas to life,—to the question: How to live.[1] But Arnold's historicism and his faith in the renovation of culture belong to a later generation. Johnson's criticism perhaps most closely resembles what Montaigne might have written if he had been more concerned with critical applications of his moral thought. And, like the *Essais* of Montaigne, it speaks to us from another age without seeming remote or obsolete. In Johnson's own language, it is "perused with eagerness, and in hope of new pleasure perused again."

One must not claim too much. There are some things that Dryden or Coleridge or Arnold can do better than Johnson; but there are others that he can do better than anyone else. He insists upon the pleasure that we have a right to expect from literature; he has much to say about the relation of literature to the moral life of both author and reader; and he teaches the thoughtful reader to trust his own responses. Johnson's individuality invigorates that of the reader, which is one reason he has founded no school of disciples—there are no systematic or dogmatic

[1]"Wordsworth," *Essays in Criticism: Second Series* (London, 1911), pp. 143-44.

Johnsonians. He helps us above all to discipline our minds and to be faithful to our essential humanity. He has his limitations—all critics do—but if we value him as he deserves, we shall not value him lightly.

Appendix

Appendix   *Congreve's Sketch of Dryden*

(see p. 178 above)

A comparison of the Congreve "character" in the *Life of Dryden* with the original shows that Johnson altered it in two ways. The first involves a number of verbal changes, few of which have much importance. Some are meant to generalize Congreve's personal emphasis by deleting phrases like "of all the Men that ever I knew." Two sentences are left out altogether, a solemn dictum ("Such a Temperament is the only solid Foundation of all moral Virtues, and sociable Endowments") and a clarification of the statement that "his Friendship, where he profess'd it, went much beyond his Professions," in which Congreve intimates that "strong and generous Instances of it" were reported by recipients of Dryden's charity. No doubt Johnson ought to have preserved this, and likewise two deleted words that somewhat change the sense: he omits "prompt" from Congreve's "capable of a prompt and sincere Reconciliation with them who had offended him" and "much" from "his Friendship . . .went much beyond his Professions."[1]

Johnson's more striking alteration transposes the structure of the piece. Congreve begins with Dryden's capacity for friendship, next discusses his willingness to communicate the fruits of his retentive memory and poetic talent to other writers, and concludes with an account of his bashfulness in conversation with anyone he did not know well. In Johnson the third topic is placed second, with important results. Congreve sees Dryden's relation to other writers as an aspect of friendship (being himself one of those friends whom Dryden had encouraged), and then represents Dryden's awkwardness in social transactions as giving a very misleading impression of the man as he appeared in his private circle. Johnson, on the other hand, inserts the descrip-

[1] G. B. Hill reprints Congreve's original in such a way as to show Johnson's verbal alterations, but without including the deleted matter (*Lives*, 483, Appendix T). The full text is available in *Dryden: The Critical Heritage*, ed. James and Helen Kinsley (London, 1971), pp. 263-66. It first appeared in Congreve's edition of *The Dramatick Works of John Dryden* (1717).

tion of Dryden's awkwardness almost at the beginning, so that
the reader accepts it as defining his true nature. In the relations
with other writers that are then described, Dryden is seen not so
much as a man among friends as a writer among writers. He
could not conduct himself with ease and confidence among
ordinary human beings, but became most human ("ready and
gentle . . .ready and patient") when engaged in professional discourse. As Johnson remarks a little further on, "Congreve represents him as ready to advise and instruct; but there is reason to
believe that his communication was rather useful than entertaining" (pp. 396-97). Whether or not he deliberately intended this
transposition to have such an effect—he may only have thought
he was improving the sequence of ideas in the manner of a
helpful editor—the effect is to emphasize Dryden's mind rather
than his personality.

It is impossible to be sure why Johnson has done this; the
treatment of preceding biographers affords no light. Samuel
Derrick, for instance, had completely jumbled the order of topics and rewritten Congreve's prose, in the interests of obtaining
a condensed version. Robert Shiels, on the other hand, had
printed it verbatim (with slight omissions, but no reordering).[2]

²Derrick, ed., Dryden's *Miscellaneous Works* (1760), I, xxxii; Shiels, "Cibber's"
Lives of the Poets (1753), III, 86-87.

Index

Index